*Happy reading!*

# Lament
## for Spilt Porter
### LONGING FOR FAMILY AND HOME

*A. McCloskey*

## Larry J. McCloskey

Published by: Castle Quay Books
Burlington, Ontario
Tel: (416) 573-3249
E-mail: info@castlequaybooks.com | www.castlequaybooks.com

Edited by Marina Hofman Willard and Lori Mackay
Cover design and book interior by Burst Impressions
Printed at Essence Publishing, Belleville, Ontario

Library and Archives Canada Cataloguing in Publication

McCloskey, Larry J., 1955-, author
    Lament for spilt porter : longing for family and home / Larry J. McCloskey ; foreword by the honourable David C. Onley.

ISBN 978-1-988928-05-0 (softcover)

    1. McCloskey, Larry J., 1955-.  2. Authors, Canadian (English)-- 21st century--Biography.  3. Autobiographies.  I. Title.

PS8575.C635Z46 2018          C813'.6          C2018-905678-9

CASTLE QUAY BOOKS

To my parents Enie & Len, their generation,
and a way of life that is no more.

# A NOTE ON THE TITLE, LAMENT FOR SPILT PORTER

WHEN WE WERE YOUNG, MY MOTHER OCCASIONALLY DRANK PORTER IN THE evening, a black, foamy, Guinness-looking drink. She didn't much like it, but her doctor once told her that it would help with her digestion problems, and my mother always did what her doctor told her to do. She never drank a full bottle, a half at most, usually more like a third. To keep the fizz from failing, she would faithfully put a plastic cap over her bottle of porter and place it back in the fridge for the next evening's medicinal.

This tale does not go anywhere. Meaningless detail 40 or 50 years old. Still, if you think about the minutiae that inhabits our mind and evokes memories of people who matter to us, these snapshots of nothingness are our fodder for meaning.

A few years ago, I managed to wedge a three-day stopover in Dublin into a scheduled business trip to Britain. I immediately went to a pub to hear some live music. The pub setting was appropriately kitchen-like, with people gathered around a big wooden table. The Celtic band was very good and featured a banjo player who gave it a cool hillbilly edge. The banjo player impressed me by playing flawlessly at breakneck speed, as he consumed three pints of Guinness in one set alone. It occurred to me that one set of his porter-like looking Guinness would have served

Mom's medicinal purposes for several weeks. I doubt his consumption was related to doctor's orders.

I liked the band enough to buy their CD. On it was a piece where the violin cries out as only the violin can do, with longing, regret, and, to this sentimental fool, bittersweet nostalgia. I play it often, and it evokes memories of—for reasons I cannot explain—home, both the one I grew up in and the other elusive one, the one we all long to return to one day. In particular the searing violin of "Lament for Spilled Porter" reminded me of my mother, her silly, innocuous routine and my inexplicable desire to return to distant trivial events now so fraught with meaning. Unable to play violin, I picked up my pen and wrote *A Lament for Spilt Porter*.

Writing requires a context—the people you are about to meet—and a beginning—the first few notes of the violin, and I am indebted to the people I have known and the many strangers in the night who have helped shape my warped mind, with a special nod to those lamenting, crying and connecting through music above and beyond the expression of mere words. Music, like faith, can neither be explained nor explained away.

# THE SECOND COMING

Turning and turning in the widening gyre
The falcon cannot hear the falconer;
Things fall apart; the centre cannot hold;
Mere anarchy is loosed upon the world,
The blood-dimmed tide is loosed, and everywhere
The ceremony of innocence is drowned;
The best lack all conviction, while the worst
Are full of passionate intensity.

Surely some revelation is at hand;
Surely the Second Coming is at hand.
The Second Coming! Hardly are the words out
When a vast image out of Spiritus Mundi
Troubles my sight: somewhere in sands of the desert
A shape with lion body and the head of a man,
A gaze blank and pitiless as the sun,
Is moving its slow thighs, while all about it
Reel shadows of the indignant desert birds.
The darkness drops again; but now I know
That twenty centuries of stony sleep
Were vexed to nightmare by a rocking cradle,
And what rough beast, its hour come round at last,
Slouches towards Bethlehem to be born?

W. B. YEATS

# FROM ODE: INTIMATIONS OF IMMORTALITY FROM RECOLLECTIONS OF EARLY CHILDHOOD

Our birth is but a sleep and a forgetting
The Soul that rises with us, our life's Star
Hath had elsewhere its setting,
And cometh from afar:
Not in entire forgetfulness,
And not in utter nakedness,
But trailing clouds of glory do we come
From God, who is our home.

WILLIAM WORDSWORTH

We are in the position of a child entering a huge library filled with books in many languages. The child knows someone must have written those books. It does not know how. It does not understand the languages in which they are written. The child dimly suspects a mysterious order in the arrangements of the books but doesn't know what it is.

ALBERT EINSTEIN, ON GOD

# CONTENTS

The modern speeded up mind is the mind of a madman; the mind that is slowed down is the mind of a saint; stop the mind and you have the mind of God.

VACILE POSTEUK, ROMANIAN POET, BUCHENWALD SURVIVOR

# THE BEGINNING IS THE END:
## A LAMENT FOR HOME

I AM AND HAVE ALWAYS BEEN A SUCKER FOR NOSTALGIA. ODDLY, THIS IS ESPECIALLY true of my parents' generation, the Depression, the Second World War, and the exquisite flowering of optimism that followed, times that I never experienced but whose shared values and ways of life we boomers threw off in the 1960s and 1970s, without replacing them with anything in particular, and certainly nothing shared. For the truly perverse, it is possible to feel nostalgia even without direct experience.

I am also nostalgic for the *without anything in particular* that followed, a time when at least some of us just assumed that the important parts of our parents' world would be carried forward. But no, we threw off the shared values and fashioned the world as we would have it, as young, stupid idealists tend to do. Forgive us, for we knew not what we did.

And so we put the memory of our parents' world into the discarded past and rapidly moved forward. Our kids move forward, and they are having kids who will move forward at ever-accelerating speeds, reaching for the next best thing, without any sense that anything, certainly not anything of value, has been lost.

For all our rapid movement, it remains true that wherever you go, there you'll be. And for all the hoopla over the next best thing, it generally turns out to be nothing more than ever-shortening periods of catching our breath and moving on again. Always motion, never still; always searching, never found.

I confess to being the world's worst offender, constantly searching for some sort of deliverance in an expected future guaranteed to disappoint. For 30 years, I've run hard miles, distance running a perfect metaphor for the constant itch to move without destination, the need to frantically keep from feeling at the core. If this seems harsh, consider Blaise Pascal, 17th century French philosopher: "All man's miseries derive from not being able to sit in a quiet room alone." Ouch. I am tempted to invoke the modern excuse for everything, "It's not my fault." Still, in my defense, my inability to sit still is tempered by this nagging voice of nostalgia. I have to move, but it is with an eye to the past, always, and with deep suspicion about the brave new world that is to be our liberating future.

Nostalgia will not win you any new friends or make you a hit at the cocktail party. The backward gaze is not something I recommend, and I've kicked myself for spending too much time in a state of nostalgia, but it won't go away. Still, lately I've had this terrible tiny thought. Maybe I should stop trying to kill nostalgia. Maybe I should sit still in a room and think about it.

Maybe I should try to answer questions like this: Why is it that we would give anything for one more solitary minute with a departed loved one, while we often ignore, take for granted, hold grudges against, or just plain don't get around to connecting with living so-called loved ones who are here, lined up to be soon among those dead whom we would give anything for one more solitary minute with? Just what are we moving toward at breakneck speed, and why do we place so much faith in frantic efforts that we could not begin to articulate without sitting still in a room for at least a few years? Why do we believe what we believe, why do we not believe what our parents and their parents believed, and what do we believe in the absence of belief? And if we believe in anything, how do we hold on to it? In this warp-speed exponentially changing world, what in the world can we believe in and hold on to?

This book has much to do with what we believe. Sounds heavy, theoretical, didactic—but, no. I am a simple creature, neither guru, able to sit quiet in a room, nor groupie, embracing the power of constant change for change's sake. Stuck as I am, it suddenly occurred to me with a blinding flash of the obvious that nostalgia, my useless obsession, is really about faith. This book is about searching and contemplating faith, with all the blemishes, wrinkles and doubts that those who cannot sit still spiritually have to contend with. What this book is *not* is the denial, complacency, and indifference endemic to the modern world.

I have no answers, but this, at least, must be true: *whatever exists, exists, and the existence of God, or not, is not determined by what we feel or believe. Wishing will not make it so, and we will find out soon enough.* I can understand why people want to avoid the thorny issue of faith. Still, I'm going to go far beyond nostalgia for this one, to the renowned Italian poet Dante, creator of "The Divine Comedy." "The hottest places in hell are reserved for those who in time of moral crisis preserve their neutrality."

My simple hunch is that there is more wisdom and more clues to meaning in the past than in the future, at least insofar as the future tends to be embraced. I am not trying to disparage our future directional thrust, since that is where we will be reflecting from before this sentence is done. Still, it seems obvious that the shift in thinking away from wisdom, belief in God and things outside of self, toward the fulfillment of individual wants and desires is bound to disappoint, not only because the messaging of real fulfillment is always at the exclusion of others but because even if one wins life's lottery, wants and desires as a belief system constantly require another level of fulfillment in order to stay relevant. Pursuing wants and desires is the addiction; death is the addict's end. Maybe we need to rethink things.

I like the fusion of nostalgia and faith, though I admit I may have deluded myself that they are related in order to justify my archaic thinking. It just doesn't make sense by modern standards—and thankfully sense is not the currency of faith—that I have always derived meaning from fairly trivial events and ordinary relationships in my life. The key for me has always been the extent to which common events and people translate into connection.

I've always wanted to write something about these events and people, but it seemed so banal, with the wilting insecurity of thinking *Who the hell wants to read about my family stuff?* The world is full of blogs and memoirs, minutia and sordid facts—what I'm doing, where I'm going, what I'm thinking about—not good, not bad, just not interesting.

Would-be writers often have multiple reasons to preserve their neutrality. It is tough enough to start writing, tougher still to come up with something substantial that holds together. To prevent going from enthusiasm to inertia, or what I call blank-page syndrome, one has to answer *What is the story?* Assuming the non-fiction writer is trying to tell what actually happened, meaning tends to be more subjective and is less likely to have universal appeal than fiction.

Still, as we peer upward from the silo of our subjective unwritten blog, we have to admit that we all grope and stumble through this life with the same challenges, with the same questions, and ultimately will face the same answer. Our lives are not the isolated silos of minutia that they seem to be in our constant obsession with movement forward. As driven as we may be toward all things future, the fact is, it is only from the past that we know who we are. Our past is where we derive meaning from. Meaning gives us faith, and faith gives us the strength to meet the moment of moral crisis, to not recoil in despair or, worse, with complacency. The past gives us the path forward.

So our stories—that is, if we forgo clever and special for connection and humility—are our myths, parables, and archetypes, less blog than biblical. If this seems pretentious, I am not suggesting that the story of your Uncle Angus replace the Gospel of St. John but that we look deeply into our own experience and the cast of characters God has put into our path and see anew the miracle beneath the minutiae.

In a Mel Gibson film *The Year of Living Dangerously*, Linda Hunt's character poignantly asks the same question as Tolstoy in his fiction: "What then must we do?" It is the elemental question, and in the film Hunt discovers, in writing Tolstoy concludes, and in our life we often find that the answer is "We must embrace whoever God puts in our path." On the surface there are no satisfactory answers for why and how things happen, including, or especially, who God puts in our path. Still, it may be that actually seeing and paying attention to those in our path will begin to reveal some answers. Sure, I may be in the grip of some grand delusion, but it is the grand delusion that pulled me from the hottest place in hell and got me writing again.

The moment I laid down the necessity to fictionalize, the story clustered around the actual cast of characters that inhabited my path and the question of what those seemingly arbitrary meetings might have to say about faith. So with that mini revelation in mind, I sat down in a café to write—a rare occurrence—a few notes about how a marriage between nostalgia and faith might look. I decided to write what little I know, as I know it, as honestly as I could. I surprised myself and furiously wrote for two hours, but then I rolled around with insomnia that night, thinking, *You have to be kidding!* The normal insecurities of a writer, but this time on steroids.

My night of sweaty doubt should have finished off any pretentions of writing this book. It had been the death of me before. Then the following sequence of events conspired against me, or for me—you decide. While writing notes, I remembered that I'd missed Mother's Day. Though Mom and Dad have been dead for many years, I usually go to my parents' grave on Mother's Day. Visiting Mom has never been tainted with obligation, since I genuinely loved her company my whole life. But I hadn't gone this past Mother's Day and hadn't been at all for over a year. I felt guilty but also understood the reason for avoidance. It was not unrealized expectation exactly, but a trip to the family plot came uncomfortably close. I go filled with memories, admire the beauty and serenity of St. Paul's cemetery, and stand looking at the words and dates on the headstone, waiting, trying to quell a sense of anticipation, even though I know nothing ever happens except for the useless welling of nostalgia.

On this day, driving into St. Paul's, I became aware that the "Wedding March" was playing on my car stereo. A bizarre piece of music for a graveyard. Beautiful, but incongruent to mood and matter. Still, it made me think. It made me think because my parents' first meeting was what I had been thinking about. So why did it strike me as incongruent?

I got out of the car and walked the short distance under shady oak trees to the gravesite. I became aware, as I always do, of separation between noise and activity outside and the disquieting quiet of the empty cemetery. And yes, the quiet was disquieting to me, because I don't sit still in a quiet room and think. I thought about my parents' wedding day. As distant as their wedding day was, it seemed as real as anything else in this life at that moment. I wondered if on their wedding day in the bloom of youth, and in the spell of their special moment, and in anticipation of lying together, surely for the first time, did either of them have a thought about lying together for the last time and for all time in this grave?

I then wandered across the graveyard to where other relatives are buried. I noticed the grave of a first cousin, Mike O'Grady, who had died five years earlier. I had not known that he was dead. We had not known him well. He was a very decent guy whose wife had died when they were a young couple. He was older than us kids and had dropped by our rented cottage in the 1960s to show us his new car. It was a tiny Honda, and, as the first Japanese car we had ever seen, it was wildly exotic, and Mike was very cool. Why had we not known him better? How did we not even know he had died?

It got worse. On the same tombstone beneath Mike's name was the name of his daughter, Kelly Anne, who had died in the last few years. We had not known that she lived; we had not known that she died. How many years had it been since I had walked across the graveyard to visit our cousins?

I thought about my Aunt Isobel. Aunt Isobel, 65 years a nun, had been our family historian and told spirited stories about family get-togethers, dating back to the 1920s, until she died in 2005 at the age of 88. Up until the day she died, mind and memory remained skilled instruments and the source of a very minor vanity. She often recalled Sundays after mass when the extended family would go on a picnic, visit a lake, or just plain visit a family member's home in town or country. These visits were the highlight of the week, organized with care, and required considerable effort to bring the large group together with limited means of transportation and communication. Still, they did it almost every Sunday. They knew each other, they knew about each other, and the thought of not knowing that a first or distant cousin had died in the city in which they had all lived was inconceivable. They did not have smart phones. I felt somewhat bewildered and ashamed. I am a product of the modern world.

Nearby, the grave of my Aunt Laura, killed in 1960 from complications after a car accident right outside her home. I don't remember her alive, but I remember her dead. I was brought to her wake at Kelly's Funeral Home, and it was the first time I had ever seen a dead body. I understood in an instant what everyone comes to know about the dead: they are not sleeping, they are not in a coma, they are not lying still, waiting until you leave the room to get a rise and rise again. They are dead, and nobody can tell you why everyone, including a boy of five viewing a body for the first time, knows the difference between death and life faking death.

Lying with Aunt Laura is her husband, Terry Curry. I loved Terry Curry. He and Dad had been good friends their whole lives—both alcoholics, lives cut decades short by the drink and tobacco. They sat together often, or at least as often as men with young broods could manage to do. They were compatible, alike in many ways, though Terry had been able to face and beat the drink, but not cigarettes. Terry's quiet was calm; Dad's quiet, intense; together they were mostly compatibly silent. Together they would sit smoking, perhaps drinking, perhaps not, not talking much, but comfortable as only men of a certain age and temperament can be. Quiet, solid, emotionally retentive Ottawa Valley Irish men, hard drinking, hard smoking, hard men, but with a distinctive soft spot they rarely exposed. They did not willingly reveal themselves. We could not see their softness, but in retrospect it was fairly obvious. Youth wasted on the young. Watching them together, smoking, drinking, not talking, but for the odd word, Terry with a kind word to us and kind eyes, and Dad more relaxed in his presence. And me, and sometimes a few others, watching, listening, compelled to be there, not understanding why.

I thought about growing up, our tiny house filled with us, filled with other people, family, friends, the endless Irish clan mostly, their presence, the hub of activity saturating a Saturday morning with something elemental and eternal but fleeting. Now gone, utterly absent from this place with their names on stone, and me standing, empty and inquiring.

Incredibly, people stand here looking down on their family gravestones, thinking, *All gone; now what's for lunch?* I can't account for what all this activity, harmony, acrimony, and presence meant, but I can't believe, will never believe, that it was nothing, even in this despondent state. That would be too cruel, too deliberate; that would be hell. Strangely, it is the juxtaposition between not knowing and being unwilling to be pulled into the cult of nothingness that gives me a modicum of resolve. Whatever it was, it was not nothing. My ignorance, lacking, and doubt, stubborn perhaps, but at least not capitulation, a glimmer of suspended faith.

Mom never liked cut flowers. She said cut flowers reminded her of death and funerals. So this time I brought some live flowers—not knowing what kind—and planted away, a little distraction from the emptiness where my parents' remains remain. Always I leave the graveyard wondering, imploring, asking, *Where are you? Are you?*

I then drove to the market area in Ottawa and wrote some more notes, hunched over coffee. I wrote about my parents, remembered details, stories, focusing, for reasons unknown, around the time in the mid-1940s when they met. I wrote energetically, with purpose, but without any confidence that my musings would amount to anything. I sought immediacy and connection, and I felt distance and doubt.

I escaped doubt to the end of the Second World War, for which there was no doubt. The world had rallied against the Nazis and the Japanese, having achieved common purpose and full resolve to win at all costs. People had made many sacrifices, for six years following the Great Depression, and the connection between people on V-Day is perhaps unprecedented in human history. People did not simply read about war, privation and victory; they breathed it and shared in the realization of final victory. It is difficult to conceive in our modern fractured interest-group world of people ever coming together as history records. The problem is, achieving shared values and common purpose is a surrendering of self, and Western democracies have become increasingly subservient to wants and grievances, with competing interests replacing common interest, and the notion of collective good a fading memory.

Ironically, the flowering of optimism that characterizes the post-war years was achieved during a time of privation. Incomes and material possessions were scant, but optimism and goodwill were palpable. You can see it in the photos, and you could hear it in the stories from aunts, uncles, friends, and cousins. Personal problems and financial status were all deemed irrelevant when reflecting on this time of victory and rebuilding. You often heard people say that in doing their small part, in making whatever sacrifices that were theirs to make, it was the best time of their lives.

I remember Aunt Isobel telling the story of her mid-war trip to Halifax. In part I remember it well because she told it often. She was a narrator for whom there was pleasure and warmth in the retelling of known stories, far beyond the recitation of cold facts. Travelling as a nun during the war was a rare luxury, but she had been granted a few days leave to travel with her older sister, Mary, and meet their three brothers, all serving in the navy.

Canada had the third largest navy in the world for that brief period, and Halifax was the hub of wartime Canada. Aunt Isobel's pale-blue watery eyes lit up and her voice wobbled with excitement when she talked about the train ride to Halifax. She said the reunion of the three brothers and two sisters in Halifax was magical; their walks and talks, continuous movement, the flow of people, purpose, secret delights, flirtations, chance meetings, spontaneous singing of wartime songs, optimism, homesickness, meeting new friends and saying goodbye to old ones, and anticipating the next reunion were beyond excitement. She never said it, but I imagined that it must have been hard going back into convent life, for my Aunt Isobell loved to be current, relevant, part of what matters and makes a difference, and though she distinguished herself in her career in medical records as a nun, the excitement level could never have equalled those few days in Halifax during the last war that people of the same country agreed had to be fought for the betterment of mankind, without a trace of irony.

I can hear the criticism about our naive, warmongering parents; how dare they associate not only good but the best of times with the evils of war? But their response to the war was not evil; not responding with resolve and common purpose leading up to war would have been the embodiment of Dante's "hottest places in hell" or Edmund Burke's "the only thing necessary for the triumph of evil is for good men to do nothing." Until 1939 the Allies had done nothing to stop Hitler and in that sense had created him, with Chamberlain's "peace for our time" perhaps the greatest lesson of history. Chamberlain, a good man intent on doing nothing, had preserved his neutrality against a man whom, as Lord Acton had foreseen, absolute power had corrupted, absolutely. Churchill's bulldog tenacity and unparalleled leadership galvanized the Western world to act according to our heritage of shared values. Churchill, not a religious man, allowed people to have faith in themselves, to have faith in their cause. This was a time of faith, and this is what our aunts and uncles meant when they said it was the best time of their lives. Cornball schmaltz that actually happened.

In our family I am the holder of family photos. In the mix are a couple of photos of my parents before they knew they were our parents, before they knew or cared about the progeny that would follow from their union. They are young and restless, absorbed in the miracle of each other, before being swallowed by obligation, a steady stream of kids, and life. Every child should understand that their parents were once fun-loving romantic fools bursting with life and adventure and not salivating at the prospect of holding their kids back from taking risks and having fun.

In one large photo, a group of young people in formal wear is striking for its gaiety—a 1940s appropriate word—and its sense of optimism. True, smiling people have problems too, but the radiating faces in this photo are all looking to a future they know they can believe in, because they came from a place of adversity where faith had been redeemed. And there right at the beginning are Irene and Len, as they were—unsure, hopeful, placing their faith in each other, but not alone, surrounded by friends, supported by family, and in the presence of God. Looking at their early photos, where they're always surrounded by their community, their lives seem secure, their union solid. Today when you drive by a blissful pair exiting a church on their big day, it's hard to wish them well without thinking of their likely demise. Couples know what their individual needs are, what their chances of success are, and are not prone to the delusion of optimism. It's hard to have faith in couples who have no faith in themselves.

It would be enough of a revelation to meet my parents when we were all young, but what would it be like to walk into this photo, them in their mid-twenties, as I grind my way through middle age? If we are no more than the temporary holding of our physical bodies, who would these kids be that radiate the beauty of youth? Who would I be, who once buried their bodies, vitality and optimism gone, forever gone?

It seemed to be *the* thing in the 1940s to dress up in formal wear and go out with a group of friends to the dance hall. This was the golden age of the dance hall, and a night out was a big deal. The earliest photo of my parents is at a dance hall, but where was it located, and what was its name? I knew it had to be fairly central—the suburban thing had not yet reared its head, and public transportation was limited.

Mom—Irene, or her nickname, Enie—and her two sisters, Kaye and Evelyn, had moved from their family farm to the city during the war to find work, and likely adventure. They shared an apartment downtown;

this we had always known. But where exactly did they live? I wondered why we hadn't asked, had never thought to ask, while Mom was alive. There are many questions left unanswered after someone dies, and I have no idea why my mind gravitated to Mom and Dad and the dance hall where they met or to the apartment where the three O'Neill girls lived during the war.

Still, I made a mental note to ask my brother Mike, who had traced our family tree, if he knew the answer to my two specific questions, knowing that he would think my questions obscure and me, weird: Where was the mystery dance hall, and where was Mom's apartment located? I didn't expect Mike to know the answers to trivia questions 70 or so years after the fact. Still, making a mental note to ask is important in view of what followed. And for better or for worse, without making that mental note, doubt would have ground writing into inertia with an inglorious, inevitable end. It seems that doubt triumphs over faith most often, which transforms us from doubters into defeatists. It is our modern way.

The next day I planned to write a few more notes. I was enthusiastic about writing, as at the starting of things we tend to be, but conscious of the possibility of doubt and inertia, always lingering, to take hold, allowing optimism and faith to steal away. For some reason—and I suppose determining the reason may be the purpose of this writing—I went up to my office and reached up for an obscure book high on the top shelf. I brought it down and, yes, blew away dust as I opened the cover. With the fanciful title *A Mountain Never Too High*, it was a biography written by my Uncle Bill O'Neill in 1977 about his multimillionaire uncle, Jack. It had likely been commissioned, and though an interesting story it has an uncritical, promotional aspect to it.

It is the unlikely story of my mom's uncle, Jack O'Neill, who rose from very humble roots in Navan, Ontario, to become one of the key players in the development of California's post-war economic miracle. He was primarily a rancher, and one of his main contributions was his leadership on the California irrigation system. In central California today, essentially emerging from desert is the O'Neill Forebay and Dam, supplying two million acre-feet of irrigation for more than 600,000 agricultural acres. It is astonishing to see the vast aqua blue reservoir and recreational lake surrounded by desert, where fresh water does not naturally exist. The project took twenty years of lobbying and planning, finally began in February 1963, and took fully five years to complete.

The murder and intrigue in John Houston's movie *Chinatown* resulted because of water shortages in Los Angeles. But the problem of water in California is and was even bigger than a case of murder and mayhem. Without water, California's development would have been permanently halted. The California that we know would never have been. The magnitude of Jack's contribution was such that on August 18, 1962, a group gathered for a groundbreaking ceremony at the dam site, presided over by President John F. Kennedy. Jack O'Neill had died the year before, and President Kennedy's address was a tribute to the person credited with being *the* driving force behind the world's biggest irrigation project.

Jack O'Neill also bought and invested in radio, television, and film and hung with the likes of Walt Disney and his good friend Ed Sullivan. In fact, Uncle Bill reported that Ed would occasionally take the liberty of sending Jack a special hello from New York during his Sunday evening variety show. Though far too square to be seen as a California rat-pack type, Uncle Bill was one of *the* elite movers and shakers of California, just as California was becoming *the* place to realize fame and fortune. Of course for most people California dreaming never became real, but for the lowly Canadian who was to appear in a 1959 *Life* magazine photo with President Eisenhower, his was an ending worthy of a Hollywood movie.

As he prospered, Uncle Jack was known to be generous. He never forgot his roots, and he wanted his extended family nearby. The central story of my mother's family is that because of opportunities her Uncle Jack offered to their family, all the O'Neills moved to California within a few years, including Mom's parents. Except for Mom and Dad and their young family. In the early fifties, Mom and Dad were flown out to California at Uncle Jack's expense and enticed with the dream, but by a narrow margin they decided to stay in Ottawa, Canada.

I didn't have any particular reason to reach for this book. I was looking for some fodder for writing because we always knew less about the distant O'Neill clan than the close-by McCloskeys. I knew the gist of the Jack O'Neill story—he was after all a much discussed mythical figure as we grew up—but I am embarrassed to admit, I had never read the book.

As I opened the book a letter fell out. It was dated June 13, 2001. It was from my Uncle Basil, the twin of Uncle Bill who had written the biography of their Uncle Jack. I vaguely remembered reading the letter and putting it into the book, with the intention of getting back to both items, but 12 years had passed. Yes, hell is paved with good intentions. Uncle Basil was the O'Neill family historian, and a very funny man, whose letter began with the following paragraph:

Hi Larry,

We visited our daughter Joan and family this weekend and she mentioned that you were starting to do some genealogy research. When I was in college (many years ago) I decided I would do that. I started with an Irish encyclopedia and the first paragraph describing the O'Neills said that they were the "belligerents" of Ireland. I had to acknowledge to myself that they were the belligerents of Navan, Ontario, Fresno, California, and a few other places on this continent. I calmly closed the book and ended my research (but not before I beat up the book!).

Your wise old uncle Basil (at least one of two is true)

The letter contained 12 pages of carefully prepared O'Neill family history. The letter also contained the obituary of Uncle Bill, who had died in an accident in 1996. Uncle Basil had taken the news of his death hard; they had been close in a way only twins can appreciate. Sadly, Uncle Basil had died in 2012 of Alzheimer's disease. The family historian, with endless entertaining family stories, had been robbed of the capacity to recognize his loved ones. Uncle Basil, fellow nostalgic, had lost the context of his life, even as his loving family surrounded him with constant context. His mind had vacated his body, a sort of death in advance of the fact. So perhaps Alzheimer's forces the issue in asking the question, who are we if not our physical form? Is life a crapshoot at the Darwinian wheel of fortune, our demise simply the arbitrary hand of disease or any of a thousand other grim reapers? Does the accumulation of lifetime experiences and relationships matter? In the absence of a past, who are we?

Even then, I did not sit down and belatedly study the O'Neill family history. I glanced at the list of names and dates, hoping more than trying to see the human stories that would not reveal themselves as lists and charts. I was grateful for the information and the care with which Uncle Basil had prepared it, but I did not understand it. I missed Uncle Basil's stories, one-part history and three parts humour. I still miss that.

So I called his widow, Aunt Marilyn, a lovely woman whom I had not talked to since her husband died. Aunt Marilyn had been the world's most dedicated teacher, forgoing becoming principal to return to the classroom long after most teachers had retired. Uncle Basil kept asking her if she was ever going to retire, and she did not know herself, even at age 70, until one day a student put up her hand and announced to the class that Marilyn had taught her grandfather. Marilyn decided to retire at that moment.

When Marilyn answered the phone, I told her that finding Uncle Basil's letter had got me thinking, and I decided to call. At the mention of Basil's letter she casually said that she had put a letter in the mail for me that day. We continued to catch up, and her letter was not mentioned again, though it was the only time in our lives that she had sent me a letter.

Marilyn's letter arrived on Wednesday, three days later. I had completely forgotten about it. Her covering note was in perfect cursive writing, as only a teacher of 45 years could achieve. She said that she had recently gone through Basil's things and had found the enclosed letter, made a copy, and thought I should have the original. So I read the original letter, and then I read it again.

The original letter Marilyn had passed to me was written from my mom to her brother Jack in California, began on March 11 and completed on March 16, 1948. It is warm, chatty and deliberate about passing on the news, in a way that email is not. Letter writing and receiving in 1948 was an occasion and an important means of communication with people who mattered, even if the tone was whimsical and easy. It was not unusual for a letter to be written over several days; it took time to gather the news and write out all the details to a waiting audience. In this letter Mom notes that their sister Evelyn and her husband, George, will have permanently moved to California "by the time you get this letter." This move was part of the exodus to California from Navan occasioned by Uncle Jack's success.

Most interesting are Mom's plans to go to the upcoming St. Patrick Day's dance with a local Irish guy.

Tomorrow is the seventeenth of March. No doubt you boys will be celebrating with your Irish girlfriends. It's Leonard Patrick Joseph McCloskey's birthday tomorrow too so Len and I, Ev and George, Muriel and Herb are all going to the Standish to celebrate St. Patrick's day, Len's birthday and Ev and George's trip. So there will be plenty of excuses for having fun.

It turns out, Standish Hall was *the* place to have fun in 1948. It was located across the Ottawa River in Hull and had been the mansion of E. B. Eddy, lumber baron, until it almost succeeded in making this provincial backwater the big band and jazz capital of Canada. Sarah Vaughan, Duke Ellington, Oscar Peterson, and Louis Armstrong all played there. Louis Armstrong barely escaped with his life during a fire in August 1951. His drummer was not so lucky and died in the fire. An ugly Standish Hall was built where the old one had been, until it too was torn down in 1975, an inglorious end to the dance hall craze with the rise of a bland government building.

So there it was, the answer to my obscure question, never asked in the previous 50 years, dropped in a Fresno, California, mailbox on the day I had noted to ask Mike. Mom and Dad had met at Standish Hall.

Though Dad was emotionally retentive and not prone to hyperbole or exaggeration, he would occasionally tell an abbreviated tale of his first sighting of Mom. Dad and a friend had gone to the dance hall, and he spotted Mom from across the dance floor, turned to his friend, and said, "See that girl there? I'm going to marry her someday." A cornball cliché sentiment and chance meeting that happened just like that. There was a time when we didn't resist cliché and convention out of some misguided sense of our own originality.

I was trying to imagine the night they first met, how their relationship might have developed, and then the St. Patrick Day's dance at the Standish. I thought about Mom and her sisters getting ready for the big night, the three of them in their city dwelling after growing up in the country, all the promise, hope, and optimism, even if punctuated by the occasional sisterly disagreement. I flipped over the envelope, which I had not looked at in my hurry to read the letter. Neatly printed was "I. O'Neill," which was interesting since we had never seen her maiden name handwritten. And there below her name was the answer to my second question. Mom and her sisters had lived at Laurentian Terrace, 360 Sussex, Ottawa, Ontario.

This address no longer exists. It was on the site of what is now the National Gallery of Canada. The location would have been a nice, easy walk to the Bank of Canada on Rideau Street, and again as soon as I thought the question, there was the answer. I wish I had the power to ask questions and receive immediate correct answers about, say, the stock market, but I don't, and I'm not rich. In fact, the stock market and I have a proven record of consistently generating the wrong answers.

It is easy to dismiss my tale of receiving answers to my questions, both their obscure nature and eerie timing. Coincidence, and not particularly interesting at that. Still, coincidence doesn't quite explain why in the world it occurred to me to ask on the day the letter was mailed, after 50 years of knowing the basic storyline. I don't know why I asked; I don't know why I received; I don't know why I felt compelled to start writing, and especially on the subject of faith. I only know this: without Marilyn sending my mother's letter, I would never have gotten very far. For reason unknown, I was propelled by faith.

It would seem easy and perhaps self-serving to conclude that my intention to write was rewarded—a confirmation, a validation, a gift, a miracle. Years of procrastination and doubt vanquished in an instant. A leap of faith, a waiting miracle. Bottom line: I really, really don't know.

But it is strange. It is strange that with infinite unexplainable events and phenomena constantly swirling around, we stand in the eye of the storm and declare, "I am a rational creature. I can explain all." We commonly deny what has just happened for what can be explained away, with a common appeal to common sense and people nodding their heads in agreement. Or best of all, science will explain this, and all things, in the fullness of time. Without a rational explanation for all things, we feel lost, even if the use of reason as justification for what we do not understand can be irrational.

Still, I like common sense, I like rational, and I am deeply suspicious of inward-looking, self-justifying, New Age, flaky explanations of things not easily understood. And I am uncomfortable with the notion of faith as it is often proclaimed, even as I believe that faith in this life is essential for our lives to be life and not a form of death in advance of the physical fact.

I choose to believe that there is something, something that matters in my mother's letter. Maybe faith is primarily a matter of choosing. Maybe faith is not a matter of sitting, waiting to be convinced (just say you have an ounce of faith, and watch the people line up and try to convince you otherwise because they have not been visited upon or made to believe in anything). The currency of nothingness today is high.

Maybe faith is a discipline requiring practice, and our waiting to be convinced is a waste of time or, worse, the reason why we fail to see what is happening right before our eyes. Maybe faith is a matter of how and what we see—that is, with the application of constant practice.

It's hard to believe that my mother's letter is a miracle, because *miracle* is a loaded word, denoting celestial happenings, and further denoting both rarified and special qualities. Our early impression from the Gospels is that miracles happened only enough times to be recorded during that special time with special people, in a faraway time and place—special, special, special. Seems unlikely.

But if God is, there is no special, there is no then, there is no recording for antiquity, and we are not living in an age during which nothing happens. I am not special, and the extraordinary event of my mother's letter is not special, but it may be a miracle. This is not a new concept. Miracles may be common, and our access to witnessing them may be a matter of—complicated, mysterious, irrational—opening our eyes. Maybe the most common experience of life is a miracle. Maybe the most delusional view we can hold is wilful, deliberate blindness or complacency, our lazy refusal to see the common miracle. Maybe faith is, and coincidence isn't.

"Faith is walking face-first and full-speed into the dark. If we truly knew all the answers in advance as to the meaning of life and the nature of God and the destiny of our souls, our belief would not be a leap of faith and it would not be a courageous act of humanity; it would just be … a prudent insurance policy."

ELIZABETH GILBERT

# CHAPTER ONE
## ENIE

THIS BOOK STARTED WITH AN ARTICLE. THE ARTICLE WAS WRITTEN IN A STATE OF ANGST. The angst was born of fear—of confined spaces, of flying, of loss, and, right up there for true sufferers of angst, of boredom. Uneven, extreme emotions, but at least not complacency, surely the one great insidious nemesis of wonder and faith, our only defense against death and its seductive precursor, modern life. This piece was published in the *National Post* in February 2007 and is the beginning.

## FINDING GOD AT 30,000 FEET

My father had it, though I know at times he doubted. My aunt—a devout nun of 65 years—had it more than my father. Still, both my father and my aunt deferred to my mother as the true believer and holder of "the faith."

I've always admired and wondered about people who have the faith, because I've never had it. And for all my life—even in today's godless world— I've felt guilty because I am not thunderstruck by the presence of God.

But it is not for lack of trying. As a child I pondered the vastness, mystery and contradictions of God and the universe—what existed before the universe, what's on the other side of it, can God make a rock so large that he can't lift it? As an adult, pondering morphed into agonizing—as adults tend to do—because I could not reconcile the world as it is with my image of what faith tells us it is meant to be. The best I could do was to will myself into numbness and not think about the presence or absence of God for long periods of time.

Of course wilful denial only works as long as nothing goes wrong in our lives, the lives of people we care for and, as we get older, the lives of many people we don't even know. On the afternoon of the Dawson College shootings in Montreal I frantically called my daughter, who one week earlier had moved into an apartment across from the campus. I could not immediately reach her, and I distinctly remember holding panic at bay by brutally reasoning that with 10,000 students at Dawson, the chances of my daughter being a victim were remote. I reasoned as likely thousands of parents reasoned on that confusing afternoon of September 13th—as likely the parents of Anastasia De Sousa reasoned before being assaulted by the insane truth of that day. Over 7,000 people attended Anastasia's funeral, and a nation still mourns the haunting death of a girl they never knew. And perhaps nothing else challenges the notion of having and holding on to faith more than the senseless murder of a young innocent human being.

Some years ago on a flight to Victoria I absentmindedly opened a glossy magazine featuring many pictures but likely no substance. I was troubled because my mother, who had been battling Parkinson's disease for over ten years, was dying. An article unlike any other I had ever read stared me in the face. It had been written by Canada's foremost intellectual, Northrop Frye, just before his death in 1991. Frye astounded the world for half a century with his dispassionate and erudite academic writing. But this piece was shocking in its absence of dispassionate distance and intellectualizing. This was Frye raw, naked, utterly unlike his former public self, a perfect metaphor for Wordsworth's "the child is father of the man."

The article was a revelation and a confession on the occasion of Frye coming to grips with the death of his beloved wife of many years. He began by mentioning a little known fact, that in 1936, before his academic life, he was ordained a United Church minister. Interestingly, he then admitted that during his entire life he had never had "the faith." Even as the author of his monumental work *The Great Code: the Bible and Literature*, Frye had not believed in God. It seems that for most of his life he was content to consider all matters of faith as academic.

Yet after his wife died, Frye was lost, and he could not sustain an academic distance from his own life. Though he had a masterpiece on the Bible to his credit, he was now required to go deeper on the question of God. So he put his giant intellectual motor to work, and this is what he came up with.

Most of all, he could not accept, could not believe, that his wife of a lifetime—what she had meant to him, the essence of her—could be reduced to simply a collection of cells that had once lived and were no more. And since this belief was his strongest impulse, it followed that he must believe that, beyond a physical manifestation, she continues to live. And if this latter belief was really stronger than his former academic belief, which was no belief at all, he reasoned that this was faith, perhaps not in the accepted pure sense of the word but what he called "negative faith"—by default—but faith nonetheless.

It was an epiphany moment. I have always believed that the nothingness and meaninglessness of the physical world is harder to believe than the world of faith, the world from which I always felt shut out. And if Northrop Frye should come to reconcile himself at the end of a life with the concept of negative faith having merit, that is good enough for me.

After a lifetime of guilt for what I have not been able to believe, Northrop's revelation was a welcomed relief. Negative faith may not be fulfilling, because it means never really knowing what we long to know. And given our obsession with knowing everything, depending on faith can be downright frustrating. Still, we are told that God and the world beyond physical knowledge are mysteries, which by definition are not to be known. So perhaps not knowing, and how we conduct ourselves in the absence of knowing, may be the point of it all. In which case, frustrating as it may be, I'll take negative faith with an open mind over the fraudulence of an atheist's claim to knowing what can never be known.

I don't know much, but what I do know is this: faith will not, for most of us, strike like a lightning bolt. Faith will not end doubt. Faith, negative as it may feel at times, is not an end and is not even a means to an end. Faith is likely just the beginning of a spiritual dialogue that prevents us from cocooning into the complacency and relativity of modern life—which surely is to live death in advance of the fact.

———————

Even after this piece was published, I generated a lot of anxiety and doubt but little faith. I forgot that gains, however minor or negative, matter. I forgot that maintaining ground, not capitulating to modern passivity and spiritual ennui, requires work, always, like a muscle, and keeping anything less than a daily exercise regime is to invite entropy. The sad truth is, passivity is how we grind what matters in this life into dust.

Writing not only happens in fits and starts at the mercy of a chaotic, overcommitted life but is subject to the slings, arrows, and outrageous fortune of a writer's belief in his own material. Today we tell our kids, who have never accomplished anything, to believe in themselves, as if inevitable doubt in ourselves is a terminal disease. This progressive modern advice produces anxiety and erodes confidence. Hard-won confidence through doubt and failure is healthy; belief in self as a belief system is narcissism. Belief in self, as an antidote to belief in something outside of self, is our empty modern answer to stuffy old-world faith. It is death.

Still, believing in my own material, writing about faith, may be less hunger than hubris. The irony is not lost on me that I may be writing a book about faith without having much to draw upon. Faith is doubt; doubt is faith. I sometimes think that persnickety persistence is all the faithful ever get to recommend themselves.

Sorry—the mood passes, but I was in a negative frame of mind as my wife, daughter and I arrived in Prague. Prague should elicit excitement, but we had had a difficult drive from Innsbruck, Austria. Prague was wilting under intense heat, and we had received some troubling news from home. We strolled along the river, a heavy disconnect between the scenery and our response to it, between magic and mood. If God isn't, it's all wasted minutiae and disconnect. If God is, miracles happen every second and everywhere, but only for those who see. Walking along the Vltava River, we watched, but we did not see.

For the living, time can dull, mute or undo the feelings you thought unassailable for a dead loved one. I fundamentally believe that love is one and indivisible and, further, that this belief is the jackpot of miracles; that is, love cannot be undone or diminished by time. But the problem is, sustaining belief can be like holding a fistful of sand. Holding our most cherished and basic belief is our greatest challenge, and on this night I had no faith. I was supposed to write about Mom the next day, and I thought, *Not right now;*

*what would I say?* Separated by time and distance I felt like an astronaut who ventures out of his spaceship to look around and wonder at the universe, only to turn around and notice that the tether has been severed and the ship is far, and falling away.

Boats cruise the river through Prague on summer nights while happy people enjoy dinner, drinks and live music. The party atmosphere of this Saturday night was somewhat wilted by the heat, but the boats cruised along and the music played on. Mostly I didn't notice what was playing; mostly the music was festive but not very good.

I doubt that Acker Bilk is an icon in the Czech Republic. His brief moment in the musical world was over 50 years ago in America. My parents had a total of three albums in our home that we played on our little green record player. One was by David Whitfield, the first British singer to have a number-one single in Britain and the US at the same time with his hit "Cara Mia." The second was by Mario Lanza, whose impassioned "Mama Mia Che Vò Sapè?" made me think that he too was a bit of a nostalgia freak. The third was by Acker Bilk, and the title cut, "Stranger on the Shore," was one big hit that evokes memories of my parents. (The other iconic piece is Bing Crosby's "White Christmas," though I don't remember us ever owning the record, probably because we watched the movie on TV once a year, which was considered enough. Besides, with a collection of three albums, who needed a fourth?) Acker Bilk was briefly a popular clarinet player, whose beautiful but conventional or square kind of music was utterly swept away by the phenomenon of rock and roll.

But not on this night. We walked along the river in silence, in a state of inertia. Until I heard the music. First floating over the trees, origin unknown, then clearly from the river, but not in sight. There, on that boat, someone playing on a clarinet "Stranger on the Shore"—to us, no longer strangers on the shore, clear and perfect, straight to the heart. Acker Bilk lives again, and more importantly so do my parents, from far away time and place to here and now. I needed that connection, and tomorrow I will write about Mom.

———————

Mom did not stand out in a crowd—though with notable exception, when Dad was smitten by the stranger on the shore at the Standish dance hall in the late 1940s and declared to his buddy, "See that girl there? I'm going to marry her someday." She was attractive but shy, respectful, on the quiet side, especially when meeting strangers on the shore. Historical note: this was a time before assertiveness training, self-esteem workshops and expectations that all things should be made equal, whether or not people want them to be or can even agree what equal means. In 1946, my mom's reserve and respectful ways were considered positive qualities in a young woman.

Mom's formal education was limited to progressing from a one-room school in the farming community of Navan, Ontario, to graduating from a nearby high school. Dad always said that people from Navan (just outside Ottawa) didn't know if they were coming or going because the word was spelled the same backward as forward. Dad had about three jokes in his lifetime repertoire, so when he made one, it went directly into the archives of family mythology.

Mom was no towering intellect (thank God), but as time went on, we learned that she had a shockingly simple, accurate and revealing wisdom. Generally, what was revealed was the folly of our own presumptuous thinking. Basically everything she said, some of which was the butt of family derision for years, was right. She was understated, her understanding of the world not marred, compromised or distorted by flavour-of-the-month intellectual and ideological debris.

She was passionately content (not an oxymoron) and eternally grateful for her lot in life. Contentment such as my mother felt, seemingly so very dull, is only possible with the practice of gratitude, a dose of medicine taken twice daily for life. This practice was a key ingredient to her deep faith. But of course there are always countervailing forces to what is good and pure and simple in life.

In one of my graduate classes, an animated discussion arose from a group of women who decided that their life mission as evangelizing agents of social change would be to change women into their likeness. Older women were to be their target, for they were both oppressed and largely unaware of their oppression. Older unaware women needed to be made aware of their terminal systemic oppression by younger enlightened women. Only in self-awareness can older women be free, never mind that awareness was to be imposed. By midway through term I had not spoken in class. Still, on this occasion I asked for clarification. I said that my widowed mother, who had seven children and no career outside of the home, was content with her life, which in this life is not easily achieved. I asked if the consensus was that she too be made aware of her terminal oppression. The consensus was yes. Historical note: this was at a time before heightened political awareness of, and fidelity to, one's group identity, and as such anticipates where we have landed. In the reigning progressive paradigm, justice and social harmony of all peoples are to be achieved by slicing us down to our exterior components, with the internal existence of character no longer identified as existing at all.

My mom found this little tale amusing. She never presented much by way of demonstrative self-confidence, as is the nature of the truly humble, but an aspect of her understated nature was that she believed deeply in what she believed. She was a woman of quiet conviction; that is, she was one of those rare people who never question faith. Yes, I know, today such conviction is considered archaic closed-mindedness. But the point of this book is to argue that much of the very public ideological conviction of today may soon be regarded as closed-minded, predictable and terribly conventional thinking, for all its presence of originality, and as such liable to be remaindered to that quaint and annoying age of political groupthink.

My parents' generation didn't embrace diversity in the manner expected today. They were commonsensical rather than progressive, but since they never said much about other cultures or religions, it may well be that they were not much interested. Still, they did regard the civil rights movement of the 1960s as an achievement, the achievement being that external identity characteristics would no longer determine access to opportunity. They also knew that the achievement was really just a step in the right direction, and they didn't kid themselves about progress ending racial prejudice. In this way they grew more tolerant, but they were never going to celebrate multiculturalism (celebrations were reserved for religious observance). They, like their bewildered minority neighbours, reasoned that if difference is no longer *the* social determinant, why continuously draw attention to difference?

Most of what we publically discuss, celebrate or shout about today from our various soapboxes would have been regarded as simply too much information. This view, regarded by today's social justice warriors as deep-seated prejudice, was actually more in line with Martin Luther King's plea to judge a man or woman by the content of his or her character. And the content of character was not determined by how loud one virtue signalled allegiance to a cause. Not only did my parents not take issue with others' political views, they generally didn't even know the views of lifelong friends. Everyone knew that talking about politics or religion could lead to conflict, so they didn't do it. They were square conformists who adhered to social decorum and religious doctrine, but in their own quiet way they remained critical, independent thinkers to a degree alien to contemporary uncritical ideologues. They were not easily swayed; they were easily defeated in an argument. They had character, and today would be seen—if seen at all—as eccentric characters to be amused by or ignored.

My lament for my parents' generation is that in the mix of what should have been cast off or carried forward in the generational give and take that determines how we become who we are, we neglected to regard their wisdom for what it was. We abandoned wisdom, character and independent thinking, which runs counter to the generational bargain that defined every generation until our own. Without the context of the recent past, with the hubris and ecstasy of believing that only we at this time have it right, we created a nihilistic world of affluence and material comfort unprecedented in human history that seduces and cocoons but cannot hide the hopelessness and anxiety that has become our de facto common value.

My mother's belief system was conventional even by 1940s standards, but its successful practice and lifetime adherence are difficult and radically unconventional compared to today's appetite-driven absence of standards. It was not that Mom was incapable of seeing life's vicissitudes, contradictions and pain. She simply believed that Roman Catholicism is the answer, wholly, purely, unequivocally and lovingly, without which all is lost. Her belief system is completely out of step with the modern world, but to quote Dr. Phil, whom I've never actually watched on television, "How's that working for you?" There is nothing more fascinating or bewildering than the human justification system. Against all evidence, as measured in health and happiness in the modern world, it's not working for many of us. We are either in pain or heading for it, dead or dying, and no amount of prosperity or New Age distraction can change this elemental fact of life. There has to be something more than health foods, yoga, Lululemon, workouts and belief in self.

Though all her children loved her, Mom's core Catholic convictions did not get much respect. No matter; her faith was not subject to approval from anyone else. (Try pulling off singular belief in today's radically conventional world.) To her many Catholic friends and the priests she knew, my Aunt Isobell, and even her skeptical children, she was a constant, and as the past recedes and modernity continues its pervasive assault on individual thinking, her radical conventions become more and more a rarity. Funny how time turns things around.

Mom's resilience was both tested and taken for granted. None of her seven children remembers Mom ever losing it or even being particularly frustrated or stressed about anything. But her life was not easy. Seven kids— well, that number says it all. And her husband was an alcoholic, which cannot have been easy for her, though apart from acknowledging this she never complained. For her generation, complaining was a character failing; today it is regarded as a virtue.

Dad died at age 59, looking 89, from emphysema and drinking, leaving Mom with long years of widowhood. The men of his generation drank and smoked; the women of her generation lived long without husbands. My mom and her Irish Catholic widowed friends were fun-loving, hardworking and resilient as hell, without exception, and if I have just reinforced a stereotype, I have also told the truth, which is more important.

Here's another stereotype; women are far more resilient than men. I remember coming into Mom's house one typical evening when she had *the girls* over for six-hand euchre—and coincidentally, the average number of children among these gals was also six. The "girls over" was a euphemism for the fact that all their husbands were dead, all with generous contributions from the drink or smoke or, more likely than not, both. I grew up knowing all these women, the husbands they had buried, and their children, who comforted them or continued to give them grief. For some of them, the death of their husbands was supposed to be more than they could bear—their lifetime partners in all respects, romantic and adventurous even under the weight of having many children and economic hardships from single-income situations, which were then common. But whatever their private grief, they bounced back, got on with it, became and remained steadfast, and, in practicing gratitude with a stiff upper lip, became resilient. The Depression, the war, their slew of kids and the rigours of Catholicism prepared them, and the formula is not a mystery. They learned early on and had it reinforced throughout their lives that it is not about any one of us as individuals. And yet here they were, individuals, personality oozing out of every pore, having the time of their lives, never a moment without laughter, not much euchre going on. Yeah, not much mystery about how they got here, but a deep, unfathomable mystery about how they pulled a working, breathing stereotype into a formula for how to live life well.

On balance Mom and Dad had a good marriage, though it would be disingenuous to romanticize life with a man whose route to alcoholism was occasioned by his need to self-medicate for severe pain. Whatever her attachment to him was, she enjoyed her autonomous life that followed. Adult children tend to miss how much their parents enjoy their autonomy, and parents tend not to show it. Though the women of my graduate class would not have agreed, Mom lived and felt liberated to the extent she ever wanted. Perhaps more to the point, she knew that what matters in this life has less to do with liberation than it does with connection.

The simple fact is, my classmates and progressives of the modern world could not see, would not hear, women like my mom because of their devotion to family and refusal to refocus devotion onto self. They had not really wanted to liberate Mom; they had wanted to social engineer who she was and what she believed in—for her own good, of course.

––––––––––

In my parents' house, we had one and only one of what we had, and mostly we didn't have much. I don't remember ever being anxious about what we didn't have; I see people anxious today about all the things that they have. The problem is choice. We didn't have much then, my parents had much less, and today people, and kids in particular, live with the illusion and burden of endless choice. Young people are anxious about making choices, and for good reason. After all, who needs the responsibility of making a single bad choice when there are infinite good choices to be had? But the infinity list doesn't exist, and people are left with death by ambiguity.

Passionate contentment, my mom's anchor, spiritual and otherwise, comes from knowing that there are parameters and limitations to wants and desires. Contentment and fulfillment come from committing to, devotion to, loving someone and something personal, specific, not a vague, ever-changing idea of perfection. Wants and desires are ironically dulled by thinking that greater pleasure, greater fulfillment, is always just a choice away. There is no pleasure in endlessly wishing for more.

Adult children chide their parents for being so predictable, and then we are shocked when they do something outside of our narrow expectations. Just as we assumed that Mom was in for a lifetime of mourning Dad, she met a tall, dark, handsome stranger and fell in love. Jack was his name, and among the many widows in his circle he was in great demand. Not exactly the Wayne Gretsky of his generation, but demographics and longevity being what they were, he had the pick of the litter from among a very big litter. And he wanted Mom, but with one minor caveat. He wanted their new, grand life to commence with marriage, followed by removal to Florida, in the social mix of all the other snowbird retirees. The irony was not lost on us that Mom, for all her predictability and contentment, was on the precipice of the ideal to which she had never aspired, but it was hers for the taking.

Mom was conflicted. She loved her life in Ottawa and had never seen herself living her life away from her children and grandchildren. Not that she put it this way. She did not see herself as a martyr in any way, even though her life was characterized by sacrifice. As a devote Catholic, shacking up or fooling around was not an option, so it was either going to be marriage to Jack and a move to Florida or the status quo and a broken heart. And that of course is the problem of love and risk, and that of course is the challenge of contentment and devotion. She chose a broken heart, and Jack disappeared to the glorious south, where it is rumoured that his bachelor days lasted mere minutes.

Mom was shaken to the core but willed herself to recover, practiced gratitude, and basically got on with it again. We assumed that was the end of her romantic dalliances. In a manner of speaking, it was. She did surprise herself and arrive at a nice, workable accommodation, though a few notches down on the romantic scale. She was pursued again, this time by a friend of 40 or so years, who with his wife before she died had played cards and socialized as a couple with Mom and Dad in their large Irish Catholic circle.

Both Mom and Archie wanted companionship, but with a difference. Archie wanted a wife. Mom was not looking for a husband. She liked and admired Archie and depended on him for companionship but considered him not quite right as a serious romantic interest. Ever self-effacing, she kidded about what an unglamorous, square couple they were. And so we thought this most unromantic of relationships would soon end. Mom was never going to marry Archie, and she did not want to be unfair.

But the relationship did not end. They became very comfortable together, like an old married couple in some respects without having put in the years, and were actually quite fond of each other. Mom still kidded about them as a couple but knew she could have done worse, and besides, she was content. Together they stayed in the game, had a regular date for social occasions, and with intimacy and marriage off the table—though Archie persisted in this regard for a few years—they more or less continued happily until they died.

First Archie. In his mid-80s he was still with it, vibrant enough, able to pick Mom up and drive to church and the restaurant, keeping the creeping black shadow at bay, keeping on pace with a life still to live. Then the unthinkable: first one son, then another, died, and he started to slide. He kept up with Mom, because of Mom, but he was treading water, slowly sinking, trying, but with little fight left.

He tried to put it all back together, continued with habits, routines, the power of the mundane, but I suspect that the pallor of death started to pull at this will. We continued to get together, he and I playing euchre against Mom and Cara, my wife, after dinner. We always won, because Mom and Cara never paid attention. But on this night Archie hadn't much appetite, didn't joke, couldn't concentrate on his cards, though he tried to be a sport. He dismissed Mom's concern; he was tired, just tired. He usually drove, but I had offered to pick them up and drop them off that evening, and he hadn't objected. I dropped Mom off first.

As we continued to his apartment, he didn't say much, except we agreed that our hockey team, the Ottawa Senators, couldn't score. He got out of the car with difficulty. There was a long stretch of sidewalk from the car to his apartment entranceway. It was not so long the last time I had been there. He walked deliberately and with effort, and I, waiting and watching, not driving away, just waiting, tried to fight off the feeling that it would be the last time I saw Archie, knowing it would be the last time we acknowledged that the Ottawa Senators could not score a goal when it really mattered. (It mattered; they were knocked out of the playoffs first round, four straight.)

Mom felt Archie's death far more than Jack's departure. It wasn't just loyalty, though she had plenty of that. Whatever she felt, it was more than romance, minus the glitter. It's funny what can evolve between two people whose most enduring quality is endurance.

I remember kidding Mom once, asking who was her favourite kid, this to a woman who never showed favouritism her entire life, with six other progeny waiting to take exception. But Mom could surprise. Without hesitation, and without a hint of irony, she said, "Whoever is around for me." I should not have been surprised. She had responded honestly, as a human being, and not as a predictable keep-the-peace mother. *Good for her*, I thought, still half waiting for her to smile and tell me she was kidding, but no, she was not kidding.

During these last years, Mom's Parkinson's disease had been getting worse. It is not central to her story, because she chose that it not become central to her life. That takes courage to attempt and guts to pull off. Both of my parents were slight, wee things. My dad once famously said about obesity, with characteristic directness, "People are fat because they eat too much." My mom probably never weighed more than 115 pounds, except when pregnant, and struggled to keep weight on as her disease "progressed," surely a most ironic connotation to a popular modern word.

As she withered and consumed daily doses of Ensure to ensure she didn't wither further still, her mind held clear, conversational inattention to euchre notwithstanding. Then, almost imperceptibly, her mind became occasionally muddled, though coated in a disarming sweetness, and even as we denied it, this was the beginning of the undoing of self that is the tragic completion of dementia.

Mom died on August 6, 2000, a few weeks shy of the twentieth anniversary of Dad's death. It is both a heavy truism and a cliché to say that it is difficult to become an orphan at any age. As well, losing your pillar of faith when you have little to draw from is not an inspiring moment. Worse, her death seemed to just pass, and grief requires expression. We don't much express what people mean or have meant to us. We often intend to, when the time is right, but it is very rarely right, and the attempt often falls short or is misunderstood.

Then one day in December, I found a photograph of Mom when she was perhaps four or five years old, say from 1928. I had seen the photo before but had not really looked at it. This day I rose above the crush of passivity and distraction and finally saw the photo for what it was. I thought, *This is unfathomable and, unlike my mother's body, cannot be buried*. This whimsical pose of a four-year-old, not so much posing as being, was very uncharacteristic of the day, and I've never seen another photo like it. The photo is of course the cover photo for this book, and it speaks of faith, for reasons someone will have to explain to me. Good luck.

Without thinking about it too much, which is to say that overthinking is the death of much that ought to get done, I wrote, at a single sitting, a piece about Mom, trying to work out the essence of who she was and what she meant to me, to us, to other people—without getting close, but with some closure nonetheless. To use the worst possible cliché about writing, the piece seemed to write itself. I would refine or wax poetic about this concept if I could without obscuring the bottom line, which is plainly stated in the cliché that stands. I sent it to the *Ottawa Citizen*, and to my everlasting surprise they published it as a feature piece on Christmas Eve 2000.

I have no doubt that "Enie" being published is Mom's parting gift to me. For me—for us—there was, is, no greater nostalgic memory than Christmas Eve. I've since written a young adult novel that takes place on Christmas Eve (*A Christmas Dragon*), another pathetic grasp at the past. Though the symbols and rituals vary, everyone's sense of home comes with a series of images that are a distillation of how we ideally connect at our best, as our higher self, with those we love.

Christmas Eve was people gathering, getting ready for midnight mass, mystery lighting up the ordinary for everyone, and holy anticipation, the closest thing to home, the one that matters, on this earth and in this life. And we watched Bing Crosby, who looked and spoke just like my dad, along with Danny Kaye in *White Christmas*, a couple of zany bachelors with nowhere to go for Christmas, but with big hearts and a couple of go-to gals, who together organize the biggest, cheesiest creation of coming home in the history of film, gathering the general's old division at the inn on Christmas Eve, one big happy family, all singing "White Christmas," just as they did at the beginning of the film, when they couldn't go home. Completion, redemption, cornball schmaltz. Next cliché: they don't make movies like that anymore.

---

"Too many people nowadays forget their mothers. But not the Irish. No not us. We never forget our mothers." Frank McCourt, *'Tis: A Memoir*

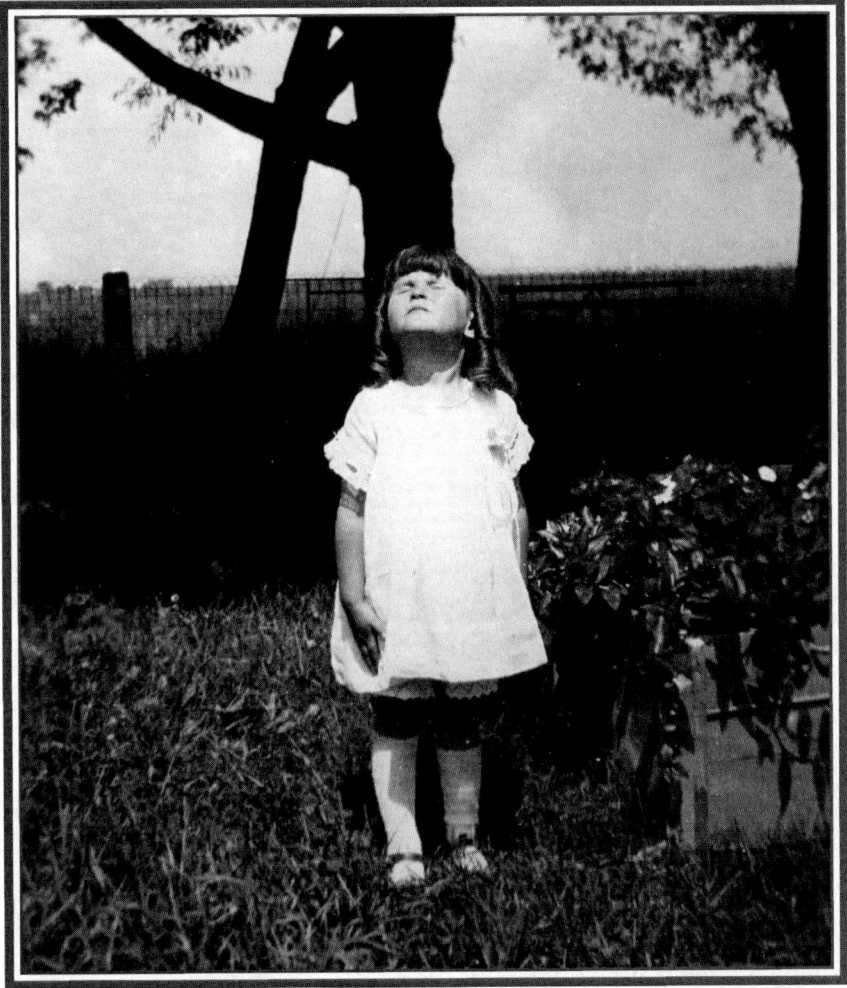

## ENIE

There is a photo of my mother. She is four or five years old. Posing in her Sunday best, hands straight to her side, hair in perfect ringlets. At the moment the camera clicks her face is raised, eyes closed, feeling the warmth of the sunshine through crisscrossing branches. A child of God.

This photo is framed in my mind beside the picture of Mom at the nursing home. Seventy-six years old. She sits in her wheelchair, posing for no one, clothes, posture, and hair no longer a concern. At the moment I round the corner from the elevator, her face is lowered, eyes open, not seeing or looking at anyone or anything.

"Hi, Mom."

She looks up and smiles, stripping away about 70 years. I lean down to hear her voice, barely audible because of Parkinson's disease.

"Oh, Larry, you'd better tell people."

"Tell them what, Mom?"

"That your father's dead."

Deep breath. "He's been dead these 20 years, Mom."

Pause. "Oh, yes, of course." She laughs. "You ever notice that I sometimes talk a lot of nonsense?"

"That's okay, Mom."

Visiting my mother in the nursing home always felt like walking past a homeless person. Eyes averted, barely noticing, taking in every detail. Guilt and shame served with a generous portion of fear.

Seems like just the other day, visiting Mom felt much different. A sprawling bungalow in west-end Ottawa was the vortex of family gatherings for our large Irish Catholic family. Though there were three from the brood with their own houses in the same city, Mom's home was where we gathered. This house is where we had grown up, where we had struck out from into the world, with some of us returning for temporary occupations as careers and marriages sorted themselves out. Always a home-cooked meal and a familiar room through the revolving doors straight down the corridor to home. And Mom. She might not approve of the reason for the return of a prodigal son or daughter, but she didn't judge, and she liked the company.

For Mom, there were no revolving doors. For over 30 years she lived in her home, and she never, ever, wanted to give it up. People said, "All that space, all that work. Time to sell. Well, at least think about it." Think about what? From a family of seven kids, she married an Irishman from a family of seven kids and had seven kids of her own. Lived in this and one other house. Where do you go from here, and who would you be, anyway?

And she wanted a house for us to come back home to. We visited regularly, but even a weekly visit left a lot of time for her to be alone. Often visits were as much about catching up with siblings as they were about seeing Mom. She didn't mind; it was just good to see the house filled again. Sunday after dinner we dispersed to our lives again, and Mom was left alone in the house. Twenty years a widow, seven mobile kids, fourteen grandchildren usually in distant locations, and Mom settled back into her house, the most constant and sustaining relationship in her life.

What did Mom and her home talk about all those years?

"It's about time you got home, Irene. I've been awake half the night worrying."

"Now, you're getting a new roof before winter, and that's it. Otherwise you'll catch a death of a cold."

"Better put rugs down on that floor, Irene. Hardwood floors are too slippery for you now, in your condition."

"I can't imagine praying at night without seeing the moon and stars outside our window."

Then, as the last of the temporary occupations ended, Parkinson's extended its insidious, unforgiving grip around Mom's body and mind. A series of caregivers, all caring but not family, could only delay the inevitable. A decision was made for Mom's safety. Home would now be a nursing home. As the Irish poet W. B. Yeats wrote, "Things fall apart; the centre cannot hold; mere anarchy is loosed upon the world."

At a conference last summer in Victoria, a chipper presenter said that centenarians generally agree upon four ingredients as being essential to their longevity. First, members of the world's most exclusive club tend not to be devastated by loss. Mom was a great example of Irish stoicism, having grown up on a farm outside Ottawa during the Depression. But she must have known. For weeks leading up to the decision, she made offhand remarks about being spoiled by all the space in the house, as if it had recently expanded. She would mention the fact that most people in the world, and lord only knows in Third World countries families of 35, haven't as much space as she hoarded for herself. Mom never complained about the loss of her house, and she refused to feel sorry for herself. She never let herself wish that all could be as it once was, as she folded her life into a small suitcase. We nostalgic baby boomers are doomed to die a thousand deaths as we cling to a world we take for granted and are devastated again and again.

Second, thriving 100-year-olds maintain a positive attitude toward life. Which becomes more amazing the longer you live. Those who are 100 years old today have lived to witness the century of greatest change, war and carnage in recorded history. But most importantly, they have outlived most human beings they have ever loved.

Such epiphanies occur from time to time. For example, there is a tombstone just across the river in a Catholic graveyard in Quebec. Chiselled on stone are the names of twins who died in the year 1923. Their father's name is recorded below the twins, him having died ten years later. The mother of the twins, and wife of the father, is recorded below her husband's name. The year of her birth is 1900, but the date of her death is blank. Seventy-seven years after the death of her children and sixty-seven years after the death of her husband, she lives and breathes and remembers from the new millennium.

But where is she, and what does she think? Does she grace the halls of my mother's nursing home, sitting, remembering? How often does she think about her dead twins, whose passing likely threatened to pull her to the grave? Or are the events of her life, once fantastical or mundane, all quieted now, the seeds of self withered and displaced by the preoccupations of bowel and bladder care? How many lives has she lived, born before air travel, insulin and email?

If she sits in my mother's nursing home, her final years will likely be filled with time to reflect on her many lives. There are many activities at the nursing home but nothing much to do. Most of the occupants live in wheelchairs clumped in corridors or sunrooms or peeking out of shared bedrooms.

The third characteristic of the 100-plus club is that although members are old and have done much, they are not finished yet. There were no intimate late-night whisperings between Mom and her nursing home. There was nothing to worry about at the nursing home. Twenty-four hours every day, staff were there to be asked all the questions and provide all the answers. The nursing home was well-maintained. It neither gave nor received care. Work and fretting over meaningless details, profound human struggles, seem to be the reasons we get up in the morning. There are no aspiring "Freedom 55ers" among the 100-year-old-club members.

Old, worn-out residents with nothing left to do watch you come and go to what you have yet to do. For all their inglorious stares, they were vital once, with places to go, people to see. They had thriving careers, complicated marriages, and people who counted on them—some made love under a full moon, stopped by regularly for a cup of tea and a smoke, were filled with jealousy, thought that the goddam job would never end, fell foolishly in love, worked passionately in the garden, waited up desperately for news of a wayward teenager, laughed uncontrollably about nothing, thought nothing about laughing uncontrollably, felt desirable and could inflict it on a crowd just by walking in a room, feared never finding someone to love, escaped poverty for the war, hated high school, despaired of acne, were inspired by a grade-school teacher, were tenderly picked up and passed around by just about every adult, were framed in many photos, just like my mom, and still know, deep down inside, that they are children of God, even if the world has forgotten.

In the nursing home my mother shared a room with a woman who was 105 years old. They never met. My mother and her roommate spent most of their time in the corridor, crowded between snoozing residents. They likely passed each other in the corridor again and again but never knew it. Perhaps it didn't matter. Mom's roommate was never cognizant, and Mom became less and less so.

"Hi, Mom. How're you feeling today?"

"Larry, is that you? I thought you'd died."

"Died? But I'm here, Mom. I just went away for a week to a conference in Victoria. How is it that you think I died?"

A thoughtful look. "Guess it doesn't make much sense."

"You don't seem to have been too upset about me dying." Said with real hurt.

A childlike smile. "No, I don't, do I?" Now a giggle. "Guess I got over it pretty quick 'cause I knew you'd be coming today."

"So Mom, how're you feeling today?"

"Pretty good. How 'bout you? You look terrible, like you've been running too much again."

During such moments, my mind tended toward the recent past. It was only six years ago when we had a big surprise party for Mom's 70th birthday. All her friends came, many of whom had known her for almost 50 years. Her sister, her brother and his wife dropped in from California. Mom drove her own car then, went to church every day and to the hairdresser every week, even travelled with her sister to Ireland. She had a gentleman friend. Though a decade older, he took care of Mom with a sense of chivalry typical of his generation. They went to restaurants together and had common friends, similar interests. Mom and Archie were partners, not in the multitasked, ambiguous sense of the word today. Archie was her no-nonsense card partner, who demanded that you pay attention to the game. Which Mom often didn't do, much to Archie's chagrin. But as long as he kept her mind challenged by the intricacies of euchre and the need to be ready at a certain time, she thrived. She had things to do; she wasn't finished, yet.

During this time Parkinson's had been creeping into her life slowly. Slow enough for us to kid ourselves that with new drugs and determination, things could go on pretty much the same way forever. She deteriorated, but with the help of a live-in caregiver, the house seemed normal again. At least until Archie died. Archie had had two sons die in the previous 18 months, became tired, and probably decided that he'd had enough, even if it meant giving up euchre.

Mom often said that she missed the old guy, but not much more. No longer would she have the arm of a gentleman to steady her through the shopping mall or down the corridor to her church pew. Her escort from now on would be a caregiver of her own gender. Her sons and daughters hardly qualified and were never available for the daily routine. Still, she continued making her daily pilgrimage to church and to the shopping mall. Once joy ended, Mom persevered stubbornly. She might never come close to joining the centenarian club, but she was determined to navigate through life without complaining. And with a touch of humour. One day while shopping a man in a great hurry brushed by Mom. After he mumbled an apology over his shoulder, Mom whispered to her caregiver.

"It's so nice just to feel the touch of a man again."

"Irene! I can't believe you just said that!"

"Well, I'm not dead yet!"

Mom's makeshift euchre parties after Archie's death were not pleasant. She hallucinated frequently, seeing a room full of people in her house that she didn't know. Later, in the nursing home, she hallucinated constantly, never quite used to the rooms full of people crowded up and down the corridors of "home." She was walking then, but the anchor of her life, her home, had been lost at sea. One day Mom, fragile and precarious on her feet, bumped into a wheelchair and fell. She had fractured her left hip.

The fourth and final feature of the 100-year-old club is that members stay physically active throughout their lives. Mom mended slowly from the surgery on her hip. Pins held the frail bones together, and after a stint in hospital, she looked and acted ancient. For a while, with some assistance and much pain, she wobbled down the crowded corridor, but for most of the day she sat alone in her wheelchair without moving or speaking. Whenever I visited Mom during the next two months, my one wish was that she would not be in the same spot as I'd left her. Unreasonably, I feared that she stayed in the same spot in the corridor, sitting perfectly still until I returned to the home. Mom was never physically active in her life, at least not in the extreme way that people define it today. But she had never been forcibly inactive, and before she could get used to the new restrictions, she fell again. Mom was not what you would call trendy, but after two falls, she lay in a hospital bed, tragically hip.

Another x-ray was taken after her second fall. There was no apparent damage, and she was returned to the nursing home without treatment. Three days later she was still in pain, and a doctor noticed that Mom's foot splayed outward, indicative of a hip fracture. The subsequent x-ray confirmed that her right hip was broken, but since more than 24 hours had passed, the opportunity for pinning the bones together under a local anesthetic had passed. She now required a full general anesthetic and partial hip replacement. Invasive surgery coupled with a full anesthetic for an elderly person in the advanced stages of Parkinson's is quite simply too much. All personal control and vestiges of dignity melted way. Nothing left to do.

The neurologist said that it was to be expected, a natural thing. Mom got pneumonia, as medically predicted. Prognosis fatal, chances of recovery nil. At first we gathered by her bedside, just like Sunday dinner at Mom's. Then we took shifts so that Mom would not be alone.

The current thinking in palliative care is to take the patient off intravenous treatment and wait. Without fluids and food Mom was expected to die peacefully within 3 days. She persevered for 16 days. We think that she was comfortable during this time and that she died peacefully, but we were all wrecks. I guess nobody told her that she could go. "The blood-dimmed tide is loosed, and everywhere the ceremony of innocence is drowned" (W. B. Yeats).

There are moments of understanding that even a positive attitude cannot will away. Whenever Mom talked about Parkinson's disease it was within the context of what she was doing about it. Before the nursing home, there were appointments to go to, drugs to take, hot new experimental ones to try, all swallowed with a sunny disposition. Until one day last winter when Mom said simply, "I've come to the realization of just what this disease means."

"Why do you say that, Mom?"

"Because I can't kid myself anymore."

"Do you not feel well today, Mom?" Sinking feeling.

"Not too bad today. Not too bad at all."

"Maybe you're just tired, Mom. Have you had your nap today?"

"I lay down for a while before you kids came over, but I couldn't sleep."

"Why don't you try to sleep now, Mom? There's still time before dinner."

"No, don't think I will. I want to watch the young ones play."

"Are you sure, Mom?"

Mom looked death in the face without blinking, as I looked away. Again and again. Every time I left the house after that, there was a moment at the door. Mom would look me directly in the eye. There were no words, no tears, just the smile and wonder of a four-year-old, searching. I would look at Mom for a few seconds, and then something of foreshadowing, exposure, seared me raw. I felt angst, guilt, impatience in the face of undistilled love. A child of God and a sinner.

"Enie, for the love of gawd would ya give a look here."

"Daddy, I can still see the branches moving even with my eyes closed."

"Lawdy girl, I haven't got all day. The O'Tooles are waiting to eat."

"Can I stand here for a few more minutes, Daddy?"

"I'll tell ya what ya can do. Ya can stand straight and look at the camera 'afore we starve, dammit."

"Daddy, the sun feels like it's burning my face, but it feels yummy."

"Christ sakes, that'll do."

"Can I make a wish, Daddy?"

———————

I mourn Mom's death. But I also lament the passing of my parents' generation, of their people. Their people, once so familiar, seem strange and distant now. Irish Catholic—didn't emote much; never complained; and for all their repression and our freedom, they had a hell of a lot more fun than we ever did; strong on religion, family and community but mighty clannish about those outside of it; tended to stay in one place, maybe 'cause of all the kids, but had lifelong friends, whatever the reason; treated us kids as a herd but seemed to know each of us enough to love each of us; and weren't big on the individual thing, so we lacked for lessons but were spared neurotic expectations.

In many ways my parents were rooted in the nineteenth century more than the twentieth. I remember family picnics with other large Irish Catholic families—a hundred or so folks, violins, square dancing, a wee bit of drinkin', lots of talk, horseshoes, cards, singing, a mass of cousins (what relation, we never knew) running wild, with the veil of discipline and order down for the day. Hours, days, years spent in church, with only the smell of incense a relief from boredom. Weekday mornings clumping through snow to seven o'clock mass at the cloistered convent, terrified. Terror as a glass of milk was spilt in front of my father's plate at the dinner table, again. My mother's forgiving word to save the day, again. Watching my parents watching Wayne and Shuster and laughing, and laughing at my parents laughing, and wishing that they laughed more often. Christmas Eve midnight mass and then Chinese food takeout before opening a few scant presents. How in the world did we ever get so excited about so little?

Because for all the faults, and there were many, the package was nearly complete. And even for what was missing, it was a place that we could return to. Parents, a family, a community, shared values, palpable and real, to be feared and respected, abandoned but never totally forsaken. Home.

We don't have or know these things today. We are free instead. We have endless choice, but this tidal wave of individual freedom has cost us. Death by ambiguity. The ennui of self.

The image of my mother standing, searching, serenely pleading at the front door to her house will always pull me back into a bittersweet past. Nostalgic drivel, I suppose. But there may be something to that lost world. Something to resurrect. Something to pass on to my kids. Something important. I'm not sure if we can find our way back home again. But the way is not likely screaming toward the promise of a bigger, more powerful and bullish exponential future. I'll have to try to figure out what it was she was thinking about, searching for, that last day.

There is a photo of my mother.

"Ask yourself whether you are happy, and you cease to be so."

JOHN STUART MILL

# CHAPTER TWO
## WEEPING AND WILLOWS

I HAVE AN IMPRESSION OF MY DAD THAT HAUNTS ME: SELF-LOATHING. HE WAS always mad about something—he was busy, work was tough, there were too many kids, who the hell spilt that glass of milk, again. This is not a Daddy dearest diatribe, quite the reverse actually. He was decent, did his best under duress, always duress. I loved him, and many years after his death I feel his presence eerily, comfortingly and strangely. Strangely because he was a distant father, whose distance has narrowed by these many years of death, though we have a way to go. He simply could not articulate what I've come to know of him. He never made excuses, never made a case for himself, died resigned to being misunderstood, I guess. Our obligation to the dead is that they not live in our minds as misunderstood as they lived their lives. I think one of our primary needs in life and in death, not given proper due in psychology or just plain human understanding, is our need to be understood, our fear of being misunderstood. We owe the dead understanding even after death, especially after death. Rest in peace has meaning.

We never doubted that Dad loved us; we just didn't know if he liked us. Dad was difficult and, I fear, lost faith in himself. He was a good and principled man who judged himself a failure. He failed to live up to his own principles, for which there would be no forgiveness. He was not the man he had planned to be. It would have helped him to see himself as others saw him; it would have helped for him to see himself as we came to see him.

Dad's counsel was much sought after by his many friends and siblings. He would sit quietly listening to someone's problem or concern or need to vent, rarely speaking even to ask a question or offer a word, just to say "I'm still here." Sometimes, when not smoking, he would chew on the ends of his glasses, which gave the impression of intense concentration. When the petitioner was done, he would offer a word or two of assessment, according to what he actually thought, without consideration of what was expected of him. People respected him for giving them the real deal, rather than bland validation or, in Irish terms, a bunch of malarkey. At the time he was just quiet; now he'd be an exemplar of listening skills. But he was not a modern man. His values and take on the world was nineteenth century Irish Catholic, Ottawa Valley, uncompromising, steadfast, and for all his fidelity to the past, he didn't have an ounce of nostalgia, that we knew of. His children did not seek his advice, which pained him. Dad never did get the *me* generation. I've often sought his advice in the years since his death. He listens, but he still doesn't say much.

Dad might have given himself a break if he had been able to feel any sympathy for himself. His was a life that certainly qualified as having been hard. He had addictions and lived in constant pain, and raising seven kids on one salary could not have been easy. Hard to say how tough, since nobody tries to support a large family on one salary any more. Without a thought for his lot in life, he would have agreed with Scott Peck's opening line in *The Road Less Travelled*, "Life is difficult."

We all lose everything, after all. Some die tragically young; others live to a great old age, losing things by increment, which, Chinese water torture as it is, is apparently the good news. Loss is the fundamental reality of life, and life's lessons of loss may just be the point of it. About personal loss in life, Dad always had one stock line, a bit facetious, mostly deflection, lest anyone think to offer sympathy where none was needed: "It's better than the alternative." I never believed it for a second.

I believe that Dad was one of those rare human beings who look death squarely in the eye and stoically accept the inevitable without existentialist angst. As the lurking beast of the inevitable cast its final shadow over his emaciated form, I think he felt some relief that the alternative had arrived. He left without making a fuss.

Which is not to say that Dad was unhappy. An analysis of personal happiness never entered into it. It may be hard for people of a certain age to understand that the question of happiness was completely alien to previous generations, only rearing its self-indulgent head on the heels of the now boomer, then me, generation, beginning in the early 1960s, progressing from the self-esteem movement of the 1990s into the present happiness-obsessed and mentally fragile bright new age. Ironically and paradoxically, it seems that the people who get closest to being happy (whatever that is) are not overly concerned with it. Happiness is not a personal goal, just a happy by-product of a life well, and contentedly, lived. Dad was not unhappy with his lot in life and felt a version of gratitude, expressed in his "it's better than the alternative" line. Between pain and obligation and the world of scarcity that characterized both the Depression and wartime, Dad would have regarded a discussion about happiness as irrelevant to the human condition and, most of all, to his own situation.

Which is not to say that Dad and Mom didn't have fun. Funny thing is, we kids all thought Dad and Mom were so square—so many archaic rules, Catholic guilt, so little in touch with the liberating new fads in music and style and thinking. But we all have to admit now that they partied harder, had more friends and more real fun, that is, deliberate and unencumbered fun, than we seven sibs ever have, or ever will. Every week they went to card parties or dances or got together with couples, for laughs, talk, food and drink; no electronic devices, political or religious debates, or discussion about causes and social justice. They had fun every time out, in a way we could never achieve, even if we had their number of close friends. I guess it pays to be square.

And there were times—not many, but I can remember getting a glimpse of Dad having fun, not old before his time, as an old man nearly broken, but as a fun-loving kid. One occasion was on Victoria Day, after the fireworks, maybe a few firecrackers and a burning schoolhouse, darkness setting in, a crush of crazed kids, and bedtime a remote possibility. Dad uncharacteristically and spontaneously joins in the ball game, doesn't move too easily but has natural coordination and ball sense, and most of all he is laughing, really laughing, like life doesn't hurt and this moment could go on forever. And for me, on rare occasions, it does. He, in those clips, are among my best memories of home.

We can revisit nostalgic moments whenever we want. Bittersweet for sure, but as for being in the past, I'm not so sure. I'm not convinced the past is past, and I do think nostalgia lives on for a reason. I don't think we are supposed to forget, to reason away the heritage of our home. Not the one we have a mortgage on—that's a house—but your home, the place from which you came, with trailing clouds of glory, and to which you will return, with less glory perhaps but maybe to something and someone familiar and loved, always just out of grasp in life, but with the promise of being whole and complete, without end.

Mom and Dad were lucky sevens, each from families of seven children, and together they had seven rotten kids. Dad was the fifth of seven, a middle child but the de facto eldest of the family by virtue of being responsible, to a fault. He was born in 1921 and was shaped by the Depression—scarcity on steroids—and the Second World War—the best and the worst of times, better than worst for most. At the expense of offending anybody with sweeping generalizations, they were frugal and hardworking, enjoyed simple pleasures, and believed in family, country and God. You know, those thing that are no longer relevant. At the expense of offending anybody, they were all like this.

Oh yeah, and worse, everyone outside of Quebec agreed that Canada needed to support Britain, and Britain needed to stand up to Hitler. The people in Canada knew this before Prime Minister Mackenzie King; the people of Britain knew this before Neville Chamberlain. For many people who had scratched and clawed their way through the Depression, "peace in our time" was understood as capitulation, and enlisting actually meant having more fun and food than they were used to. Combine the reality of the times with commitment to the common cause phenomenon—once assumed, now utterly lost—and you have a generation unrecognizable to the one that exploded in its wake.

As a teenager in the 1930s, Dad exited his centre townhouse by 3 a.m. under the stars and walked the streets of Ottawa to begin his horse-drawn milk run. At the end of the week he gave his mother his money, all of it, and received back cigarette money, and that was it. Ottawa is a cold, desolate place in winter darkness, especially when lugging milk bottles until dawn. With high school following the morning milk run, it was a very long day, even before factoring in homework and other chores. So when the war broke out, my dad, all 125 pounds of him, enlisted on September 25, 1939, without hesitation or moral ambiguity, and likely without reflecting on his pre-dawn drudgery with regret.

Which is not to say that September 1939 was the demarcation between a life of hardship and a life of liberation. Life in the armed forces during war was not easy, just easier for many than what their life had been before the war. Life during the Depression, hardship notwithstanding, was not without having standards. During his very limited time off before the war, Dad hung with "the gang" at Gladstone Park. This was a rough part of town in the 1930s, though the gang never thought of their world as such.

So what standards did these kids adhere to? The following article was published in the *National Post* in February 2010 and is a tribute to my dad and his gang.

## LAMENT FOR STYLE IN A CARTOON AGE

"Style is the man himself." Georges de Buffon (1707–1788)

There is a photo of my father, age 17, taken in 1938, posing with "the gang" at Gladstone Park in Ottawa. "The gang" designation captioning the photo in my father's navy album was a term of endearment, unlike the sinister connotation of today. These friends did not look like gang members, even by the standards of the 1930s, since they seem to be enjoying each other's company too much to look tough. Actually they all look like a million bucks, even before inflation, and more now than ever in consideration of the entropy that has characterized style since that time.

My father is the guy in the bottom right-hand side with the severe expression, wearing the stylish fedora. Notice that every member of the gang is wearing a shirt, tie and suit, some with hats, others not, each according to his particular sense of style. I have other pictures to prove that this was not just a one-time photo op. These guys regularly dressed with style to show who they were and, more importantly, what they were intending to become.

What one could become in a tough Ottawa neighbourhood during the poverty and unemployment of the Depression was highly questionable. And yet these guys convey a sense of optimism, almost a swagger of possibility. Or maybe these tough and resilient Depression era graduates were just determined and dressed to play the part.

It was entirely likely that these stylish young men only had one suit, and upon close inspection, it probably was a bit tattered. For the sake of clothing longevity, they expressed their self-reliance by pressing, sewing and stitching their own shirts and suits. They had the brains and self-respect to do the best with what they had and may have been willing to sacrifice a meal or ten to get what they were wearing. What mattered most was this—the hunger to be someone was literally more important than the gnawing at the pit in their stomach. The hunger to be made the man.

So what was the connection between style and aspiration? In a world small on wealth and opportunity and big on self-reliance and shared values, one came to regard style as substance. Just because you didn't have much money didn't mean you had to act or dress poor, since money was not the thing that built character anyway. So style, the putting together of a considered and timeless exterior to show what you were made of, was serious business. If big dreams didn't pan out or were slow in coming, a fella still had to make a show, just in case that girl he'd been waiting for should stroll on by. If the job opportunity or the girl did show up and you were dressed like a chump, you might never get a second chance.

Regrettably, I don't know who any of the other members of the gang were. I only know that they had at least two things in common that marked their generation: a sense of style and poverty. Today, we live in the most affluent time and place in the history of the world. The deprivations of the Depression are mostly forgotten and would not be understood by people today even if presented with the facts. Indulgent baby boomer parents have over-indulged their children with inflated notions of self, and entitlement is the natural, if regrettable, result. Entitlement—otherwise known as expectations without responsibility or gratitude—is a terrible legacy because it robs a young person of curiosity about the world and a burning ambition to do something in it, the stuff palpably reflected in my dad's photo.

The consequence of this seismic shift are perfectly reflected everywhere today in the expression of style. If the world is coming to you and for you, why make any effort to fit oneself into it? Why borrow a style when you are free, totally free, to express yourself in any way you please? Of course the problem of complete freedom directed at none other than self is that it can never be satisfied. Non-conforming individuals have necessarily sacrificed style for attitude. Thus, stylistically, people today feel compelled to continuously up the ante, from out there to extreme. Small wonder then that clothing has morphed from casual to grunge upon grunge, with the potential for a pants' waistline to be literally below the crotch. Body piercing has gone from discrete pinpricks to large gaping holes or, depending on one's sense of style, the potential for mutilation of any and all body parts.

Still, it may be the cartoon world of tattoos that best exemplifies the end of style. Scary snakes, spiderwebs and barbed wire, the spectrum of Disney characters, profound oriental symbols, menacing Harley Davidsons, and an array of Celtic borders all speak to a crude need to express who or what an individual intends to be known as for all time. Apparently, irony is no longer in style. Norman Rockwell captured the illusion of living for the moment in his famous tattoo-parlour painting. In it, a tattoo artist (if ever there was an oxymoron) strokes off yet another sweetheart's name in anticipation of a new name to be branded on the arm of a young man still not accepting the inevitability of change.

One cannot help but wonder if in the future a whole generation will be seeking expensive treatments to rid themselves of an ill-advised fad that keeps them frozen in another time. I don't think tattoos quite meet the romantic sensibility expressed in John Keats' "Ode on a Grecian Urn" wherein the constancy of love is reinforced by the never-changing image painted on the urn. Certainly if I'm being hard on young people today it is not because I hold my era, the 1970s, as a time of high style. It was hideous. Still, we did not commit to wearing bellbottoms and long hair for life when we thought those were the *in* thing.

It is fascinating to me that 70 years after the fact, the Depression era gang still exude a classy sense of style. My dad and his chums looked great a year later upon entering the service, throughout the war, during the post-war era, and certainly into the 1950s. Interestingly, it was in the 1960s, with emerging emphasis on the individual, that style, with any discernible sense of class, slipped away. When John F. Kennedy made his famous 1963 plea to Americans—"ask not what your country can do for you, rather ask what you can do for your country"—the world had already tilted away from such old-world sentiments. My dad always maintained some of his 1930s style, but even he could not resist the entropy of style throughout the 1970s into the 1980s (try finding a 1930s fedora like he's wearing in the photo today).

Style isn't about money. Style isn't about me, myself and only my expression of the world. If my dad's photo and others like it teach us anything, it is that style is a subtle and respectful refinement of self within a limited range of possibility. It defines not so much who we are—for that takes time, depth and relationships to determine—but rather what our place is in the world, either held or aspired to. Style does not say the world is about me, but rather says I am interested in and about the world so let me come in and make both a statement and a contribution. Style may be the man himself, as our friend George de Buffon says, but it is not about the man. The razor sharp distinction between the self and one's style is precisely everything.

———

As both a nostalgic and sentimental fool, I have come to be the holder of our family albums, mostly of my parents' generation and of us as kids in a series of photos in familiar youngest-to-oldest lineups. It is only in having a record of us when we are young that our kids can half believe that we ever were.

My favourite and most cherished possession is my dad's navy album. The photos, neatly laid out and labelled with superb cursive writing, comprise an important historical document, though to me it is a portal into a world we would never have guessed existed if left to Dad's storytelling. My dad was part of the Canadian navy convoy crossing the Atlantic Ocean to protect against German U-boats destroying the merchant ships bound for supply-starved Britain. Though mostly he is taking the photos, occasionally there he is, a muscular lad of 160 pounds, with an additional 30 or so post-Depression pounds of muscle, no doubt the result of distance from the 3 a.m. milk run and the introduction of three square meals into the equation.

Young Len stands on deck with his mates, flexing his newly acquired muscles, or on shore, taking in the sights with a couple of sailors at the hub of the Canadian navy in Halifax. There are also a couple of poignant photos of Dad with his close friends, having their portrait taken together in a studio. In a couple of frames, both in the studio and in taking in the sights, Dad is hanging with his portly friend Happy, and there is no denying his look, that one we never saw on him growing up, in photo after glorious black and white photo. He is not only with Happy; Dad is happy. The young man we never knew.

The young carefree man we never knew was once an adventurer. Being carefree or seeking adventure were not qualities that we thought Dad ever cared about, let alone tried to be. The careworn Dad we knew would not walk a single block to get cigarettes when a car could easily make the journey. Dad didn't do things unless there was a good reason. Sailor Dad the adventurer apparently used to love to be up on deck by himself during a storm to see and feel the fury of wind, rain and ocean swirl.

But as all sailors know, the ocean is an indifferent lover. During one raging storm on the Bay of Fundy, where ocean tides are highest in the world, Dad's lover threw him unceremoniously backward into the guardrail. In that instant, ocean and metal teamed up against adventure and human spine with predictable results. Dad's back was broken, and almost 80 years later it is no stretch to say that on that day his spirit was broken, too.

Dad was taken to the Montreal Neurological Institute and operated on by a renowned surgeon, Dr. Wilder Penfield. He needed multiple spinal fusions for broken vertebrae, a form of surgery then still in its infancy and rather barbaric. After several surgeries, Dr. Penfield decided that he could not continue for fear that further fusion might make Dad a paraplegic. Given the pioneering or barbaric nature of the surgery, Dad's case was in the medical textbooks of the day. Dad never claimed fame and certainly would not have wanted infamy.

There is no doubt that the surgery saved his life, and it is equally true that it cost him some of his life that is life. He lived in pain, always. My Aunt Isobell told stories of Dad in the early years after the surgery, sitting, gripping the railing of his bed, unable to move, unable to let go for the pain, the railing his only pathetic defense against what the ship's railing had inflicted. Dad lost two inches from his height of five feet seven inches, could not turn his head, and walked with a monstrous stiffness that only those with true perpetual back and neck pain can emulate.

So Dad learned to cope. Without a word of complaint, for which there was little tolerance at the time, he completed a year of rehabilitation, buried his recently acquired muscular and cocky self, and returned to Halifax and the navy for active duty as a flagman and disabled veteran. We know nothing about Dad the person during the next few years. The scant facts are he served in the navy and was based in Halifax until the end of the war. But there are no longer pictures chronicling his naval journey. His photo album records no more adventures at sea, no more group photos on ship, shirts off, muscles flexed, attitude and confidence hanging in the air, no more strolls around Citadel Hill in Halifax, no studio photos with unknown close friends, or the two of them, he and Happy, happy no more. He was a land-lover now, a signal instructor, useful but no longer a player. I often wondered if in addition to everything else, Dad was ashamed of his non-combatant, highly avoidable injury. He paid a lifetime price simply because he liked to experience storms at sea. In later life Dad was neither a risk taker nor a pursuer of whimsical fancies. He had lost that capacity during a storm at sea. We often praise the risk taker but less often acknowledge when the risk goes badly.

But Dad's story is not all about pain and loss. Much of his story through the late 1940s and '50s is the story of people in all the allied countries who had beat Hitler and, though bruised and battered, were eager and confident to rise again, to collectively get on with it. Hollywood films reflect a kind of cornball naiveté of the times, which, being Hollywood, has to be taken with a grain of salt. But in talking to people who lived through the war and its aftermath, there is an element of truth to the portrayal of palpable shared values or what would later be regarded as conformity and naive optimism, to be forever abandoned. For all the bumps and warts of any time in history, this was a period of great hope, before we lost faith.

I remember sitting around our pale-blue linoleum and metal kitchen table, then utilitarian and Spartan, now mid-century chic, listening, our place mostly listening, happy to listen to guests who revealed something of Dad's buried world to our eager ears. Some guests revealed interesting tidbits; others reinforced Dad's inscrutable nature. Dad sat listening, not always looking comfortable, if for example his brother, Uncle Ernie, was talking about navy days or telling us about what a mistake it was to get ships tattooed on his forearms during days at port. The tattoos were amateurish hulking smudges, only qualifying as ships because Uncle Ernie said so. Dad repeatedly grunted acknowledgement of Ernie's reminiscence or diatribe against the folly of youth, with increasing annoyance but without comment. We grew up knowing that Dad did not did not necessarily admire people who talked too much, though he never said so. I think I learned from watching Dad and Uncle Ernie that brothers can be brothers without being friends. Dad smoked and grunted and occasionally fumed through the fumes, sitting rigid, chewing on the ends of his glasses, feigning attention, his mind far, far, away.

But there were others whom Dad really listened to, and whom he actually talked to. Well, not in so many words, but in a few short sentences he talked to the privileged few. Nothing personal, but stuff that we could puzzle over, trying to make sense of the complicated tapestry of family and friends. We never missed sitting at the dinner table when Art Brennan dropped by. Growing up we never knew what the relationship was between our parents and their friends. It turns out that they were usually a blood relation, but we didn't know that until we were adults.

Art was a giant. When he was young he had actually tried out for the Ottawa Rough Riders professional football team. He was 6 feet 7 inches tall, and when he tried out for football, he weighed 300 pounds. In other words, he was the biggest human being who had ever lived. Today his size is fairly commonplace, but then we used to marvel at the gentle giant standing beside Dad. Dad was an emaciated slice of maybe 5 feet 5 inches, down to 120 pounds, and yet there they were, Art talking to Dad as if he were the bigger man. Watching Art sitting with Dad, huge hands cradled in his lap, I learned that respect was not measured in the number of words spoken. Art was soft-spoken, slow and deliberate, and together they covered common ground, spoke the same language and liked each other's company.

I wish we knew what Dad did after he turned to his friend at the dance hall and declared his intention to marry Mom. Did he walk up and introduce himself or hang back and wait to ask her to dance when the music was just right? How did he pull it off? And then what? Dating was serious business; there was either potential for marriage or nothing. Hooking up was not an option.

And the litmus test for forming a relationship with an O'Neill girl was meeting Joseph O'Neill out at the Navan farm. Both men were wee things but strong, silent, principled, tough as nails, without a hint of ego. Joseph O'Neill and Leonard McCloskey were serious types, and Dad knew exactly what he wanted. But at some point during the courtship his confidence waned and his sense of duty got in the way. Today, choosing a partner is often defined by how the other person can serve one's wants and desires. In 1948, Dad loved Mom but felt duty bound to break off the relationship because he did not think with his injuries he would live long enough to provide for a family. It was more than that. Dad wasn't just worried about providing for Mom; he wanted to make sure that her one shot at having a family was the best possible chance a girl could get. For all the difficulties and occasional acrimony in their marriage—alcoholism will do that—they loved each other, and in this they never fully lost faith.

We seven would not even have made it as a glint in Dad's ultra-responsible eye if not for fortuitous advice from someone with a fortuitous name, one Father John O'Neill. And since Mom also had a part to play in our existence, we were twice saved by an O'Neill. Though Dad never talked about how the advice session transpired, Father O'Neill must have listened to Dad's need-to-be-responsible argument and then freed him to follow his true heart's desire. So marriage in 1949, followed by six of us in short order between 1950 and 1959, with the last unexpectedly in 1968 to complete the lucky seven trisect.

After the war, Dad worked as a civil servant and took university courses—makes you wonder why he was worried about his war injuries when it was obvious that a whack of kids and courses could just as easily kill. Dad was determined to do his best to provide for his family and did not think he had the luxury of time. Everything he ever did, and everything we ever saw him do, was directed toward this goal. This unselfish urgency to provide much while the slender clock was ticking is fundamental to understanding the man of a thousand words—in his lifetime, that is. With the me generation on the horizon, Dad's personal urgency and general fidelity to God, country and family was about to relegate him to the dust heap of ancient civilization. A man forever out of step, the king of uncool.

It is an interesting 1960s phenomena that kids from large families, common at the time, could exist, thrive, be invisible, stick to basic family rules, make an appearance at church, be known as, in our case, one of the *McCloskeys*, though first name remained a mystery, and not really have much conversation or contact with one or both parents for long stretches of time, and everyone thought everything was just fine, and it probably was. Today, parental hypervigilance may be contributing to mental health problems for adversity-adverse kids who never develop resiliency. We roamed the streets and neighbourhood with liberating savagery, occasionally confronted with toughs when real gangs were fairly common but not worrying about what to do or how to report *bullying*. And that is the difference between resiliency and fear.

In 1955, the year I was born, the fourth bundle of trouble in five years, we moved from a small rental semi in the centre of town into a single family home on a double lot in Westboro—a trendy west-end neighbourhood now, not then, and oddly for a northern Canadian city, it was a tiny post-war California-style bungalow. There was a reason for selecting this particular house.

After the war, all of Mom's family moved to California to join or live in the shadow of rich Uncle Jack O'Neill. As the only Canadian holdouts, my parents had an offer from Uncle Jack that they couldn't refuse. Except, alone among the O'Neill clan, they did just that.

Uncle Jack flew Mom and Dad to California to see the wonders and surrender to the sun, as all northerners do after countless northern winters. But for reasons we never knew, possibly Dad's civil servant job, they decided to stay in Canada, the black frozen sheep of the family. When they bought their first home, Mom's dad, a retired subsistence Canadian farmer, then raising peacocks in Five Points, California, gave them the entire down payment of $1,500, a princely sum in 1955. Dad wrote a heartfelt humble letter of gratitude to Joseph O'Neill, a man like Dad is so many ways, which to this day moves me. And so for the tiny California-style house that became home, the expansive double lot and the neighbourhood slumming ground, we owed thanks to the feisty little grandfather we never met.

For better or worse, the decision to stay meant that Mom was essentially cut off from her family. However they arrived at the decision to stay in Canada, there is no doubt that a central tenet of our family mythology is Dad's promise to get Mom to California every year of his life, which he managed to do, seven kids and one salary be damned. This was a big deal in the 1950s. Given the need for economy, Mom only ever took one of the two girls with her, since how do you choose one among five rangy boys?

But early on, with a brood of wee bairns, Mom visited her California family alone. We like to think of the modern dad as hyper-involved with his kids and the 1950s mad-men dad as distant and disconnected. And our recollections of Dad from our teen years would confirm this stereotype as being true. Still, long after his death something was revealed of the early years from the dad we never knew. We have exactly one letter in our family archives from Dad to Mom during one of her early annual California visits. This one, dated July 29, 1954, in perfect cursive writing, was completed just after he put Mark, age one, Mary Donna, age two, and Pat, age four, to bed for the night.

Dear Irene,

I've had so much idle time on my hands I don't know why I haven't written sooner. This job is a cinch now that I've got things "organized." For example, after I finish the morning chores, and before it's time to start getting the dinner, I have lots of time to light a cigarette and sometimes I even get to smoke the whole thing.

Seriously though, everything is going okay and everyone is fine. Pat had a good birthday. Mother gave him another truck and Mary a sports shirt. He was really tickled with all the cars and trucks—hardly went out of the house all day. Mary and Mark are giving Pat a bit of trouble in sneaking off with one of the vehicles.

I sure enjoyed talking to you all on Sunday evening. I would have liked very much to have been in that gathering. As I told you on Sunday I haven't given Mark a bottle since you left. I didn't plan it, but he just didn't seem to care, so I just give him a cup of milk when he's going to bed and the old pet just lies down and drops off without any fuss.

Yesterday I made a lunch and took the kids to the Experimental Farm and this morning to Gladstone Park. Pat really enjoyed the swings and slide—but Mary was content to "look." This afternoon while Mary and Mark were asleep, Theresa kept house while Pat and I went for a haircut and to the bank.

The cooking has been going fine—but I must admit that when I went shopping Saturday I bought quite a few cans of "canned dinner," beef stew, etc., but good, mind you. The washing is okay too. In fact all the women in the neighbourhood have been coming over to admire my white washings. I think I'll fool them tomorrow and hang a diaper all covered in "sa," just to let them see the evidence.

Well, Enie, as it is now 10:30 p.m. and I still haven't read the paper I must close off. Give my best to all your folks—especially your mother and father—and tell them I was glad to be speaking to them again—if only by phone. By the way when you get back I think I'll go up to Pine Lodge for three or four days. I'll probably go on Thursday, Aug. 12, and Wilf will join me on Friday evening for the weekend.

Well, Sweetheart, there is no point in me saying I hope you are enjoying yourself—I know you are, and I am glad. We all miss you and will be glad to have you back.

I was also glad to hear your trip down was okay and hope the return trip is too.

Enjoy yourself, Sweetheart, and all our love. Len

This letter does not seem likely from the man who once called off the relationship for fear of being unable to fully realize his duties as husband and father due to poor health. This letter does not seem likely from the man we came to know or, more accurately, we came to conclude could not be known. Who we are cannot be reduced to a fixed time on a continuum. Dad was not only this letter; Dad was not only our later memories of him. But we did not know this letter, these moments, this version of Dad until after he died. And these moments, echoing 60 years after the fact, are poignant testimony that Dad was tender, fully engaged, funny, content, loving and not only knowable but wanting to be known. The simplicity and sincerity of this letter, written in calm stolen moments between when everything was finally done and when everything had to be done again, somehow exonerates all the complexity and acrimony of a life that takes us away from our higher self and our holy moments. With another baby the following year, and in consideration of the fact that the fourth little troublemaker was me, the complexity and acrimony of life was ramping up. Poor Dad.

We boys were intrigued by the idea of California and the "other" family we never knew, but we didn't much look forward to time alone with Dad. Not that Dad's fried baloney, headcheese or blood pudding wasn't something to look forward to. Like everything else when we were kids, we learned to love the one and only choice offered at each meal. The golden rule of the day. Today, choice is everything, and a kid might have the nerve to prefer filet mignon over animal entrails. But choice also leads to anxiety, and we were spared that malady.

The real problem was that Dad's normal preferred distance from schedules and chores was replaced with military precision and attention to detail while Mom was away. And combining chief cook and bottle washer duties for seven kids with his job and private demons, he was under a lot of pressure.

The way we coped was to go outside. In fact, except for meals and sleeping, we weren't actually inside most of the day, any day. Even in winter I would go outside after dinner into darkness playing, often by myself, in the snow or on the ice, with one eye to the glow of the activity in the house, and the other looking skyward to the shards of icy stars.

Even though we travelled the neighbourhood far and wide, until a certain age we mostly played on our double lot. Our swath of dirt was a neighbourhood mecca; it might have had some green once, but gardening had likely been abandoned with the McCloskey occupation. In the 1950s and 1960s kids were supposed to stay outside, and neighbourhood parents were probably grateful for our dirt-packed gathering place, which allowed them to preserve a modicum of green on their ordered single lots. It was not unusual to hang for years with one of the kids from the green lots and never to have been inside their house. We didn't care; outside is where we wanted to be in any weather, in any season. Freedom was not defined by forecast.

Meanwhile, Dad fulfilled his responsibilities and duties while emitting a low-grade constant and palpable anger. This growing-up stuff was apparently serious business. But—first incrementally, then pervasively, and still hauntingly—I came to understand that Dad felt completely alone. How can it be that a man with seven children, a wife he loved and who loved him back, friends, church and standing in the community felt utterly alone? At seven years old, I learned the existentialist dilemma of human experience.

The most memorable and contrasting feature to our potato-famine-like dirt lot was a collection of giant weeping willows stretching across the entire front of the yard. Broad, gnarled, twisting trunks, deep, deeper and deepest green impenetrable foliage, held together by bright yellow whip-like willow strands. The trees were quite close to the house, so today the first instinct would be to cut them down. Liability, danger—oh no, what if? Things happened then too, but there was less obsession with what might happen and a bit more connection to what was happening, even without mindfulness workshops. Less liability, less bubble-wrapped living, less standing, frozen, on the tracks, staring at the train of life bearing down. One very rarely sees a giant weeping willow in the city today, and I lament their passing, especially as, as with most of the iconic memories of childhood, they seem to have vanished without notice. Weeping willows in calm, willows weeping in chaos. The sound of the willow branches swishing across our open screen windows is a powerful recollection. When windy or during a storm the willows openly wept, the air electric with climatic mood.

One hot summer evening when Mom was away in California, and just before Dad made his bedtime sweep, I hid under the family linoleum table in the front room with windows open, willows swaying, that swishing motion the heartbeat of our lives. I wasn't stupid or brave enough to think I could get away with it for long, but kids are playful and want to play with just about any dance partner unless they lose faith. As I waited under the table for the predictable eight o'clock call, the wind picked up and the sky darkened, foreshadowing a summer storm. Eight o'clock came, but there was no call, only the sound of the willows gathering momentum.

Dad came into the room but did not speak. He thought he was alone, always alone. I stifled a giggle, which had no chance of being heard over the weeping outside. Under normal circumstances, Dad's anger did not feel particularly personal, unless you happened to be the one—and I often was—who had spilt the milk, again. And a milk incident was short-lived, volatile but forgivable, until the next inevitable spill.

So when Dad suddenly erupted, smashing pots and pans and emoting something vocal, something visceral, I learned the sound of pain. This was not spilt milk. This was no lament for spilt milk. Dad smashed pots and half growled, half shouted disappointment, frustration, anger—outward sounds, but I knew and never forgot that the source of his pain was inward, deep, deep inside, and that I could not touch it, and he could not escape it. What was it, and why couldn't Dad be who we could see?

In the literature, children of alcoholics suffer low self-esteem. That makes sense, but my bias is that there is too much emphasis today on esteem, too little emphasis on recognizing and moving on from childhood experience. True, some psychic wounds may be too deep to recover from, but a point of maturation is understanding that life is less what happens to you than your perception of it. As Dad and the willows wept, I understood that Dad, who we loved, did not love himself. The willows outside were weeping, but the Dad inside could not. My understanding of Dad was sealed and has never changed, my forgiveness absolute.

The next day Dad seemed normal, maybe less mad, certainly not sad, just Dad. I knew that I could not fix whatever haunted him by being good, by making jokes. Still, I think I am probably a lifetime clown, bad puns and all, an Irish affliction, and I made an early and pervasive attempt to make Dad laugh, to undo that thing in him.

And I am certain that my lifetime as clown has been an ill-conceived attempt to escape boredom. Our family sat in church long hours over the years. We said the rosary together during Lent, eight of us on our knees, hours passing between ticking seconds, and boredom as palpable and real as life and death. Inexplicably—well, the reason is clear, but committing the act given the punishment is right up there among stupid actions of all time—during one particularly claustrophobic rosary rendition I carved my initials into the coffee table I was kneeling beside. Note to self: when boredom makes you do things to occupy the mind and pass the time, it's probably a bad idea to leave *your own* initials on a family heirloom if you want to live to fight off boredom another day.

But there are other aspects of childhood memory—whether real or imagined—not weeping, not boredom, but home. Home is Christmas Eve with family, at least the good memories, and the haunting, never fully forsaken desire to be there. Faith is understanding that this image, anyone's image of home, however unlikely, corny or contrived, is an echo from the trailing clouds of glory and hope of return. Dad looked and spoke like Bing, singing not so much. His musical repertoire was limited to occasionally playing "Turkey in the Straw" on the harmonica, which made the dog howl, and not with delight. He was grumpy and impatient when putting up the lights on Christmas Eve, but we didn't mind, because he took us out for Chinese food after midnight mass.

And there were times when he could shift from seeing you as part of the group and look you in the eye, however briefly, and speak to you, knowing you. He called me *Lawrence* sometimes, the only person to ever do so, which when you are stuck with the name *Larry* seems remarkable. He could soften and say a few words, kind and inquiring, if you were to visit him in his basement workshop. This was in the bigger bungalow we had moved to after the California dreaming bungalow was deemed too small. Newer suburban bungalows were all basement, and Dad's lair was a windowless, aesthetically unpleasing space, not a man cave to be desired. As well, he was always easy when he talked to the dog. So many of us can talk to a dog with ease and then falter when we try to translate to people. Less a human failing than a flicker of hope. Looking back, it is important to remember that the flickers of hope are closer to who we are, our higher self, than the recrimination of our failings.

Our California bungalow had some unusual features. There was a three-season sunroom over the garage that you could only get to by going through our parents' bedroom. Six kids, with another unexpected one to greet you in the future, and your bedroom is a corridor. I suspect the architect's career was short-lived. When I was nine or ten, as I was walking through the bedroom corridor I spotted a five-dollar bill sticking out of my mom's wallet. I hesitated only a moment and then put it in my pocket. Kids are often asked why they do things and just as often respond, "I don't know." What adults have difficulty understanding is that they often do not know and cannot explain. Decades later, if I think about it at all, it's obvious that my one-time theft was my middle child jumping up and down for attention.

I had no idea what to do with the money, and none of us kids had experience buying things with such a magnitude of cash. So I asked my brother to come along with me to Beamish's department store on Wellington Street to spend the moolah. We picked out a few cheap plastic toys that I didn't really covet and went home, and within minutes I was ratted out by the same brother, who kept his stash of toys from half of the fiver.

In the days of the basement-less California bungalow, Dad's workroom was a double garage. I was told by my mom that Dad wanted to see me. I knew from her face and the strategic absence of my brother and his toys that this was trouble. In our family we had a means of discipline called the Persuader. It was a solid and well-worn wide piece of lumber about two feet long. Under normal circumstances the existence of the Persuader was enough deterrence to prevent the need for its use. But there were exceptions.

Dad didn't waste many words. He knew I did it, I knew I did it, and there was a price to be paid. Dad's use of the Persuader was fast and furious and went on far too long. I remember him saying something about the evils of stealing as he smacked my behind, but I did not understand the significance of his rant for another 40 years. My backside burned all night, my shame longer still. As I lay in bed burning, Mom took a look at my backside, and I could see concern in her eyes. She was gentle, and I knew I would be forgiven—not then, but someday. I think I understood, even then, the cliché to be true. It hurt Dad more than it hurt me. My shame burned for days; his, for a lifetime.

Dad was not nostalgic. In this respect he was almost modern, divorced from the past, eyes focused forward, never looking back. But it would be disingenuous to associate Dad with much of modernity, since his values were clearly rooted deep in the past. We don't know the truth, but I believe that central to his tough pioneer mantle was a refusal to live with regret. Things happened, and, without permission or inclination for psychoanalysis, he let the past fade into the distant past. It may be that he consistently and successfully evaded regret, or else it ran too deep and painful to ever acknowledge.

We know that he had not always been without a past. Dad's navy photo album is poignant testimony to the great divide between the kid—posing, flexing for posterity, meticulously recording the grand adventure, and Dad the responsible veteran—returning to service, in pain, determined to be useful and to put all vestiges of the past behind him. There are no photos taken after the accident in 1940, although he served in the navy until near the end of the war, officially discharged in 1945. There is a gap of years until a photo of Dad exists again, redemption received at the Standish dance hall on the evening he met Mom. Still young, he had lost his navy muscle and something of his vitality but regained some faith in the future. Solace for those who cannot face the past is the fact that we are always moving from it. The same fact is less comforting to nostalgic types.

Not surprisingly, we didn't learn anything about Dad's past life or family history from him. When we were young, he didn't say; we didn't ask. My pathetic nostalgia may have been incubated by the vacuum between not knowing and emerging curiosity, fed piecemeal from other sources. We knew we were Irish, in the "wear green and celebrate St. Patrick's Day on March 17th" limited kind of way. We didn't know that on both the McCloskey and O'Neill sides we were among mid-nineteenth century destitute potato-famine Irish who came to Canada aboard the coffin ships from one of the most devastating human calamities of all time.

We didn't know anything of our arrival in the Ottawa Valley. For years we drove through the small town of Aylmer, Quebec, on our way to our summer holiday at Norway Bay. We never stopped, but as we passed under the shadow of the grey limestone Catholic church, Dad always made the sign of the cross. I was never sure why he did that, but I found it reassuring, proof, I guess, that Dad had not lost faith. When he died in 1980, we learned that most of his family was buried in the same St. Paul's cemetery that we always passed. Whatever his thoughts as he drove past the church and family plot, he never revealed a word. It remains a deep, impenetrable mystery. The family plot thickens.

Even more puzzling was this: growing up in Ottawa, especially for families without cottages, day trips and picnics to Gatineau Park were common. The national park is minutes away from the capital, natural and accessible wilderness on our doorstep. One day my parents took a walk with my brother Michael—a rare occurrence indeed—along the dirt road from where they had parked at Champlain Lookout. The lookout is where all residents of the capital region bring visitors, as it features the best view and is the demarcation between rough shield hills, rock and lakes, and the flat fertile valley, the majestic Ottawa River, and beyond. Mike tells the story of Dad stopping under a signpost and picking up an old discarded handmade sign, now replaced by a new shiny metal job. Both signs boldly and inexplicably proclaimed "McCloskey Road."

Even receiving a sign from above, both literally and figuratively, did not elicit an occasion for storytelling from Dad. Checking with other sources— mostly Aunt Isobell, possibly Aunt Mary, and inevitably cousin Ted, some research, and later from an official plaque marking the site—we learned something of our history ... that we had a history.

The crossroads where Dad picked up the old McCloskey Road sign is directly across from the old McCloskey farm, Dad's grandparents' farm. The road was so named because the McCloskeys had been the lead family for a group of approximately ten Irish families who had vainly and valiantly tried to pull crops and sustenance from the rock, roots and infertile soil underfoot. Walking the farm perimeter today, it is hard to imagine that an acre, let alone an entire field, was ever cleared; that a single potato, let alone a crop, was ever pulled; that a person, let alone a family, was ever fed. Despite the loneliness, despite the deprivation, despite the hardship of cultivating and extracting subsistence roots from an inhospitable Canadian Shield landscape, they persisted. Not that the Irish are stubborn.

The thought about history that nags me is this: if trying to research our family's recent past mainly draws a blank, with all the tools of the modern world, what do we really know of the "historical" events that shaped our lives and our civilization from the deep past? History chronicles long-ago battles, treaties, the comings and goings of kings and queens, but the history that matters is rarely recorded, exists between the cracks of recorded history, and may make a mockery of recorded history. Social history—the words and relationships between humans—that is where history actually happened; that is where the mystery lies.

The historical fact of the Second World War did not cause Dad to abandon his past. It is unclear, but it is likely that he never looked back because of the fact of his broken back. His personal history, our personal historical omission, may have been decided as he sat on the side of his bed in pain, willing himself to recover. We never knew the young guy in the pre-accident photos; he was missing in our lives and did not register in our family history as the image in those early photos hinted was possible. Dad chose the Great Leap Forward and chose his unchronicled way between the battles, without glory and without feeling sorry for himself. I still have his navy photo album and that the old wooden sign proclaiming *McCloskey Road*. We know where the road is high up in the Gatineau hills, and I know where the photo album is high up on my office shelf. We just don't know what they mean.

When Dad took early retirement in 1975, he went into a three-week rehabilitation program, and the secret was exposed. I always thought it revealing that none of his many good friends knew or even suspected that Dad was an alcoholic. He was just too responsible, smart and high functioning to let alcohol get the better of him. Of course part of the answer is that alcoholism was fairly common among the Irish Catholic men of his generation. Drinking was an everyday practice, and Dad held it together remarkably well, for remarkably long, until likely concluding that "the centre cannot hold." As a man of secrets and a man of integrity, he suffered the exposure of not pride but moral failing.

People today would have a hard time understanding this dilemma. For most, when things don't go well, they conclude they have been hard done by. But they were not forged by the expectation of moral fortitude and self-reliance, the Irish Catholic Depression-era moral code. He smoked, he drank, he deserved to pay the price. And of course, with those thoughts, he could not stop drinking again after rehab, and his last naturally aspirated breath was through smoke-filled emphysema-ridden lungs.

Regret hangs flaccid and mournful between opportunities not taken and words not spoken. Dad could never admit to what he felt and, as a consequence, was misunderstood as a lifelong condition. But this is not only Dad's story. I am my father's son. When I was 15, Dad inexplicably tried to bridge the gap between words never spoken and words forever intended. I remember sitting on our front steps, cold stone, hard on the backside, especially for those with boney backside syndrome, my lifelong affliction. We didn't do comfort in our house. The Irish like discomfort as a means to assuage guilt.

Dad, master of the unspoken word, sat down beside me *to talk*. Apparently, I'd been silent and brooding lately. I didn't know this about myself, but my mother told me so, and even at that age I didn't doubt her. Dad never did get teenagers, could not understand that while they might check out for a number of years, they remained salvageable. Still, he had something on his mind and, in a rare and deliberate moment, seemed determined to say it. His words were intense and halting; he knew what he wanted to say but really didn't know how. The gist of his discourse was that he had noticed that I had become quiet and distant (just like my dad), and he wondered if it was about something he had done in the past. *Here it comes,* I thought, but I didn't speak, for which in our family there was precedent. He continued, painfully saying that maybe I still harboured feelings over the fact that some years earlier he had taken our dog away to the pound.

So that was it. No mention of the Persuader incident. I hadn't thought to blame Dad for the dog, and I never blamed him for the Persuader. Sitting on our stone steps, discomfort in my backside, discomfort in my brooding mind, I could not, did not, speak. Dad had likely thought about the Persuader a great deal during the past years, and he obviously felt guilty about taking our dog to the pound. But I did not understand then that this intense, haunted man was asking me for forgiveness. I have of course embraced Dad and given not only forgiveness but unconditional love a thousand times since that inarticulate time, but at that moment I sat, trying not to feel but feeling numb nonetheless, unable to speak, unable to explain why. I didn't harbour any grievance, could have given Dad some comfort and forgiveness, but sat head hanging, rear end hurting, waiting for him to finish, to stop trying to put something into words, a little different each attempt. I sat waiting for him to leave.

At some point the words "I love you" did escape from his throat, more like a cough or guttural retch than words, but, God love him, he had spoken. I could not, did not, respond. After an awkward time, he did leave, likely believing that it was a wound too deep to forgive, that thing I had utterly forgotten, and once Dad had departed my head lifted back up, and I returned to the brooding thoughts of my 15-year-old angst-ridden mind. The passing of two ships in the night.

The father truly is child to the man. That scene of inertia fermented for the next ten years. In the summer of 1980, Dad's fragile health deteriorated. There was a photo taken of Dad then, at age 59, which I later destroyed because it is of a man in his 80s suffering.

Dad was suffering—laboured breathing, low energy, general wretchedness; he looked and acted a man adrift. In September 1980, Dad was the first patient admitted to an entire floor of the newly build Ottawa General Hospital. Ironic, that the man least wanting and needing attention in the entire world should have an entire floor and nursing staff at his disposal. Before the drive to the hospital, he sat in a chair waiting for Mom, on the same hard stone porch where we had not had a conversation ten years earlier. We chatted—that is, I babbled, as much as I was ever able—to deflect from the fact that his pending journey was one way only. But neither of us said those words. In fact, he did not respond at all, which for all his quietude was not like him.

Still, I was not the same brooding, inarticulate boy of 15, and words needed to be spoken. Desperately and painfully I forced words through the impasse between us. Mom stepped outside for a moment and announced that we were just about ready to go. There were no other chances, the hard-assed front steps were not going to make it any easier, and I took the plunge. "Dad, I love you." I needed to vindicate myself for not responding when he tried to say the same ten years earlier—sitting on the edge of my seat, racing heart, he trying to get a heartbeat from a reluctant dance partner. The irony was not lost on me that he was just like I had been then, that 15-year-old who could not respond, waiting for the moment to pass.

I had convinced myself that I needed to say "I love you" to him, to finally convey feeling, to give forgiveness. But Dad wasn't stuck, didn't struggle; it wasn't that he couldn't find the words. Whether from sheer physical pain or spiritual and psychological resignation, it was not the right time. He was beyond all that. I hadn't forgiven him; I had tried to forgive myself, for which I was ashamed.

The last words I heard Dad say were to a doctor who was wandering the vast, empty hospital corridors and dropped by to ask how he was feeling. To which my dad answered, "Fine, thanks, Doctor." But of course he did not feel fine. He was wretched, his Irish Catholic Depression-era breeding not permitting him to say otherwise, and the doctor wasn't listening anyway. We then learned that his breathing had worsened, emphysema laying final pillage to his lungs, and he was put on a respirator.

A respirator is an awful intrusion. It is inserted down the throat, forced mechanical breathing, no talking possible, all gesturing from the intense disembodied eyes of a drowning man. And the irony of enforced silence for a man for whom much remained unsaid was not lost on us. The respirator causes a constant parched throat, a thirst that cannot be quenched. We took turns feeding him ice chips, like feeding a baby Pablum. I was tired of thinking *The child is father to the man*. Drugs, further resignation, and eyes once wild, now calm, went dull, the need to crunch ice chips the only constant. Each day a challenge to find some one-sided conversation, to keep something flowing, desperate not to lose the thread.

Dad had been a lifetime news junkie, each day reading the *Montreal Gazette*, the *Ottawa Citizen*, and the *Ottawa Journal*. People in this town tended to render their fidelity to one of the two rival local papers. Not Dad.

He read both papers, cover to cover, for decades. So it was a surprise on August 27, 1980, when it was announced by its rival paper that the *Ottawa Journal* had gone under. I told Dad the news and watched his dull eyes register recognition and interest—an effect that telling him I loved him ten days earlier had not had. Which is just fine, thanks. For all our mutual inarticulate speech of the heart (one of Van's best albums), I'll take his eyes coming to life, hanging on my words as I detailed the reported story, registering curiosity and acceptance, with perhaps his patented response to the vicissitudes of life—*"Well, wouldn't that frost you"*—if only he could have talked. I knew that he knew that trying to say I love you was just a matter of finding the right words, with "I love you" being too direct, too clumsy, too much. Who knew that love was best and finally expressed with the words "The *Ottawa Journal* has gone under"?

These were the last words I said to Dad. Limited as our words were, we felt much; that is our way. Well, until I decided to write a book. For this stifling end is not the end. And free of the constraints of this mortal coil, we have grown. We debate, we doubt, and though faith's ebb and flow is often low, it is never quite gone. Low marks: unquestioning faith; high marks: persistence.

Dad never had Mom's ethereal and complete faith in a loving and merciful God. He and I shared the notion that we do not deserve mercy, that pain is our birthright, and that scarcity is what this world has to offer. Dad was forged by the Depression; I am my father's son. Dad once described himself as a maverick, which I define as freethinking, healthy skepticism. It caused him some problems in his career, because doing and saying the right thing regardless of popular opinion do come at a price. But most of all, his heathy skepticism kept him from believing that he was worthy of grace, divinity and, as Springsteen sings, "taking in the forgiveness this life has to offer."

Dad missed the experience of his many grandchildren. Still, in my mind, with a modicum of faith, I see him there for all the events that matter. For all his emotional retentiveness, he loved and was unabashedly expressive with babies. I can see him holding Shannon, my eldest, as a baby, born three years after his death, and talking to her as an adult, her common sense and intelligence exactly what would have appealed to him. He really liked Kristen's playfulness and corresponding childhood name, Punky, until she banned us all from its use. He comments on Cate's high sense of style but thinks she should cover up and put on a sweater. He loves sports and followed my brother Mike on his path to the Olympics. Many examples, mutable time circling, close the distance between us.

It is true that the mind can compensate for loss and embellish fleeting feelings. But the thing is, my mind, like my dad's, tends the opposite way. I think there is mystery beneath the minutiae, but I don't embellish. I doubt: I doubt what cannot be seen, and I doubt what is right before my eyes. I am the prisoner sitting in jail, languishing for years without noticing that the cell door is unlocked, has always been unlocked.

In 1996, I attended a university student services conference in Halifax. The night before leaving, I had a dream. Dreams are, of course, hard to make sense of, harder still to communicate to other people. And I tend not to dream, that I remember. But this dream was different. Vivid, focused and real, undream-like, and though not nightmarishly haunting, it was hauntingly euphoric, imprinted on my mind as if accessing something that is not to be revealed but inexplicably was.

I had not been thinking about Dad and had not made the connection that Halifax was where Dad had hung during the war, both in happy times with Happy and later, crushed in spirit and in spine. I was worried about Mom, she ever sinking into the morass of Parkinson's grip, but that had been a constant for some years.

In the dream, Mom and Dad are sitting together at a small table, holding hands, old and failing both but both still alive. I am standing watching, and I recognize the table as the fold-up card table, for several decades a family fixture in both bungalows. I sit down, occupying the third chair, with my parents, and we three sit, holding hands and crying, surely a death watch for Mom, and maybe me.

And then there were none. There is a tap on my shoulder, and turning around I see Dad, standing behind me, tall, straight, radiant, no back problem, no pain, at peace, a young man, the one we never knew but whose essence I never doubted, which surely is a facsimile of faith, though that is not what I am thinking. I am thinking nothing, am suspended, looking up and waiting, and he simply says, "It's okay." There it is—not profound, not flush with insight, just simple reassurance, hope and a reason for faith.

I know that it was only a dream. I know the psychology, why I conjured it up, am familiar with the intellectual orthodoxy and why I should dismiss it, but I don't care. I know that it is a thing separate from all else. I have had few dreams of any significance. Even with the significant few I have thought might be significant, I would think about what it might be telling me, only to forget it the next day. With despair always lurking and faith antithetical to my skeptical nature, this dream could not have graphed onto my consciousness easily, but for whatever reason, 20 years later it is still there, front and centre, Dad standing strong and tall, no more weeping and willows, because "It's okay." And mostly, it is.

"God has a most wicked sense of humor."

MAUREEN O'HARA

# CHAPTER THREE
## AN AWFUL IRISH AFFLICTION

HE DOES INDEED. IT MAY BE THAT HUMOUR IS AN ACT OF FAITH.

Life fundamentally is loss. Not maybe, not sort of, not if you're unlucky. There is no escaping—it is loss, subject to timing and awareness, from the cradle to the grave. But this is not the bad news. The bad news is that if you do not have faith, if it is your belief that oblivion follows upon inevitable loss, if in the absence of belief you have capitulated to the modern cult of atheism and parked your faith in nothing, though you may be in the trendy majority, it will be enough to drive you mad.

I know, I know, people will say "I don't believe in God and am perfectly content, happy actually, in my lifestyle choice." And it is funny, in a black humour kind of way, to think of everlasting oblivion as a lifestyle choice. It may be self-serving for me to say this, but what a dung heap of overripe modernity. The fact is, our most primal archetypal impulse is that we, in our transient human form, fear death. It is the fundamental curse of consciousness that humans—alone among animals—have foreknowledge of and anticipate our death, not peacefully in the fullness of time but like a freight train hurling toward us, frozen in body but not necessarily in spirit.

Intellectuals claim that faith is merely an opiate for the people, a pathetic and humorous defense against our fear of death. Even for those who have faith, a much maligned minority, death is to encounter the great mystery of which our cautious and predictable lives are mere speculation. I have met some few people whose faith saturates every aspect of their being—my mother among them—and they genuinely do not fear death, even as they may be saddened by its inevitable arrival. Modern atheists place their faith in the certainty of complete and inevitable obliteration, which seems an odd thing to place faith in. Many further claim to be comfortable with this stark version of the "reality" of death, the implication being that we who do not regard physical death as obliteration are not facing up to reality. But to proclaim being comfortable with death while confidently claiming to know the reality of what cannot be empirically known is to float down the river De-Nile into the heart of darkness. Faux confidence in the modern sense equals fear. Those whose lives are defined by fear tend not to allow their lives to be refined by humour. Still, faith gives us a modicum of hope that there may be something more, some meaning to this life that taken at face value is a humourless, definitive end. Faith gives hope of something beyond, and humour helps get us from modernity to eternity.

Humour in general and having fun in particular, not unlike those who struggle with faith, hold that there is more to life than exists on the banal surface—even if the mini mystery is just a bad play on words. If, as Winston Churchill asserted, "a joke is a very serious thing," the thing is this: *life is short, life doesn't end well, life adds up to a dung heap, so either there is more, much more, which makes our self-importance in this life very funny, or else there is nothing more, and we are the butt of the biggest, albeit cruellest, joke of all time.* Humour then is what we have to work with before the mystery of death, the mystery behind life, is revealed. Not much maybe, but it will have to do.

By pointing out the playfulness and absurdity of life, humour says that truth exists outside the common view, offbeat, out of focus. It practices a healthy, absurd skepticism and, like faith, advises the practice of insanity or nonconformity if you want to stay sane. Humour refuses to accept the vale of tears as commonly written and defiantly cries, *Better to go down with a peal of laughter at the mad, mad world that we live in than to pretend everyday insanity to be all well and good.* Serious humour doesn't take itself too seriously and doesn't know a thing.

There is something to be said for having to entertain yourself—no, no, not doing anything that can cause blindness in adolescence—but I happen to believe that humour is one of the highest forms of creativity and that the creative impulse needs a push. Innovation is wrung from desperation, and necessity truly is the mother of invention. From Michelangelo to Groucho Marx, the accomplished, the best in their field, have in common hard work and bloody-minded persistence. The genius, often put on a pedestal for having unique talent, is usually at her craft for 15 or 20 years before such recognition is given. And without doubt, one of the great human motivators of all time is boredom.

Boredom happened regularly in school and church. There was no chance we were going to squander time outside of those bastions of boredom with more boredom. And at the risk of coming across like a Monty Python skit ("You lived in a shoe, luxury!"), we didn't have much ready-made distraction, so escape from boredom was of our own making. Kids today are endlessly entertained, expect entertainment to be outside of self and technologically driven, and if by chance they should find themselves in a car or airplane that has had a technological glitch, are lost. In fairness, most adults are tending that way. With sheepish honesty, I admit, so am I.

But it wasn't always so. We worked with ferocious intensity to create not passive distraction but active play. Good fun required some real work. Play on our dirt-packed yard; semi-organized play in our roughhouse schoolyard; alone play on a winter's night tunnelling through a snowbank; indoor play, improvised hockey on the basement floor; and most of all, the Irish affliction other than alcoholism, that mind-numbing play on words. As kids we called the banter *corny jokes*; as adults who refuse to grow up, *puns*. And listening to our puns today, you would really have to conclude that the childhood name was more accurate and honest.

Our California bungalow was small, the architectural reasoning possibly being that size doesn't matter for those who spend all their time outside. The California style didn't really jive with the Canadian reality. The bedrooms were tiny. I shared a room with two brothers, with a bunk bed flanked by another sliver of a metal bed with a dip in the middle that almost touched the floor. Years later I got a regular flat bed and remember feeling that it had a weird hump in the middle. I have no idea where we put our scant stuff, but I do re-member that we had the perfect set-up for late night corny jokes. I like to think this is where I honed my skill; others like to think this is where I must have contracted my terrible affliction. I like to tell them to shut their gob, and then we get into it, toe to toe, pun for pun. Occasionally, the fate of the Western free world hangs in the balance, or else the meaning of life is decided.

We lived in a serious world that gave us a hunger for humour, both corny and pathologically subversive. Best route to inspiration is suppression. School and church were not supposed to be fun. Around the table a kid's place was to be spoken to, mostly. No *duo purposeful parents gang-grilling only child while fascinated by every meaningless detail* exercises. Thank God. Kids today are often passive about a life they are always pestered to report on and to receive praise for how great they are doing, for doing nothing in particular, just like the day before. The family dinner had parameters, the classroom had strict rules, and in church it was sacrilegious to do anything except pray to God and prepare for confession.

Getting off a joke in a confined environment, say at the dinner table after a milk spill, in Sister Aloysius's presence anytime, or during mass while the bell rang for holy communion and everyone's head was reverently bowed, required stealth and was subversive as hell, which is where we figured we'd likely go. Such is the power of getting off the punchline, completing the subversive joke. Some things are worth suffering for, even eternally, and though often punished for the act of completion, I don't ever remember feeling regret.

Sitting at the head of the table in front of six squirrelly kids, before the late last arrival, Dad might have been mistaken for Queen Victoria, as in, he was not amused. For Dad, meals were strictly a utilitarian function. Predictable food prepared, grace said, food eaten, dishes done. Talk, questions and jokes were tolerated as long as not too loud and not disruptive to the pattern. Most of our pathetic attempts at humour are mercifully forgotten, but a few have made it into the family lexicon of humour. Such as the innocuous question asked at the table one Saturday lunchtime in the mid-1960s.

"Dad, what does the word 'f——' mean?" one of us innocently asked (knowing perfectly well the answer).

"Nothing, that word doesn't mean anything," Dad growled, impatiently and dismissively.

Another of us, capitalizing on the innocence theme, "So, if it doesn't mean anything, it doesn't matter if we say it, does it, Dad?"

Dad doesn't answer, suspended between the logic of the question and the potential for unlocking forces he does not want to unleash. The question is asked again. Big mistake; logic wins. Which unleashes an immediate wall of sound from six knowing hyper-sources. But Dad has ruled, and so the unruly behaviour reigns supreme for a couple of minutes.

"Pass the f——ing ketchup, please."

"Do you want to play f——ing football after lunch?"

"Are you kidding, it's going to f——ing rain, f——er."

"Where's my f——ing fork?"

"Right beside your f——ing plate, for f—— sake."

"I said, pass the f——ing ketchup."

"Is there any f——ing dessert?"

Until Dad pounds his fist on the table, sending the f——ing forks flying, and thunders, "Enough! Don't anyone say that word again, *or else*."

*Or else* always meant business, and we were mischievously silent, never said the F-word again in my parents' hearing, and tucked this little episode away for posterity. Saying the F-word has lost its lustre. I mean, what fun is it if it's allowed?

On their own, Mom and Dad could be a tough audience. But things really opened up whenever people came over, which was pretty often. Dad in particular was more relaxed around his friends. He wasn't cross at all, and he even laughed sometimes. How about that? Drinking alcohol was common then, and we didn't figure in its mellowing qualities, though we too felt the effect. Dad relaxed was a good thing, and we responded with pent-up goofiness. We liked it when people came over. The mood changed palpably, and with it permission to be a clown. Make the adults laugh, and you had it made. It is no exaggeration to say that more than anything else, this is what made me the poor excuse for a human being I am today.

As the adults sipped their whiskey-and-ginger-ales, my brothers and I danced around the wooden coffee table, not sure how to entertain, just of the necessity to do so. The more they laughed, the more we danced, and especially me, the over-compensating middle-middle child (two older and two younger brothers, one older and one younger sister) and the most desperate and pathetic clown. I tried to move and talk and mimic and clown my way into the hearts of adults. As a kid you understand that when adults laugh, they aren't mad. It isn't much, but kids often offer themselves up in ways that adults don't fully understand. Thinking back, guests were an easy audience, and we weren't nearly as funny as we thought we were. As an adult, the same applies, and the self-deception continues.

Even a whiskey-induced comedic success could end in an instant. Since it was true that the faster you danced, the more the adults laughed, to stay funny you had to continuously dance faster. But since the physical world has its limits, I was confronted with the finite nature of my clowning routine. As often happened, just as the clowning reached a crescendo, one of my brothers or I would fall, not backward but always forward into the hard-edged coffee table, and never hitting an arm or leg—too simple, not sensational enough— no, always one of us hit our head, and the intended crescendo was replaced by wailing, gnashing of teeth, possibly blood, and the dramatic transformation of genres from comedy to tragedy.

Dad was not a fan of drama. Still, for all the restrictions of family, school and church, there were plenty of chances to get into trouble, make jokes and have fun without adult surveillance. Sure, today the world is more permissible, but kids—or little parental projects—rarely get any time out from under their project managers' thumb (I can hear the objections), where kids are far more creative. Do parents really aspire for their kids to be great at everything, which is a formula for doing nothing in particular? If parents think the worst that can happen to their kids is to experience an hour of boredom, the possibilities for creativity are truly at risk. Bubble-wrapped kids constantly lectured about safety, appropriate language and inclusiveness are unlikely candidates to dream up the most subversive, best-timed, hilarious zinger. The difference is, we were always aware of the great divide between what we said to adults and what we could say between ourselves, whereas kids today seem to have internalized ideological, socially acceptable adult responses for all situations. The media seems to love when kids take up big predictable social causes—social justice, ethical animal treatment, fair coffee, and of course causes green, greener, greenest. Just say the word and feel good about yourself, or your kid. I always think that the celebrity kid probably hasn't been allowed to be much of a kid and likely has a limited sense of humour. What about the reintroduction of allowing kids to be kids, including goofy humour as their cause?

For all their seriousness and fidelity to rules—common beliefs and shared values is more accurate—our parents and their friends understood the distinct difference between behavioural requirements of their belief system and play. Kids and adults understood and generally respected the parameters of the code—house life, school or work and the Catholic Church—and sought subversive refuge in reading between the lines. My dad wore a laundered, crisp white shirt from Hillary Cleaners, a smart tie and an immaculate suit to work every day for the duration of his thirty-year civil servant career. His colleagues only knew his professional side, and the existence of family only peeked out one afternoon a year when the civil servants brought their wives and kids in for the departmental Christmas party. Even then, suits were worn and no personal information was exchanged as couples sipped punch and watched their numerous progeny accept the requisite gift from Santa.

But among the Irish clan, friends and family—and as it turns out most friends were also family, cousins distant or close—subversion reigned supreme. More laughing than at a comedy show, stories, real involved, well told and mostly clean, though for those used to listening and being invisible, some bawdy humour. Especially as we got into our teens, I liked the way our house mood changed when adult gangs gathered, and we saw a spark of childish humour in Dad. Mom and Dad unplugged meant they went with casual clothes too. Mom wore a slightly less formal dress (the difference from a church dress escaped us), and Dad put on a slightly worn pair of dress pants and traded his white laundered shirt for a comfortable Viyella plait. Even during our two-week summer holiday in sweltering heat, Mom and Dad's casual look maintained a higher standard of dress than most working professionals today. Still, shrouded in rules, conformity and superstition, they simply had to figuratively sneak outside and have some real fun, and we, living as precarious shadows to the adult world, had some real joy.

Especially those two weeks away in summer. Norway Bay is a crowded, highly social clustering of cottages along the Ottawa River, an hour from Ottawa. The cottages were simple, Spartan even, and mostly arranged along streets, perpendicular to the river and far removed from the water. Cottages in the suburbs, with about the same amount of space between buildings. Still, our two weeks at the bay were the best two of the year, every year. If I could go back in time and watch from the outside, as I have tried to do my whole life, one of my favourite places would be Norway Bay in the mid-1960s. I'd watch my parents and their friends—with all their kids never fully accounted for—having fun, completely separate from their responsible workday world, in a way we in our grim, multi-tasking existence can't begin to imagine. The concept of a day of rest had meaning then. For all the quantity of bodies and close quarters, we were completely unfettered, free of adult censorship or restriction of any kind. Rules were suspended, relaxed to non-existence as an unspoken temporary social pact, and it worked.

As soon as we arrived at the bay—eight of us then, nine in later years, all our luggage and a large quantity of food—we threw off our shoes, a fitting metaphor for freedom, and began the process of hardening and blackening the soles of our feet. We took to the gravel and dirt roads, covering great distances, between the golf course and the pier, any number of beaches, Pop's Confectionary, the sandpit, into the bush, and all over again, for no particular reason. That was then, and it was acceptable, unaccountable fun without purpose. Not a lesson to be had, but plenty learned along the way.

Most of the adults connected to our clan didn't even know our names. We were one of the McCloskeys, and far from being offended, we enjoyed the anonymity. What they probably didn't know was that though we likely knew their names, we were equally clueless about how they fit into our tribal web.

Much as we played, the adults played more. Golf every day, horseshoes the same, euchre and forty-five every night, drinking and smoking every hour. As happened every year, the end of the holiday culminated in a friendly little fiercely contested rivalry. Dad and Lorne Kelly teamed up against Bernard Stanton and Irvin Laughern for the tournament title, consisting of golf, horseshoes and euchre. The original triathlon. While wives feigned interest, mostly glad to get the men and kids out of the cottage, the hoard of us followed the progress of the games with keen interest and rival bets. The men were lighthearted, good sports, but the tournament rituals and desire to win were always front and centre.

Golf was first up in the morning. Each man had his caddy, a son, while the rest of us followed like groupies on the professional tour. In preparation for two rounds, 18 parched holes (the players, not the greens), cans of beer were carefully wrapped in newspaper and stuffed into the sleeve of a golf bag. Out on the course, around the fifth hole, under giant white pines, there would be a beer-and-cigarette break. The men would sip and talk, and the young hoard would wait and listen. The men joked and postured in a playful way while retaining a degree of formality—familiarity with respect—common to men and women of that generation. These were lifelong friends who retained a degree of privacy as a matter of course, even on the golf course. They knew each other without knowing things about each other and would have been baffled by our penchant for telling all to all people. We use the term *too much information* today but rarely mean it. Waiting in the wings, not part of the contest, pulling for our dad's team, we never felt left out or excluded. We were happy to watch it unfold. It was not about us, which was just fine.

Later in the afternoon, the second phase of the tournament took place at the horseshoe pit in front the Kellys' cottage. This was the match that mattered, since the evening euchre game did not have the open-air feel, enthusiastic audience and drama of the former. The number of wins over the years was about even, though for all the intensity of the tournament no one really cared. Still, the tournament end had a tinge of bitterness because it marked the end of summer and the inevitability of another dreaded school year.

I've owned several cottages since that time. Much better buildings, more amenities, preferred locations, beautiful private spots on clean freshwater lakes. I designed and built a post-and-beam house that had the unique distinction of being twice featured in the *Ottawa Citizen* Homes section. Everything superior to our little two-week rental shack, except that nothing has ever been able to compare. Norway Bay was about community; cottage life today is about fending off community. People want privacy over all things, including, or especially, people. Nothing is regarded as more compelling than the prospect of owning nature without another human being in the universe to contend with.

Personally, I'd trade it all away for five minutes back at the bay, on the sidelines as always, watching my dad and mom and their friends dance their way through another crowded day in another crummy shack. I'd watch my mom drink a cup of coffee—before she gave it up—without having anything else in the world to do. I'd watch my dad stiffly bend over and pick a newsprint-wrapped beer from his golf bag and then a can of pop for his eager, grateful caddy. I'd watch us at the dinner table, the only half-hour of the day all together during our two weeks of freedom, stupid stories, corny jokes, next-day plans, Mom and Dad more relaxed than back at home, ignoring the black bare feet under the table, connected to each other and as close to home as you ever get in this lifetime.

Truth is, we don't really have faith in ourselves. We're told to, but it doesn't work that way. The self-esteem industry has corrupted young people into thinking they can do anything if they just believe in themselves enough. We may at times muster confidence, but, disconnected to the reality of *if not for the grace of God*, it is denial and hubris. Humility is an acknowledgement that we cannot do it on our own. It is the only sane way to view our little lives in the grand scheme of potential connection. We believe in, place faith in, the community of spirit, and that is not achieved in the ecstasy of isolation.

I still watch the holiday scenes unfold in my mind, summer and winter, and from this film series the excerpts feature Dad more than Mom, because his was the life furthest removed from finding, being, home. He wanted it but struggled with his own isolation, as so many of us do. Since Dad looked and sounded like Bing Crosby, my excerpts are mixed up with scenes from Bing's films. *Going My Way* is a perennial favourite, with Bing as Father O'Malley tending to the old priest, superbly played by Barry Fitzgerald. The old priest is back in bed with a wretched cold, happy to know he is not about to be cast out of the parish he has tended to for 40 years. Father O'Malley gives him a stiff drink and kids the old priest but does not patronize him. Father O'Malley sings, surely the most dated and tender moment in film, "Too-Ra-Loo-Ra-Loo-Ral, That's an Irish Lullaby" as the old man falls asleep. Soon after, having restored the parish to order, Father O'Malley must leave, a reminder that he has merely peered into the temporal world and is called to move on. The fun has ended. Such is nostalgia.

---

Without doubt, the funniest person who ever lived was Joe Brennan. (No relation to Art Brennan, Dad's giant friend, though for two people with the same Irish name in the Ottawa valley not to be related strains credulity.) Some people might take exception to my presumptuous claim regarding Joe Brennan. They might argue that humour is highly subjective, subject to linguistic and cultural considerations and varying opinions. And then there is the necessity to not offend. Sorry, you can't prescribe humour; you can't regulate laughter.

Joe Brennan is the funniest person who ever lived for the simple and compelling reason that he could make my dad laugh. I don't mean a curled lip or a giggle; I mean an uproarious belly laugh, which from my stoic, emotionally retentive and painfully serious father was a thing of beauty to behold. Joe cracked the world's toughest case, every time, as naturally as anyone ever took a breath of air. Actually, Joe Brennan made everyone he ever encountered in his lifetime laugh, every time. I know; I've checked the record.

But the truth of my claim will not be recorded in these pages; you really just had to meet Joe Brennan to understand. Still, while the essence of his humour may remain elusive, a few words about his life may give a clue. He did not have a comedic routine. He was not practiced. His humor wasn't even quick improvisation. It was simply that he lived and breathed funny utterances, and he could not be other than what he was at all times in all situations.

Joe was Ottawa Valley Irish Catholic, and yes, there is a serious lack of diversity among my parents' friends. He came from farming stock, and unlike the McCloskeys across the river who tried to farm high above the valley in the rock-filled infertile forest, the Brennan land was a flat, fertile dairy farm. But for reasons unknown, Joe chose to live in the city—probably to guarantee having a perpetual audience—and raise his slew of kids with his lovely, and incredibly patient, wife, Loretta. No bank teller, waiter, police officer, priest or nun was ever able to make a serious point or have a point of view without Joe Brennan turning it on its head. Another proof of genius: people laughed too hard to ever be offended.

Like when he got pulled over by the police in his two-block-long red Cadillac. He'd had a loud cow horn installed and had the cop belly-laughing instead of ticket-writing in a second. His description of the look on the cows' faces when they were likewise serenaded by his passing car was as classic as the bent-over cop. Neither the cop nor the cows ever knew what hit them, because Joe's humour didn't have any of the attention-seeking, Irish slagging, laugh-so-as-not-to-cry humour that I among many are commonly guilty of. In the company of Joe Brennan, you laughed so as not to pee your pants, only to later discover that you had peed and crapped your pants and were wildly entertained for it.

You can study and analyze your favourite comic's comedy routine. Consider style, timing, anticipation, originality. Some of it you could probably do yourself with practice. But how do you analyze or emulate someone whose every utterance is unrehearsed, perfectly timed, original, egoless, comedic genius? How do you figure out his shtick when he is completely unaware of his next utterance until he says it? How do you solve a problem like Maria?

Example: Joe Brennan often dropped by our house, back when spontaneous visiting was not only permissible but welcomed. Joe usually visited with his wife, Loretta, who, God love her, never ceased to find her husband funny. But on this occasion he seemed to be alone, which meant at least two ryes on ice. The cow horn announced his arrival, and my parents always felt good around Joe Brennan. Dad poured drinks, always hard liquor, with an extra ice cube as a nod to the intense heat of the day. Joe talked in his heavy valley accent, and my mom worked in the kitchen, adding to the conversation and laughing occasionally, sight unseen. Joe lit another Player's Plain with blackened nicotine fingers, he still robust, pushing 70. Dad, smoking wimpy filtered cigarettes, belly-laughed, head back, mouth open, false teeth shifting ever so slightly. Time passed quickly, maybe an hour, the intense heat barely noticed for the intense humour.

Without warning Joe Brennan switched gears and asked my mom if she could spare a glass of water. My mom said, "Yes, of course," though puzzled by a man who never even allowed water in his rye, let alone drank water on its own. Then Joe, turning to me, knowing me without knowing me, pleading, "Son, would you have the heart to run this cup of water out to the car for my wife, Loretta. She'll be gettin' awfully hot by now." My mom jolted, at first believing, my dad in another spasm of laughter, and me grinning, knowing a Joe Brennan when I heard one and glad to be noticed, even if only as a prop for the punchline.

My parents could appreciate a funny story. No sex, no f-bombs, no putting people down, but stuff that actually happened, without malarkey or manipulation. My parents were un-Irish in their aversion of embellishment, at least in the stories that made their way into family mythology.

They had few un-Irish friends, so I remember this couple well. She was a likeable, well-meaning French Canadian ditzy blonde, dumb as a bag of hammers, he a forever frustrated, bewildered policeman, never quite believing after 30 years of marriage what his nutty wife was capable of doing or saying next. Their relationship was like a sitcom, with the entire audience able to see it coming, except for the poor, perpetually unsuspecting husband.

It seems their car had an annoying rattle. It is not clear if it bothered him or her, but it seemed to originate from the trunk and would not go away. So he had the bright idea of hauling his middle-aged bulk into the trunk to check it out. But that was not enough, because it only rattled when the car was moving. So he says to his wife, "Just drive the car a wee bit so I can hear precisely where the noise is coming from." Did I mention that everyone except for the husband could see it coming? She gets in the car and starts the engine but not before decisively slamming the trunk lid down. He, confused, not quite comprehending, surprised against his better judgment, again. She assumes that finding the source of the noise, not unlike finding the source of the Nile, is going to take some time. With trunk lid down, clear view, she backs out of the lane, he not hearing the rattle, she not hearing his screams. She rarely drove the car, and when she did he was very critical, which, he being a cop and she being a terrible driver, was easy to understand. So now without the criticism, she decides to take a real drive, but being unpracticed, she stops and starts the car inordinately, but hey, you gotta learn somehow.

And then the Queensway. She doesn't usually drive on the big imposing highway, but sometimes you just have to go with the mood, rattle and roll. Her driving erratic, a few swerves, and *I hope they don't expect me to drive fast like that!* Driving, concentrating, she thinks there's some reason why she is doing this but can't quite remember, while the pesky rattling sound has become different now, louder, has acquired a distinctive banging sound. An hour later she pulls into the laneway, pleased with her driving lesson, and vaguely wonders why the rattling, er, banging sound continues after the engine is turned off.

It would have been spectacular to witness the moment she opened the trunk of the car. Which reminds me, how do you determine who loves you more, your wife or your dog? Answer: Put them both in the trunk of your car for an hour and see which one is glad to see you when you open it up.

I don't know this to be true, but when Joe Brennan died, I'll bet he went out laughing. Any nurse or doctor or orderly he encountered would have laughed, would have been made light by the perfectly timed joke he managed with his dying breath. For all the forces pulling him to the grave, Dad was lightened and made whole for a while when he belly-laughed with Joe Brennan. Around Joe you never saw the vale of tears for the peal of laughter. Humour gets us through hardship, but it is more than some dopey opiate dulling our sense of the inevitable. Sure, we need to accept death, but we also have to get over it, and the best way to do that is get over ourselves.

If we have faith that we are more than our short-lived human husk, it follows that our best shot at transcendence is to connect with others, any and all others, whomever God places in our path. Humour can be an immediate electric shock to complacency, bias, power imbalance, pettiness and conceit, taking us out of ourselves in the moment of punchline delivery. It is evidence that we are not alone. Irish stoicism is rooted in black-humour fatalism at the silliness and tragedy of it all, but with a nod to faith that our fate may be all right if we go to church and look after our mothers. So it turns out, I wasn't constantly acting badly in school when I was young; I was seeking connection, that commonality between faith and humour, a touch of divinity. Yup, that's my story, and I'm sticking to it.

It is true that everyone who met Joe Brennan was better off for it except, sadly, those few who did not have a sense of humour. I contend that humourless people are more common today than a generation ago. My parents' generation were serious people, adhered to strict rules, but did not take themselves too seriously. Most people whose identity was forged by the Depression did what was right, rather than talk about social consciousness. Today many people do not believe in rules but take themselves very seriously. They believe in themselves but take on the collective mentality of causes without consideration of personal values, and don't seem to know the difference. We live in the age of ideology, a serious social force absolutely antithetical to humour. My parents always told us to stay away from talking religion and politics if you wanted to keep a friendship. People's views on politics and religion were not only irrelevant to friendship but largely unknown. All the advice they gave us that we ignored has turned out to be right. We forget a simple truth: we admire but we are not drawn to someone who is right or has taken on the right cause; we are drawn to and like people, most of all, with whom we can share a laugh. Most of our destructive notions that consign us to our lower selves—resentment, grievance, pride—do not hold while we are afflicted by humour. There are solutions to our problems, even the ones that haunt us. It is for good reason we have faith in someone who can tell or receive a joke.

Like my Uncle Basil O'Neill. My mom's ten-years-younger brother and his twin brother, Bill, were a force to be reckoned with growing up in the sleepy farming community of Navan, Ontario, in the 1940s. As teens, they often used their likeness to mischievous advantage, writing a test while posing as the other or presenting one to the other's girlfriend, just to see if she would notice. When it came to a fight, taking on one was to incur the wrath of both. They represented double fun for those who wanted to play and double trouble for those who preferred to fight.

The boys came by their spunky attitude honestly. Mom's father, Joseph O'Neill, was known both in Navan and later in Five Points, California, as a *character*. Being and having character is little understood today. Before the homogenizing of the world, people had to be more resourceful, independent and free thinking in order to survive and thrive. We defer to the government today to do our thinking, take our risks and ensure there is food for the winter. Joseph O'Neill was old school, a man who seldom spoke but meant every word whenever he did. Uncle Basil recalled evenings when visitors such as the O'Tooles came over for cards. Joe liked cards, but once done he was done and wanted to go to bed. Social decorum be damned; whenever it suited him, which was often enough, he would announce, "Well, I'll be going to bed, so you folks can get going home." And that was that.

And it was a bit of a surprise that Joe felt the need to go to bed early, considering his favourite drink. Mom remembers watching him experiment by dipping a tea bag into a strong cup of coffee. He sipped his new brew, carefully smacked his lips and announced his approval: "That makes a damn fine drink."

Joe also had a propensity for making shrewd observations. He wouldn't seem to know you were even in the room and then would make a direct and personal comment. Often rude, occasionally insightful and always offbeat, uniquely Joseph O'Neill. One day to Mom when she was quite young, "Enie, you got a real narra' head." Once the pronouncement was made, he felt the need to remind Mom ever so often of her head-width deformity. In our family we often comment on each other's narra' head. Could be that our familial narra' head accounts for our narra' views.

Later in Five Points, where the family had moved to seek their fortune, and where Joe finally received some relief from the asthma that plagued him during cold winters in Canada, he took on a part-time job at the local cinema. His brother, rich and successful Great Uncle Jack, owned it, and Joe was not going to let it be compromised in any way under his stewardship. So he performed his lowly job—taking the movie fare and giving tickets— seriously. By this time, Joe was no longer young and was, like my dad, about 125 pounds soaking wet, so low on the intimidation factor. But fights are not necessarily won by the strongest opponent. Fights are most often won by the person truly willing to put himself on the line. A big young guy, full of attitude and testosterone, pushed his way into the theatre without paying and challenged Joe to make him pay. Big mistake. For a while, Joe let him sit and watch the movie, with a sense of victory over the scrawny theatre clerk. Then with a polite tap on the shoulder Joe called him out, they exited the theatre, and Joe finished him off with about three well-placed punches.

Uncle Jack was rich, religious and responsible to a fault. But even he had a sense of humour, though the recipient of this practical joke might have disagreed. Jack had two close friends in the Imperial Valley. Deep in the desert, far from city, town or prying eyes, a brothel was established and was doing well. One of the three close friends became a brothel customer, and Jack and his other close friend decided to play a trick on their fallen pal. They knew that the brothel building was portable and on stilts, and Jack was skilful at handling mule teams. After an evening trek into the desert, the mule team was hitched to the brothel building and unceremoniously pulled it into the centre of Calexico, the nearest town. Brothel patrons exiting into the desert was one thing, but exiting into the centre of town to an audience of stunned people was altogether a different experience.

Uncle Basil was both the family historian and a man for whom a joke mattered. As Mom's ability to travel waned with advancing Parkinson's disease, I travelled with her and became acquainted with the California side of the family. Basil and I both had a competitive streak and an affinity for delivering the best punchline. This sickness is the Irish affliction; the drink, a distant, lacklustre second. Fortunately, it is untreatable. Basil's wife, Aunt Marilyn, deserves a Noble Peace Prize for patiently enduring our slagging and, if I do say so, brilliant exchanges.

Basil and Marilyn's son Matthew had the Irish affliction in spades. Matthew also had cystic fibrosis, difficult to live with and life-threatening, but it was his sense of humour that was the affliction. The remarkable thing about people who are truly challenged is that they tend to have a wicked sense of humour. I think there is something in this, profound even, that we tend to overlook. Humour is freedom of sorts, a pact to not be tied to the smallness of the world most of us are drawn into, a perspective that does not allow for delusion about what this life is about and has to offer. If, as Samuel Johnson is reputed to have said, "When a man knows he is to be hanged in a fortnight, it concentrates his mind wonderfully," nothing gives perspective more than knowing, fully and viscerally, the reality of this finite, limited life. Matthew knew this always and lived it every second.

I didn't get to know Matthew. He is one among many from my mother's O'Neill clan I know by reputation only. The California O'Neills always held a fascination for us distant winter-bound Canadians, more for what we didn't know than for what we did. For years, we listened to Mom talking about her people. Mom always said I should meet Matthew because we had the same sense of humour. I hadn't the heart to tell Mom that mine was a one-off. Still, I was intrigued. But not by his sense of humour as much as by his courage.

Matthew died in 1994, just shy of 30. It was no surprise; it was always going to be this way. Matthew lived with the knowledge but not the attitude of certain death. And to help assuage people's natural sympathy, which, well-intended as it is, can create distance, he used humour. A wicked tease to his siblings, nieces and nephews and a competitive punster to all others, including and especially his dad, Basil. Most of us kick the concept of death far into the future, one we never expect to have to face. We talk the talk and then strategize for delusional deniability. A roll of the dice says chances are that we have time, and statistics tell us so, so we act and plan certain of the time still owed us. Our facade is contingent upon this assumption, and for most people, denial or not, it sustains us. Good health helps to sustain the illusion. Which raises the question, if one of the primary reasons for this life is to pull back the curtain on human conceit and find meaning in mortality, is our quest helped or hindered by good health? If suffering has meaning, maybe it's not such a dumb question.

People with cystic fibrosis have shredded lungs that fill up with mucous, less easily with air. They struggle for breath; they require daily pounding on their backs to clear the mucous to find their next breath. And then there is the certainty factor, their only one, that death will come early in life, however well lived.

Dad also had the certainty of physical struggle followed by early death. He walked like Frankenstein, was racked with pain, and suffered the slow suffocation of emphysema. Basil and I shared more than an affinity for bad puns. Watching people we loved slowly drown, we frantically paced the shore, holding a life preserver, though we knew it would never be thrown. Still, we paced, always pacing. Basil habitually rose with the sun and walked long distances every day. I have been a distance runner for over 30 years. As long as we move we are not standing still, not standing and watching, useless. We know the outcome, but to stop would be to lose faith. So when we're not moving, we move the conversation along by telling jokes, brilliantly and badly.

Matthew showed up every day; that is, he lived life to the fullest, and yes, clichés can nail truth. He doggedly pursued and almost finished a master's degree in biochemistry. Takes guts, inner resources and a strong dose of humour. Toughness alone can't sustain the grace under pressure of true courage, so humour really helps. And if that is not enough, those who live under the cloud or clarity of human mortality often worry about the effect on others more than on themselves. Matthew assuaged worry from others with humour. He and his dad joked and laughed. We joke and laugh so as not to cry. Our cry is both a pathetic and holy communion. A good joke is serious business indeed.

Most of the family lexicon of humour features true stories. Here is one of Basil's best. A first cousin of his father, Joseph O'Neill, was a widower who worked long winter months in a lumber camp in the Canadian bush. His son lived with him in the camp, but when he was about ten years old, his father thought it was about time that the boy got a proper education. So he enrolled his son in a school, and the boy dutifully showed up on the first day and stood on the threshold of the credentialed world. At the teacher's beckoning, he entered the one-room school, took a seat and lit up his corncob pipe, as was his custom. But the teacher objected, saying that his pipe was not allowed, and he would have to choose between his pipe and an education. So naturally the boy chose his pipe and left the classroom, never to return to that or any other school in his life. Despite, or possibly due to, him having no formal education, the boy successfully made his way in the world and had a good and prosperous business career.

I love that story. Tough for some to identify with the pipe choice. Chances are, he decided that placing faith in something outside of his own making was a bad bet. He didn't quit; he walked away from something he couldn't believe in, in search of something he could. The triumph of self-sufficiency over credentials, when personal qualities still had a fighting chance. Kids today are graduating from university with expectations that will never be met and with no idea of how to dig deep inside and find their own way.

My Navan-bred O'Neill grandparents never lost their self-sufficiency. In Five Points, California, without a dairy herd to look after, Joe raised peacocks, both as a sign of true eccentricity and a proof of self-reliance. Gramma fretted over the cold her grandchildren had to endure while she and Grandpa ended their days in the sun. So every Christmas for years, she painstakingly made us—that is, all of us—flannel pyjamas. Lots of work, lots of pioneer initiative, lots of crotch. Sorry, it had to be said; it is, after all, part of our family mythology. Frugality was hard to give up, once forged by the Depression. And Gramma's pyjamas were well made and bound to last. She made them big, hulking US marine big, so that we could grow into them, I guess. Of course since she sent a new set every year, it made us wonder why the need to supersize for the future. Anyway, one remarkable feature of Gramma's largess was the elongated, trench-coat exposed, nicely embroidered open crotch. I used to regret that I never met Gramma, but I was consoled by the fact that if she ever met and saw the size of me, she'd be really disappointed.

Then again, we did meet, that one time. I don't quite remember all the details, since she was waiting for me when I popped out. I was the fourth wee thing born in five blitz years, and Gramma came back to Canada just one time to help Mom manage. There is also a rumour that my reputation preceded me, though notoriety at birth would be a record. Gramma being a roll-up-your-sleeves-and-pitch-in type of gal, picked me up sans diaper, or open crotch pyjamas. Not wanting to be shy on a first meeting, I took careful aim and peed all over her. My theory is that Gramma made the flannel crotches extra big to accommodate my projectile peeing, or else to humiliate me for my lack of inhibition. Not knowing the answer has kept this little episode in our family scrapbook.

Mom and Dad shared their parents' utilitarian streak. Make pyjamas to stay warm during cold, cruel winters. Slap a diaper on that kid before he pees again. Apply work toward required completion of task. Run a marathon? No. Our parents' generation worked bloody hard and did not have the luxury, time or energy to add a workout to their day for fitness, love or money. So it's no wonder that in the 1970s when the running boom hit North America, they were perplexed. My torturous decades of running in competition had not started yet, and so I suffered a kind of hyper-ennui without release. Running had occurred to me, but being my parents' son, I had to get over the idea that exercise was child's play and not a serious activity for a man all of 21.

I remember driving through Carleton University on a Sunday morning with Dad. It was raining, and coincidentally runners were gathering for a big marathon. Inside the car we sat enveloped in cigarette smoke, as was his custom. The concept of second-hand smoke for non-smoking passengers, coughing, hacking, gasping and wheezing, had not yet kicked in. The smoke inside the car combined with the humidity and rain outside made it hard to see. Dad slowed the car as windshield wipers flapped across our vision. Through the mist and vapour a middle-aged fit-looking man appeared, making long running strides in preparation for the race. And just as I thought I might try that one day, Dad made one of his rare proclamations: "What a stupid thing to do, at his age, out in the rain." God love him, I've run with Dad in mind for over 30 years now, him gasping for breath to drive another mile, me grasping for breath to run the same. I still grasp to live, and he breaths easy now. Now we both split our lungs at the irony of it all.

Running for me has been as much about exorcizing angst as exercising my various parts. I run, therefore I am—able to sleep at night. But early on and for many years, I wanted to compete. And of course doing a marathon, especially your first, is supposed to be a big deal. So I thought. But Mom was unimpressed by sporting events and focused her concern on the well-being of her son. I had been injured coming into race day, and by the time I came past Mom, 25 or so kilometres in, sitting in her lawn chair and wearing a plastic hairnet, she noticed that I was running slowly, struggling with one leg straight, about as efficient as a hermit crab. Mom, with a dose of both common sense and concern, looked up and said, "Oh Larry, why don't you quit!"

Mom didn't get that the role of a spectator in a marathon is to encourage, to tell runners who look like hell that they look great, to perpetuate the illusion that the outcome actually matters. No, you just couldn't count on Mom, cause she had this pesky concern thing going on that got in the way of important things like finishing 2037th versus 2054th, or whatever it was that first pathetic year. We used to kid Mom that she would make a great motivational speaker sitting in her lawn chair, quietly and undramatically telling truths, discretion be damned. But the thing is, she was right. I should have quit that race, and because I soldiered on with a sense of faux-destiny, I was sidelined for six months before I could run again. And the deeper revelation came when I had to admit that she was right about this and, well, everything she ever said. Without exception. Humbling and true.

Mom was a snappy dresser, and having seven kids never changed that fact. She, like many women of her generation, often went to the hairdresser, and her hair always looked perfectly coiffed. If she went outside at any time of year with any chance of wind, she covered up with a plastic head scarf that protected but did not muss up her do. One might be forgiven for thinking that Mom's plastic headgear would at least be restricted to warm weather—especially since in winter her signature stylistic statement was an elegant long fur coat. But in addition to fashion sense, Mom believed that people caught colds from exposing themselves without protection to cold or wind or precipitation of any kind. Mom would not have joined PETA, and she loved the warmth of her full furs. So she regularly combined wearing her $5,000 fur coat with her year-round 50 cent clear plastic accessory. From the neck down, Mom was a portrait of elegance; from the neck up, she looked like she was wrapping leftover meatloaf for the fridge. Mom, a study in contrasts, saw no contrasting style statement in this, and as I said, since everything she ever said turns out to have been right, this too must have been a true style to emulate.

Not so my dad—straightforward, decisive, no time for contrasts. Kids get loose teeth; there's no sense beating around the bush. Once one was identified, we would meekly follow Dad out to his workroom and watch as he pulled the old familiar pliers from their accustomed hook. Open up. Which one? One pull, one extracted tooth, every time. Tell this little episode today and people want to call the Children's Aid Society to inquire about retroactive child abuse arrests. But it was fine, mostly. When it comes to pulling teeth, you want decisiveness; when it comes to interesting winter attire, you want a hint of contradiction. All the dentist journals and fashion magazines say so.

It was rare to see Dad belly laugh outside of the company of Joe Brennan. Humour comes in surprising twists and turns. He and I loved Jim Unger's Herman cartoons, but for Dad humour was more a passing amusement than uproarious laughter. So if he cracked a smile, you had nailed it. But one day he saw a Herman cartoon, one of Unger's least funny really, and he started laughing. It featured two men standing in front of a wall display adorned with manly hunting trophies, antlers and the like. One trophy was decisively unmanly and had a limp skinny tail drooping from a big wooden plaque. One man says to the other, "I don't know what it was, but it sure could run fast." And Dad laughed and laughed and, for the only time in his life, seemed as if he couldn't stop. Yes, I became a clown for this moment, with credit and thanks to the late great Jim Unger.

There were other times, many actually, when laughing with my parents was commonplace. Thank God for TV. Before social media made us all anti-social, we gathered for shows at designated times, and if you missed it, you missed the social gathering. And yes, I am making a case for television bringing us all together. First of all, there was only one TV, so no personal screen time, downloading, choosing from among infinity, getting exactly what you want when you want, without anyone in the world peeking over your shoulder. Some of my favourite family moments, all compromise by today's standards, were watching comedy and variety shows together, without any thought about wanting to be, do or watch anything else. We were that dull. The Carol Burnett, Andy Griffith, Red Skelton and Lucy shows were memorable, with big, real talent, now rarely seen in the age of reality TV, cheap, crass humour and obsession with youth culture driving all things entertainment.

One character on TV had an effect on Dad equivalent to the Jim Unger hanging tail cartoon. Dad loved the antics and comedic genius of Don Knotts. Don Knotts absolutely made the *Andy Griffith Show*. I remember one movie with Don Knotts, *The Ghost and Mr. Chicken*, that made Dad laugh out loud, head back, dentures shifting, tears in the eyes. It was nice to see. The lighter moments, the ones that connect, always outlast strife and tension. In rare instances when I see a clip from one of the oldies it does stir memories of my parents, in their lighter moments, in that brief time between when everything was done and when everything had to be done again.

Mom made the best apple pies in the world, and that was no laughing matter. Her reputation was such that accomplished pie-makers deferred to her omnipotence, and finally, 18 years after her death, I can divulge her secret ingredient: 7-up. Now the singular skill of pie-making cannot be offered up to the public trust, but she allowed that the secret to her superior flaky piecrust was in adding a dollop of this holy beverage. Mom knew that I loved her apple pie more than life itself, and long after she quit making all her other dishes, she soldiered on with apple pie. Even as her Parkinson's disease tightened its grip and her mind wavered between normalcy and a ghostlike, demented version of herself, she enlisted the support of her live-in companion and continued to come over for dinner with homemade pie in hand. Cara and I always gratefully received the gift while admonishing her for taking too much trouble. I for one was blatantly insincere. For Mom and those of her generation, arriving empty-handed or, worse, bringing something store-bought was not an option. She wanted, desperately in her understated way, to remain useful.

And there was something else. For all the losses she was absorbing, she held her quivering chin high, dressed up, hair perfect, out to church, seeing friends and family, and still making apple pie. Normalcy equals pie rounded. But the companion was not a world-class pie-maker and could only follow instructions. Mom remained the brains of the operation, and her brain had lapses that could only compromise the delicate art of pie-making. On this last pie-making Sunday evening dinner, something went terribly wrong.

Mom wanted the pie to have oven freshness so saved pairing her renowned piecrust with her equally scrumptious filling until after she had arrived at our house. But the piecrust was not light and flaky as had been her fifty-year tradition; it was heavy and concrete-like. Too little, too much 7-up or any other ingredient, who knows, but the outcome could not be denied. And I could see accumulated loss hovering in the periphery of her mind and in her eyes. So I put the piecrust on my head like a First World War helmet and ordered us all to march around the dining room table. Which we did, and she laughed—surely one of the greatest joys in my life—and all was right with the world, and the storm clouds faded from her eyes, for the eternity of that small space of time. No one wanted pie anyway; we just needed a good laugh.

Life, circumstances and time reshape and distort, for ultimately, for all of us, the centre cannot hold. The wonder of it all is how bloody well, on balance, most humans hold together what cannot be held together. We don't wither in the shadow of death; we don't die from the reality of life. Nostalgia is reaching back for the trailing clouds of glory; faith is belief that we will return again.

As Mom hung suspended between being herself and the lurking shadow of what she would become, she would ask what was real and what was not. The realization of becoming what you are not, of losing who you are, is surely frightening. But when she reflected on what she had just said, from the fictitious world that had invaded her living room to her sorry role in the tragic drama, she would always laugh at herself, and that I will never forget. More than courage, more than I can understand.

The curse or blessing of old age is that we become more ourselves. Dementia is a bit of a wild card, reinforcing one's higher self for some and unmaking one's true nature for others. Most of us are not comfortable in own skins, let alone with the possibility of unedited exposure. Mom's sweet, self-effacing nature became more acute as she treaded water, submerged, resurfaced briefly, and then slipped below the still, murky water. Details fell and scattered like November leaves on a windy day, but you could always bring her back for a few seconds with a joke. For my parents, whose final days were both horrible and holy, humour gave momentary reprieve from any and all of life's vicissitudes. They were serious people who didn't take themselves too seriously. They were straitlaced squares who loved a good laugh.

I often walk around the dining room table with Mom's piecrust on my head. I really do miss that pie.

"False words are not only evil in themselves, but they infect the soul with evil."

SOCRATES

# CHAPTER FOUR
## FAITH AND INNOCENCE

I MISS THE WORLD OF LARGE FAMILIES AND SHARED VALUES—INCLUDING MUCH maligned Christianity. This is a lament, after all, not a knock against diversity or other religions. Diversity and inclusion of themselves are good, but the politics of identity is often unnecessarily divisive. The problem is the palpable disparagement from likely Christian-born but long vacated progressives who never miss an opportunity to express their loathing for Christianity and tolerance for anything that is not Christian, sometimes including disturbing cultural practices that have nothing to do with religion. Most of all, we who have not capitulated to self-hatred of Christianity and all things Western need to fully embrace that speaking up for something is not speaking against something else, as seems to be the confusion of the day.

It is true that my parents were not tolerant of other religions in the modern sense, which is to say that it would never have occurred to them to be. They were respectful and distant while acknowledging the important shared value of belief in God. But to apologists my parents' great sin was that they happened to believe Catholicism was right. People seem to have a hard time with those who actually believe in something particular and distinct rather than adhere to relativism. My parents weren't afraid of or against other religions; they just didn't believe in them, for that would be to not believe in Catholicism. They didn't disparage belief, though they did non-belief, or atheism. Tolerance of all things and belief in nothing, though a winning formula at a cocktail party, seem vacuous and a bit dull. I will understand if I don't get an invitation to speak at the next atheist convention.

I know and respect people of conviction from differing religious backgrounds, and the thundering irony is that people of the believing minority are very unlikely to be threatened by adherents to other faiths. Feelings of exclusion are difficult to muster from those who do not want to be included. Relativism—the pressure to flatten, make dull and invisible all reference to our religious heritage—comes from apologists, most likely well-educated, usually of the conforming majority, and always worried that a shared value might leave someone out. Increasingly, belief in nothing is believed to be the de facto formula for acceptable full inclusion.

A few years back a friend and colleague organized our office Christmas party to break through sensitivities and achieve, in this case, having fun. She is a practicing Muslim. To their credit, most adherents to minority religions in Canada are confused by rather than interested in the vacuous majority.

Part of the justification for the apologist view seems to be out of concern for young people who need to be spared the indoctrination that they were once subjected to and—no, they do not thank God—rejected. So to compensate for religious indoctrination they ban belief and religious context, which means that a whole generation of young people are growing up having nothing to believe in, reject, criticize or return to, and they have no idea what they are missing. The self-esteem industry has negated religious belief for belief in oneself, but placing faith in oneself creates a likely scenario for psychological and spiritual disillusionment. The human heart and soul yearns and, with the passing of time, aches for more. Maybe, just maybe, the curse of consciousness, the haunting angst we feel—if we feel, the mere discomfort if we deny, is a stirring of the soul. Seems strange, I know, because we don't know our soul. But maybe our soul knows us.

If so, does our soul recoil at our deepest, darkest thoughts, our unspeakable crimes, the things we don't admit even to ourselves? Does our soul have faith in us, for us, even as we lose our faith, lose our humanity?

We did not know it then, but our neighbourhood of the 1960s was a bit freewheeling and rough. We were constrained by both parents' and teachers' controls, such as they were, but we were remarkably free to roam and explore on our own. It was a time before hyper-regulation and risk aversion in the name of safety in all things. It was also a numbers game; seven kids will disperse parental vigilance, which is probably the real reason an only child wants a baby brother or sister.

Still, many will argue that the present age is the exemplar of freedom. So were we more free then, able to leave in the morning without restriction or parental knowledge of whereabouts, or are kids today more free with their unlimited choices and ever-present-adult supervised world? I think we were freer then in a way that really matters—free to make our own way, including repeated failure—whereas young people today live with the illusion of endless choice, which leads to anxiety and inaction.

We were streetwise, whereas kids today don't venture out into the streets much. We were free to seek adventure at an early age. At 16 turning 17, I travelled across Canada, often hitchhiking, often staying in unsavoury places, which just as often included unsavoury people. We got into trouble, slept in fields and alleyways, but got by somehow, without love or money. The idea is not to glamorize living on the street—I knew I would rejoin my middle-class family soon enough—but to illustrate that this cross-Canada trekking, a rite of passage in the 1970s, would be regarded as absurdly risky today. And I would agree, but I'm glad I did it. It was a time suspended between childhood and adult responsibilities. It was freedom from planning and expectation. It was treading water and looking into the dark, murky waters below, feeling a flutter of doubt, taking the plunge and coming back to the surface again, out of breath but exhilarated and wanting more. The exhilaration of wanting more did not generally lead to greater risk taking. Family values and the knowledge that no one was ever going to make it in the world for us served to reel us in.

After five weeks away without contact and three days on a bus non-stop from Vancouver to Ottawa, I showed up at home two days before school started. I had had nothing but a single loaf of bread for the duration of the bus ride. When I walked in Dad said hi and Mom said that supper would be ready in ten minutes. It was not indifference; their reaction was not any different than expected. Their universe had not ended with my departure;

their universe had not resumed upon my arrival. They were interested in what I had done—once dinner was served. Some of it, I would even tell them.

I would not have fared well under the thumb of today's hypervigilant parents. Still, there was an underbelly to our freewheeling, less-regulated world—kids were less protected. Seat belts, second-hand smoke, only sissies cared about those things during the mad-men days of the 1960s and '70s. More insidious and often denied were the actions of sexual predators. Especially if they were social pillars and close family friends.

Father Dale Crampton was more than just the neighbourhood kid who had done well. He became a priest, returned to his own neighbourhood, then proceeded to become a star in his own city. He was tall, good-looking, had the longest tee drive anyone had ever seen, was a recognized expert in canon law, represented Canada in Rome, and had a popular TV show called *Something to Think About*—this only becoming ironic in retrospect. Suffice to say, his pretense of faith and capitulation of trust gave him something to think about for the next 40 years.

We tend to think of the loss of faith as a passive thing, God being vague and nondescript. But faith is not obscure dogma; it is active in pursuit of a singular fundamental dilemma: God either is, or isn't. The examination of this conundrum, far from being passive, should be the most passionate pursuit of our lives. Of course our egos, appetites and complacency get in the way. And singular to our nature is our uncanny ability to justify and deny what we know to be true, even or especially at the expense of being true to ourselves.

Father Crampton was considered charming. I think my mother and all her Catholic friends secretly loved him. He was a romantic lead, a taller, better-looking version of Bing Crosby in *Going My Way*. He also was personable with us kids, knew our names and even had some semblance of where we fit into the family order.

One day, far, far away, Father Crampton was at our house as he often was, and the conversation turned to his status as a local TV celebrity. For some reason that led to talk of the priests' cottage, an hour outside of Ottawa in a small town called Pendleton. I can't remember exactly how it came about, but some weeks earlier he had talked about a small patch of land near the cottage the priests owned that they hadn't any interest in keeping. He had offered it to me for a dollar if he could manage it, and I was thrilled. But on this day, the good man had to deliver the bad news. It wasn't to be. Petty rules, small-minded people, getting in the way of a kid's dream. Still, he wondered, if my brother and I might like to be his guests on the next episode of his little show. My parents were in seventh heaven. I was excited by the thought but terrified by the reality.

I distinctly remember Father Crampton talking to us in a certain way before the show and how completely he was able to transform himself once the camera started to roll. The show was live, so his television performance had to be just so, and it was. He was in control, he was interesting, he was charming. I learned that adults can instantly change who and what they are.

Father Crampton did not tell us what questions he would ask. For most of the show he talked about stuff that had nothing to do with us, and I hoped he had forgotten that we were there. But no, he told the audience that young people were important, and suddenly he turned to us and smiled. First, to my brother, "What do we want to be when we grow up?" Naturally, he answered, "A priest," leaving me without an answer. Ten-year-olds tend to be short on career options. Still, I untied my reluctant tongue and said, "A lawyer," without any idea what it is they do. Nothing has changed on that front.

The show ended. I knew I hadn't given anyone anything to think about, but when we got home Father Crampton had another thought. Something for my parents to think about. He assured us that we had done well, and since I couldn't have that little patch of land, he wondered, by way of reward, if we wanted to go to the priests' cottage for the weekend. And of course there was no question of parental approval; it was our reward, after all.

We drove up to the priests' cottage listening to the radio. We listened to a popular song at the time by Diane Warwick called, "Do You Know the Way to San Jose?" Father Crampton improved on the lyrics and sang, "Do you know the way to Pendleton?" He sang the word *Pendleton* loudly, so that it sounded like Diane Warwick was singing *Pendleton* too. It was funny, and he was clever and charming even to us kids, especially to us kids. Other kids didn't get to go to the priests' cottage. We were lucky.

After supper, we watched the hockey game on the monsignor's old springy bed. Bill Hewitt called the game, a classic, between the Leafs and the Habs. Father Crampton was busy doing something for the first part of the game, but then he came and sat between my brother and me on the bed. He asked about the game and we told him who was winning. We were wearing our pyjamas. They were not ordinary pyjamas but the flannel pyjamas that Gramma made us. These were the oversized pyjamas for the under-sized kid that Gramma had not seen since I had peed on her when I was first born. She made them big so that we could grow into them, but in middle age I'm still not big enough to fill her super-sized pyjamas. Long as the sleeves and legs were, the crotch opening was relatively bigger. An odd stylistic signature for an elderly and modest Catholic woman.

You can see where this is going. The open crotch feature, a point of embarrassment to us, was a source of access for Father Crampton. Sitting on the bed between us, he watched the game feigning interest and then slipped his hand easily though the gaping flannel onto my vulnerable thigh. That moment taught me something about children that I have never forgotten. Things of a sexual nature were never discussed in our Irish Catholic home. My mom once confessed that she didn't even quite know what a lesbian was until she was 40. God love her, this was probably true. But what we know is not always drawn from experience, instruction or even rumour. There is knowledge of the world kids don't need to be told about to know about. No idea how I knew that there were people in the world who wanted to do terrible things to children, but I knew. So I squirmed as only a hyper 10-year-old can squirm.

I don't know what he expected, but he left the room soon after. I knew after that. I knew what Father Crampton was; I knew I could never trust him. I also knew I could never tell my parents, and so the underbelly was exposed.

Father Crampton didn't come over to the house much after that. He was a busy and popular celebrity, so no one took much notice. People were just grateful when the good man had an occasional minute to spare. I think the real story is that Father Crampton had not yet capitulated and was in the process of choosing the man he would become. In this, his choosing is the dramatic story of every man. We are not only free to choose; we are required to choose. In the absence of faith, our choices tend to cluster around appetites and self-interest.

It may be that Dale Crampton became a priest in order to hide his sexual tendencies. Or he may have intended for faith and devotion to trumpet appetite and desire. His life does not add up to a benefit of the doubt scenario, but early on, it has to be considered. Maybe he had some faith; maybe his intentions were not always dishonourable. Maybe he lost his faith; maybe he lost himself.

It is also possible that he wilfully and strategically used his position of trust to lure and abuse children. Maybe he was tortured, at war with himself, fully understanding the implications of the divergent paths that would define his life. His choice may have been less a surrender than a Faustian bargain.

We know enough to speculate on the trajectory of evil. *Evil* is a loaded word and makes people uncomfortable in the secular world of relativism. We prefer to deconstruct evil and relegate it into clinical, sanitized language, contained and categorized according to the ever-expanding *Diagnostic and Statistical Manual of Mental Disorders*, now in its fifth edition. But *DSM–5* cannot explain the essence of evil that we see in the world, any more than science can explain the meaning of life.

Years ago I saw a documentary on serial killers. Most people do not want to understand psychopathy or the cause and origin of serial killers. We can't and don't want to find the source. Throughout the documentary, a wise older psychiatrist provided information and insight into the workings of the serial killer's mind, but she was emphatic that our collective and her professional insight were limited.

We use the term *psychopath* to describe narcissistic, predatory behaviour, but this only describes 1 percent of the population. Most psychopaths are not violent and never murder, let alone join the rarified club of serial murderers. There certainly can be contributing factors in the early lives of serial murders, but there is no empirical evidence to show a causal relationship between the incidence of psychopathy and early environmental factors.

At the end of the film, the psychiatrist extended herself and consciously exited her professional persona in order to divulge her strongest informed opinion and deepest feeling on the matter. She said that 35 years of studying and working with psychopathic killers had not provided her with a satisfactory answer as to why or how the condition exists. Further, she doubted that clinical experience and psychological expertise would ever accomplish that. Therefore, she concluded, as the documentary concluded, that the explanation lay outside of psychology and human understanding. She deduced, not based on religious conviction but on careful study and gut instinct, that evil is real and that this acknowledgement is necessary in order to have any explanation for what science can never explain.

Attempting to grope a vulnerable squirmy boy after a premeditated set-up is an evil act. But Father Crampton was not necessarily evil, yet. Why?

Because he stopped. He may have been conflicted, able to see his actions for what they were, still within the possibility of redemption. That possibility was likely remote, the route back too difficult even if a small part of him craved meaningful redemption. I was lucky. For others, when they met Father Crampton's irresistible charm, the dimming light had gone out.

Fifteen years later, I was in a wedding party and attended the wedding rehearsal. The presiding priest was Father Crampton, whom I had not seen or thought about much in all those years. But I remembered him and at this chance meeting wondered if he would remember me. I was no longer the vulnerable boy who had feigned wanting to be a lawyer. I considered whether I should say something. Not exactly a subject to enhance the mood of a wedding. The rehearsal began, the party gathered close together in the expansive church. I watched him; our eyes met. He knew. It was enough.

A few years later Father Crampton was arrested and charged with multiple counts of sexual misconduct with young boys and, significant for me, for acts beginning in the early 1970s. So when he had accessed my open crotch pyjamas in the mid-1960s, he may not have irrevocably chosen his path. It is entirely possible that he held back then purely out of fear of being caught. I suspect that whatever the reason or reasons, it was more complex than fear alone. The underbelly of that time made it relatively easy to get away with predatory behaviour. The fact that a priest could victimize many boys over the years is testament to that observation. Before this time, he may not have been completely subservient to his narcissistic desires, suspended between desire and a modicum of conscience. These are not forces that can coexist easily or for long, but my experience as a ten-year-old suggests the possibility of their coexistence at that time.

In rare instances, committing an evil act may provide a cathartic opportunity to confront and expunge an evil aspect of self. Or committing an evil act may set up a trap, whereby the bottomless pit of self-justification rears its ugly head and declares itself immune to all judgment, most of all its own. This is the transformation from committing an evil act to becoming evil, from which there is no going back. Once self-justification is loosened upon the world unfettered, evil follows, for it is a truism that true evil does not recognize itself.

The problem of evil remains complicated. Though we do not understand evil, we tend to put it in a simple, convenient place as far away as possible.

Father Crampton was tried, convicted and given a suspended sentence, which the prosecution rightfully and successfully appealed. In his favour at sentencing was the fact that he had sought treatment before being charged. It seems highly likely that he knew charges were coming and so seeking treatment was a good strategic move. He served only eight months in jail.

At sentencing, Father Crampton apologized for his actions, which the trial records spanned 10 years (1973–1983) and had occurred in the rectories in Richmond and Nepean, Ontario, and at his cottage. The courts and public opinion had not yet adjusted to the reality of pedophiles. Father Crampton's trial was one of the first high profile cases involving priests that swept across North America, and in the early years, the church attempted to manage the problem, rather than treat it for the horrendous crime that it was and is.

Perhaps more complicated than how society adjusts to evil crimes is the answer to this question: after you have been convicted and exposed and face empty time in the terrible and lonely company of yourself, *who are you?* Criminologists will tell you that for many of the worst criminals, the self-justification system remains intact; in their minds, they are forever victims, not victimizers. But at some level, buried in the you that you cannot face, you do know, at least until evil hardens into permanent pathology. Time may not give relief so much as allow the cancer to fester.

Over the years I wondered occasionally what Father Crampton thought about, how he saw and judged himself. Did he judge himself? And did his version of himself change over the decades? I imagined that it would be hard to sustain an innocent version of himself. I imagined that it would be hard to face a guilty version of himself, leaving the convenience of complete denial.

Is evil nuanced or absolute? Absolute evil certainly exists. There are people who commit acts that are, as the phrase goes, soul destroying, both for their own and for the souls of others. Hitler and Stalin are the great examples of the twentieth century. Murdering literally millions became as easy and commonplace as breathing, but without even the purpose of breathing. Even darker, if that is possible, they inspired millions to follow—to be complicit in their crimes, to share their darkness, to judge evil as good and good as evil.

Listening to Clifford Olsen's and Karla Holmolka's versions of evil is instructive. (The former sexually assaulted and murdered 11 children; the latter did the same to 3 victims, including her own sister.) Olsen basked in the glory of his accomplishments and the extent to which he was able to continue to manipulate from prison. He gloated and chided the parents of his victims, once saying to the father of a child he had murdered, "What's the big deal, since you have five others?" Karla's version is testament to the banality of evil, or perhaps to the banality of life after evil. Karla dismissed the deliberate murder of her sister, who she had offered up as a sexual prop for her murderous husband, as an accident and then proceeded to get a university degree in prison and, once freed, have three children. Neither ever lost faith in the evil narcissistic version of themselves. Surely, this is the evil twin of faith in God.

Still, most people do not fit into an absolute portrait of evil. Dale Crampton committed evil acts and became evil, though there may be evidence, at least at the end of his life, that his version of himself does not fit absolute evil, for I believe he may have suffered some insight into his crimes. This is not to regard him or his crimes with sympathy, nor to suggest that his victims suffered any less than what they say they did. This is not an attempt at judgment but an attempt at understanding.

The look in Father Crampton's eyes in the early 1980s was not that of a man blind to his crimes. I believe he recognized and understood the depth of his depravity. As a social piranha, he consigned himself to a lifetime of isolation, with a lifetime of something to think about. In this sense, he lived in hell in advance of the fact. How do I know this?

After his conviction, Father Crampton disappeared from Ottawa, and nothing was known of him. But he came back. Back to the scene of his crimes, or back to his lonely, diminished version of home. On June 9, 2009, in Ottawa, another civil lawsuit was announced against Dale Crampton. It is unknown if this lawsuit was related to his subsequent actions. On October, 13, 2010, in Ottawa, 25 years after his conviction and having accomplished 25 years of sobriety, Dale Crampton jumped from an apartment balcony 24 stories in the sky. But of course he didn't simply jump; no one simply jumps. All who share the communion of violent self-harm and death have to live their darkest hour of the soul. The thorny path to this moment must have been forged in excruciating pain and self-loathing. All the reasons, longing, desire and warped intimacy gone; all recourse and possibilities at redemption long since expunged from his self-damning, withered, blackened soul. This is not my condemnation but possibly the measure of his own self-worth, though once again, we just don't know.

The aging, decrepit vessel of his wasted human matter, barely able to climb onto the railing, perhaps hung suspended for a second or two, long enough for a searing knowledge of the gulf between who he had become and who he intended to be, long enough to relive the moment of final surrender to appetite, anticipate the final moment of his obliteration and maybe ask for the last time with disgust, Who am I? Self-hatred, as with aging, in a soulless state is not for the faint of heart. This is what faith looks like when it has been displaced and utterly lost.

"Everything can be taken but one thing: the last of the human freedoms—to choose one's attitude in any given set of circumstances, to choose one's own way."

VIKTOR FRANKL

# CHAPTER FIVE
## SPECIAL KAYE

FAITH IS NOT A GIVEN; IT IS A GIFT, COMPOUNDED BY BLOODY HARD WORK. LIFE-changing experiences, big divinely inspired moments for a select few, a touch of grace, subtle and as imperceptible as morning dew, for the rest of us, maybe. Perhaps nothing is more poignant and instructive than watching someone transcend the cards they are dealt. If ever the cliché, *easier said than done* has application in this life; it is bluffing a royal flush while holding a house of cards.

I met my Aunt Kaye no more than six times in my life. Not a lot to go on, but there was something about her life—how she lived it, held up and had fun—that was both mischievous and miraculous.

Like all our California relatives, we knew more of her through Mom's stories than actual contact ever warranted. Mom and Kaye were close and sustained each other for over 50 years, apart except for Mom's annual pilgrimage to her family on the west coast. Together they steeled themselves and stared down the many and various vicissitudes in their respective lives, and incredibly, they were determined to share a laugh between, and sometimes during, tragedies. These no-nonsense Depression-era Second World War graduates were resilient and funny as hell and fun to be around, at whatever point on the circle of life they were to be found. Both icons of faith, just for the way they smiled.

Character is how one interprets the world in the face of adversity. Aunt Kaye endured tragedy throughout her entire life but was not a tragic character. She was in the play of her own choosing, and it is in her choosing that the miracle of her faith exists.

My earliest memories of Kaye were overhearing concerned whispers from my mother to my father. Kaye and her husband, Paul, had visited Ottawa from exotic California and had made quite an impression. She was glamorous and kind, and best of all, she was my godmother. Paul's parents still lived in Ottawa, which is why we saw her more than others of the California crew.

I remember on one early visit, without much fanfare she gave me a miniature tool set. Just the thing for an overactive boy. I remember feeling both joy at the unexpected gift and a reluctance to touch it. A gift outside of Christmas and birthdays was unheard of, and the reaction of the other siblings had to be considered.

But Mom reminded me that Aunt Kaye was my godmother, a now defunct, meaningless role, and with that I let the magic in and grasped my tool set. The starkness of this inexpensive one-time, off-season gift misses the point. The gift was all the more important for its singularity. Who knows, if I make it rich, by the end of my life it might be my version of Rosebud.

Mom was pretty even-keeled, but you could see worry in her face for her favourite sister. Soon we learned that Kaye's son Terry, whom we had never met, had died of cystic fibrosis. Mom travelled to California after that, as she did every year, and little else was said.

Fear and anxiety distort time in a child's mind. Soon after, it seemed, there were whispers again, more often and less hushed than before. Kaye and Paul's second son was diagnosed with cancer. Mom made arrangements to meet Kaye in New York, where Anthony was scheduled to see a specialist. But the news from the specialist was not good, and surgery was scheduled immediately. The surgery, both necessary and brutal, amputated his arm up to and including the shoulder socket.

I remember Mom talking about how difficult it was for Anthony to adjust to school with only one arm. We were about the same age, and I tried to think of what was more difficult, getting used to doing things with only one arm or getting used to people watching you struggle with only one arm. I decided that getting used to people was more difficult, and after working with persons with disabilities for over 30 years, nothing has changed my mind.

Mom said that when Anthony went back to school, some of the kids were cruel. I wanted to fight those kids, but being the size I was, and 3,000 miles away, it was a bit unrealistic. So we said the rosary for Anthony, and then we found out that he too had died. Mom said it was cruel that Anthony had to go through with the surgery to save his life, only to die. I still wanted to fight those kids. Mom flew back to California. The year was 1964, and Aunt Kaye had lost two sons in five years from unrelated diseases, both with an infinitesimally small chance of happening to any human being. On the day Anthony died, Kaye's brother Bill and his wife Verlee's only child, Peggy, was born. Welcome to the lottery of life.

Kaye had a wicked sense of style. And for all her tribulations, she lived a grand life. Whenever Mom returned to California, she took an extra suitcase for clothes she would return with, courtesy of her sister Kaye. These were Aunt Kaye's castaways but were always better than anything else Mom ever had. Sometimes Kaye would mail great packages of clothes, and we would all go and admire Mom's new exotic wardrobe. When Kaye visited or Mom visited her in California, Kaye dazzled everyone with her infinite array of interesting, stylish clothes. We were of course northern hicks, and Kaye was the Hollywood star, and we were all happy to play our role. Kaye had a wicked sense of style.

And a sense of humour. Life was always a thing to be enjoyed. Hell was a private thing, to be endured when it had to be endured but to exit from as soon as another human being came on the scene. She didn't just laugh; she made everyone laugh and was remembered for laughing and smiling.

A few years later, Kaye's husband, Paul, died suddenly, age 42, heart attack. Kaye recovered, and in another few years she married a very decent businessman, Tom Heffernan. They bought a grand house on a golf course and lived a grand lifestyle, and Mom got grander clothes. Then in rapid sequence, Tom received news that his estranged daughter, who worked as a hooker in L.A., was found murdered. Then Tom died of a heart attack. Kaye, who never paid any attention to their finances, discovered that her grand lifestyle was grand on paper only. Tom, the highly successful businessman, had more debt than assets. My Uncle Basil had the misfortune of having to convey the fact that after the dust settled, my Aunt Kaye, with a lifetime of both high style and high income, was now completely broke.

So, after more than 40 years of not having to worry about paid employment—not since she and sisters, Mom and Evelyn, had worked at the Bank of Canada during the Second World War—Kaye went back to work. Without either job experience or education, the best she could get was working the cash register at a drugstore—bad shifts, low wages, always standing, but no complaints. She was almost 70 years old, doing the best she could, but life was not done with her yet.

She was diagnosed with breast cancer. She was told that a mastectomy was the best means of treatment. She must have thought about Terry and Anthony often during this time. She may have consoled herself that what she was about to endure was easy compared to Anthony's surgery for cancer. Anthony had returned to school, and Kaye planned to return to her standing position at the pharmacy.

As with Anthony, the centre would not hold. Kaye was told that she required a second mastectomy. After surgery there were complications with infection. She did not, could not, heal properly. She was in constant pain but had to return to work. So there she was, age 72, post double mastectomy, in pain, broke, standing at the cash, trying to get through the day.

Then one day, a couple of punks come into the pharmacy. One draws a gun and points it at her face, and she faces death, as even-keeled as she faced anything in her life. She doesn't die, but again something vital has been taken. *It's not what happens to you in life but how you handle it that counts*—this is the reality and poetry of her life.

I've often wondered if throughout her life, especially at the end, Kaye asked herself, Why me? Not in the random "Why did my number come up?" sense, but "Why particularly me, again and again?" Anyone would have to ask the question about the death of not one but two children. Knowing Aunt Kaye and my mom—similar strong, stoic, resilient, fun-to-be-around Irish Catholic women—I doubt she spent much time dwelling on existential questions. For women of their era, the question of why was particularly indulgent, even if to the rest of the world it was the most natural question in the world.

Fortunately, Kaye and Mom did not suffer from inward-looking expectations of the unfolding progressive world. They had much sympathy for others and little pity for themselves. They did not have ideas about how the world should be; rather they had acceptance for how it was. They had faith—deep rooted and inscrutable and not something that can be fully accounted for by either the virtue or vice of religion. Maybe their faith lay between the cracks of their many and various contradictions: they were gentle friends, mothers, sisters, with characters that were tough as nails; they were prone to innumerable habits but able to easily absorb the most profound and disturbing change; they were egoless but cared with persnickety precision about their appearance; they had great integrity but didn't really care about what people thought; they were stoic about life's vicissitudes but didn't take themselves too seriously; they seriously laughed loudly and often, even in tragic situations, and saw no contradiction in this at all. And while navigating the prevailing winds of life that saw them marry and bury, manage a slew of kids, and circumstances that meant they were to live most of their lives 3,000 miles apart, they remained the best of friends.

Faith. My inability to understand it, let alone articulate its essence, is pathetic. But I sometimes see it. Mom and Kaye's last words together are both a testament to faith and a poignant example of the inarticulate speech of the heart. Inarticulate because though they felt deeply and wore their emotional hearts on their sleeves, neither actually acknowledged that this would be their last meeting in this life.

Mom had travelled to California by herself most of her life. But with the progression of Parkinson's disease, she needed help to keep up her annual pilgrimage. Funny word, *progression*. My wife, Cara, and I loved doing things with Mom, and a trip to California was an adventure in itself. We flew to San Francisco and then drove Mom to Fresno to be with Kaye before leaving on our coastal journey. Mom and Kaye were happy at Kaye's apartment, and barely a word was spoken about the golf-course house and opulence of her previous life. That was then, this was now, and in both times Kaye felt gratitude. Most of all, the sisters felt gratitude for being together again.

Cara, Mom and I inwardly knew that this was to be Mom's last trip to California, but that was the sad inarticulate speech of our thoughts and not the happy narrative of our journey. Yes, a fancy dressing up of denial. Still, we worried about Mom seeing her siblings for the last time, her friends, places she had been, had visited every year for the past 50 years. We toured the Big Sur with an awareness of things last, but with Mom all we ever talked about were things next. Still, at some point during the visit—when leaving Ottawa, upon arrival in California, while staying with Kaye—it must have occurred to Mom just what *last trip* meant.

Before our two-hour drive to the San Francisco airport, we drove from Basil and Marilyn's house to pick up Mom at Kaye's apartment. For once we were not in a hurry. Cara waited in the car, and I waited inside the front door as Kaye and Mom fussed with the details of departure. Everything was light and cheery between the sisters, as always. They told amusing stories of people they had visited or encountered during the past ten days, no doubt for the umpteenth time. They laughed and fussed, fussed and laughed, doing what they always did to get from the present to the next holy moment. Only as the fussing gave way to pretense did the tone and gestures between the sisters and lifetime friends imperceptivity change.

All packed, clock ticking, all the reasons for fussing diminished and unceremoniously ended. With me silently, and for once patiently, waiting to take Mom's luggage to the car, the reasons for delay leached out of the room, and we—that is, they—were left with just the fact of departure.

I felt an oppressive weight, an indecency of witness, seeing the intimacy of the moment, but I could not leave—Mom's suitcase had not been closed, and neither of the sisters wanted me to leave, neither wanting to be alone with the other for this naked moment. There had rarely been a moment in their entire lives when one or the other wasn't talking, but when *the* moment came neither spoke. They hesitated, both of them, but neither spoke. Neither had planned for or practiced this moment; neither was wired to look back with sadness; neither had the capacity to feel sorry for herself. I had witnessed their departures before, jovial, talkative and with definite plans for their next visit—talking still as the door was closed, the car was started and final, final goodbyes were made. But now, each looked up at the other for just a moment, without words, with an expression inscrutable, impossible to discern and, though absolutely unrehearsed, exactly the same. A look half-amused, searching, verging on tragic, close to tears, but no tears, no tragedy, just goodbye, an understanding beyond words, inarticulate speech of the heart, articulate speech of the soul.

I wonder still what they thought about: their lives together and apart, the Navan farm, people who had passed, the roller coaster of life, their wish for more time? I have no idea, though I doubt that, like me, theirs was a lament for spilt porter. That indulgence of nostalgia is a thing for our, spiritually compromised, generation.

I understand Northrop Frye's dilemma, trying to reconcile his academic lack of faith with the greater impulse of negative faith, the revelation that his wife's essence existed beyond the physical life of biological cells. His lesson of negative faith is negative in name only. His negative faith is powerful and palpable. If ever I had to distill my faith, limited and weak-kneed as it is, down to one discernible moment, it is the moment when Mom and Kaye's eyes met for the last time—knowingly, lovingly, intimately, and with finality, beyond this life and yet not quite rid of it, finally and barely admitting to what each felt in the other's soul.

"Preach the gospel at all times, and when necessary, use words."

## ST. FRANCIS OF ASSISI

# CHAPTER SIX
## NATURE OF THE BEAST

MODERN PARENTS OF YOUNG CHILDREN ARE NOTORIOUS FOR WORKING THE subject of their precious progeny into every conversation. This is not a formula for making friends and influencing people. Once the children of these parents grow up, their dog can be inflicted upon any audience, at any moment. This astute observation comes from long hours spent in a kids' park that doubles as a dog park. You get to see the progression of obsession from kid to dog.

Dog owners know everything there is to know about each other's dog, they know what each other thinks about every conceivable topic of conversation, and yet, oddly, they rarely know each other's name. The dogs are Tofu or Diesel, or in our case Sonny, and the owner's status is wrapped up with their dog's appearance, behaviour and popularity with the other dogs. Dogs, everything; dog owners, nothing. This is an unspoken ritual between dog owners who have time to kill while their dogs take their own sweet time conducting their necessary business. Important business transactions cannot be rushed.

As far as I know Sonny doesn't know that he inspires faith. He doesn't go to church much, and I am not a PETA devotee. Adherents of Persons for the Ethical Treatment of Animals like to think that animals are people too. Actually, they think animals are better, far better, than corrupt humans.

PETA derides our human-centric world and wants equal status to measly man for gerbil, python and ferret. The modern world is all about equality, and with Pamela Anderson as spokesperson, people—that is, men—listen, which is after all what we do.

But there is a problem. I am a dog guy—don't *get* cats—and my guy Sonny is the cat's meow of the canine world. I just don't see that PETA's enlightened notion of equality is speaking up for animals as much as putting down humans. The clever deconstruction of human to animal, or elevation of animal to human, is to say that we have no soul.

The foundation of my faith, negative as it may be, is that the essence of any human life cannot be explained or understood as simply biological cells that live and die and are no more. My belief is both logical—try getting a scientist to give a satisfactory explanation for the *essence* of things—and illogical or beyond logic, that which I cannot explain but resonates, permeating everything I think and perceive. I cannot explain the existence of the soul, though in appealing to my higher self I speak from it. Atheists regard such statements as weak, proof of nothing. I regard the existence of the soul as a self-evident truth.

And now the trick question. Yes, humans can be despicable, and yes, being a dog guy I am about to espouse Sonny's many qualities, so how come humans have a soul and dogs do not? I can't claim that a dog or any animal is soulless, because like most things, I just don't know. Sonny's soul is not self-evident, but it is evident that his life and animals' lives have meaning, both independently and in relation to humans, though the how and why remain a mystery.

I can hear animal activists screaming that we cannot define and value animals according to their ability to serve humans. True enough. My dog, Sonny, is a Portuguese water dog who neither speaks Portuguese nor is interested in water. According to the human-generated literature on PWDs, he should be able to swim 8 kilometres in open ocean and dive 15 feet deep. My wife, Cara, has kept the faith, embracing the human literature as she has embraced Sonny every summer for 14 years, gently carrying him out into the lake like a babe being readied for baptism. But Sonny, not buying into the human-centric PWD literature and having ideas of his own, when released churns back to shore as quickly as possible. So repellent is the prospect of being and remaining wet that as soon as he plants his paws back on hallowed ground, he shakes himself while still submerged in water, then bolts for shore, dripping wet. Baptism by desire. He then rolls furiously around in the sand until he brings his fur and natural curls back to their normal dry lustre. On one of his many rotations I saw him kiss the ground with gratitude, not unlike our venerable late Pope John Paul II used to do upon landing in a new country. Then again, that tidbit might just be my overactive imagination searching for a miracle. Still, Sonny does not allow humans to define him.

It has been said and written that humans have learned everything important in life from their dogs. Cat owners may disagree. It has also been said that in the process we have stripped away all dogs' natural instincts. Sonny is more likely to marinate, baste and barbecue a steak from the fridge than fend for himself in the wild. The thing is, humans tend to be more concerned with intention than action, but dogs are action-oriented and nothing if not true to getting the job done. Their affection is real and immediate and not something they'll get around to someday. Their ability to forgive, instant and absolute.

Still, Sonny's vigilance to our human ways has cost him. He barely notices the presence of another dog in the park anymore. (Of course it has to be considered that he may just be a great big snob and considers his PWD pedigree superior to other dogs'.) He puts up with all our collective and many moods, always even-tempered, tail wagging with unflagging enthusiasm. You could literally kick your dog around when you're in a bad mood and expect and receive instant forgiveness. We have imparted the concept of forgiveness, but who, may I ask, is doing all the forgiving?

So have we stripped dogs of their essential canine qualities, or have they simply become better human beings than we could ever dream of? Dogs aren't just more emotionally connected to humans than any other animal. Oh no; the full truth is that we are weirdly dependent on them to allow us to exceed, bypass and otherwise avoid many of the less than stellar human relationships in our life. I'm thinking of starting a business renting dogs out for the Christmas season to discriminating people who want to stay at home and avoid family.

One would think that on the communication front, at least, we would be superior to canines. Alas, no. Canines are not only superior to humans in communicating; it is one of their great strengths. We humans place far too much value on our point of view. We forget that the core of communication, much like the realization of faith, comes not from pontificating but from taking in, preferably in silence, what the world has to say. How can humans compete with a loyal canine who not only listens but finds everything you have to say simply fascinating?

Cara likes to single out our dog's listening skills as exemplary. Sometimes I think she's trying to tell me something, but I generally don't stick around long enough to hear. Cara spends hours talking to Sonny as he lies in full-recline position, which he tends to do when he's napping, between naps or just listening. He is so sensitive to her every emotional nuance that she can change the tempo of his ever wagging tail by the slightest, barely perceptible, modulation of her voice. She loves him to death because he hangs on her every word, which apparently I am remiss in doing. Most of all she loves him because he really knows when to shut up, which again, apparently, I do not. I told Cara that her voice modulations together with her wagging finger don't make me want to wag my tail, which didn't seem to help. I am beginning to formulate a theory that all counselling and psychotherapy should be done between clients and therapists who do not speak the same language. Obviously, knowing the meaning of words interferes with effective communication. So I'm being a bit facetious, but the truth is, dogs connect with humans better, much better, than humans connect with humans.

We recently went to Europe for three weeks, and my colleague Amanda offered to look after Sonny. We were relieved to spare Sonny the horrors of having to spend all that time with other canines in whom he had no interest, and we were also worried that he simply couldn't bear to be without us. This is a dog who waits in the dark at the front door, peering out for any sign of our return after a long day. This is a dog who will not dine alone under any circumstances. If we leave as he is eating his breakfast, he will stop and wait until we return in the evening and then rush into the kitchen to finish his stale breakfast before being served his slightly less stale dinner. This is a dog who will wait outside a screen door at the cottage and cry until allowed back inside with us rather than romp outside in the woods the way actual dogs are supposed to do. We have corrupted Sonny. He is no longer a dog who does dog things; he is a persnickety little man who has us all beat on the human interaction front and doesn't even give workshops.

So naturally we assumed that when we abandoned our special relationship with Sonny and placed him in a stranger's hands without an explanation, it would be difficult for him, if not traumatic. Turns out, Sonny settled in as soon as I left. Not sort of, anxiously, but fully, comfortably and luxuriously. Cara couldn't quite believe the text message reassuring us that our pooch was feeling quite at home away from home. This did not seem like the ultra-loyal dog who waited all day for us before he would finish his breakfast. This dog wasn't weirdly dependent on us; he was a social butterfly.

But then again, maybe Sonny was just teaching us another lesson in human relations, of canine mastery over supposed human qualities. When Sonny instantly forgot about us and adhered to Amanda, he was simply opening himself up to whoever God placed in his path. He doesn't need mindfulness workshops to be in the moment; he is a master practitioner, completely, deeply and madly in the moment and present for all relationships as they unfold, without the possibility of resentment or hint of expectation— except for breakfast and dinner. So, with only a tinge of disappointment, I have to conclude that Sonny is not a social butterfly but an exemplar, making sacred all of his human relationships in a way that we mere mortals can only dream of.

It isn't only Sonny who has taught me faith. As a kid I was always bringing stray or wild animals home, to try to make them family, to try to include them in my attempt to go home. A trip to the Ottawa River usually meant returning with a frog or a snake or a turtle. I once caught a rather large turtle, and, not knowing it was a snapper, I introduced it to the stray dog I had picked up a few months earlier. The turtle bit the curious dog on the tongue, and the poor thing ran around the yard with the turtle hanging off his tongue until the turtle decided he had tortured the dog enough. I returned the turtle to the river.

I once spent all day, even forgoing lunch, trying to catch a baby chipmunk. To my delight, I finally was able to do. It was cute beyond words, but when I got home Dad said it would die if I didn't return it to its mother. I pulled the knife from my chest and returned my baby to its rightful home.

Still, the most memorable pet acquisition was our first dog, Bunny. On a hot Saturday in August around 1964 our family loaded up the 1959 Ford, with eight of us sardined in, and drove to Luskville, Quebec, to the old Kennedy farm for the annual picnic. We loved this event, with 20 or 30 adult relations and at least three times as many kids swarming the field, all getting ready for music, hayrides, games, food and drink. Once we left the car, kids and adults did not have to associate again until the drive home in the late evening. This was a slice of Ottawa valley life—once common, now all gone.

It was fun wandering through the various adult camps, invisible but seeing fiddlers, men smoking and playing horseshoes and women laughing and preparing food. Shy with those who could actually see us, we became reacquainted with kid cousins—reason for being related unknown—as spontaneous feverish games broke out and we travelled far afield the picnic area.

I ended up at the Kennedy farmhouse and barns. I loved the old wood barns, smell and all, and especially the farm dog, who, once encouraged, followed my brothers and I wherever we went. She was old and mangy, but that didn't matter; she followed, slowly wagged her tail and had a good heart. So it seemed a bit strange when one of the Kennedys noticed how taken we wee city slickers were with Bunny and asked, "Would you like to keep her?"

Never was a more generous offer made in the history of the world. Of course we wanted to keep her, but there was a bit of a problem: Dad. He had this strange idea that there was enough activity in our tiny house (with an unexpected seventh kid on the horizon). He never saw most of the outdoor pets I had gathered, since they were kept in the garage, but a dog would be tough to hide. Also there was the matter of the transportation of a large dog in a car with eight people, assuming we didn't permanently lose anyone during the picnic. I was pretty sure that a stowaway attempt would not work.

But we knew something. The sun was setting, and we had been at the picnic for many hours, out of sight of adults except when filling our empty plates. During the picnic—during all gatherings actually—the men had a wee bit of the drink. And the wee-ness of how much they had had to drink had been stretched out for a considerable time. So if ever there was good timing to ask a bad question, this was it. Better yet, we asked if we could keep Bunny while in the mix of jocular relatives who were watching and relaxed, and weirdly on the side of the kids, with a Kennedy on hand to ensure it was okay. Dad's guard wasn't down very often, and his usual unequivocal *no* had just a whisper of possibility in it. Which the crowd, his friends and cousins, helped to exploit. Dad finally just said, "Alright," the most wonderful word ever spoken, and his role with our family dog was mostly over.

It would be fun to see a video of our ride home, two too-mellow adults, six over-excited kids, and a large mangy farm dog used to great spaces and privacy. I don't remember the actual drive home, but I do remember that family drives into the country often involved one of us lying across the top of the back seat, face glued to the window, watching the world recede. It felt safe. Different world.

This canine acquisition broke every rule of successful dog ownership. No designer dog food, scheduled walks or dog licence for our mutt. Still, Bunny was a lovely dog and seemed to make an instantaneous transition from lonely farm dog to swarming-neighbourhood celebrity. It was not unusual for 15 kids and a newly energized older dog to run wildly through the neighbourhood on one of our huge games of chase. Who says you can't teach an old dog new tricks?

But running wildly through the hood was a new trick she should never have learned. All dogs ran loose then, but Bunny did not have street smarts and ran in front of a car. She didn't die, but her legs were mangled, and she crawled under the dark stairs in our garage and wouldn't come out. When I got the news I crawled under the stairs in complete darkness to comfort Bunny and was shocked when she viciously growled at me. I did not understand.

The next day my dad had Bunny put down, and I felt a terrible grief for this aged, discarded, misfit dog. The experience of grief for the young is very intense, very real, and never to be forgotten. I remember being inconsolable, though there was no one who would console, the flip side to the invisibility advantage of being in a big family. Most of all, the growl under the stairs had felt like betrayal.

We don't see our parents' vulnerabilities until we are older. Dad hid his well, as anger tends to do. That time when I was 15 and he sat beside me, wanting to talk, was painful for both of us. I just wanted to avoid, he just wanted to make amends, and the gulf between us widened. He had thought I was mad at him for giving our dog away years earlier. That had never occurred to me, and I felt bad that he had carried this thought for years, but I still didn't want to talk about it. I held my silence without malice. But there was more.

When I was about 20, I confronted my parents with the fact that my girlfriend's allergies were severe and that if we didn't get rid of our dog she would no longer be able to come over to our house. And of course, implicit with this little gem was the threat that I would no longer be around as much. We had a little Chihuahua-mix, not much fur to sneeze at, but I was at an age and in a state where the choice was obvious. Mom immediately agreed

Tammy had to go. Dad had never shown any feelings for any of our dogs, one way or the other, but he resisted. His reasons were unclear—which was odd because Dad was always clear—and he held out until the issue had been raised several times. Finally, he relented, my girlfriend was appeased, and a crisis was averted.

I didn't think about this little episode for years. But after Dad's death, I had a creeping thought. He had retired and spent a lot of time at home. Maybe, just maybe, Dad had been resistant to getting rid of our dog because he had grown attached to her. And worse, maybe he thought I had pushed the issue because he had given away our dog years earlier. Odd thoughts that we have decades after the fact, or fiction, of our lives. I don't know what the fact is, but regret easily seeps into relationships in which there was much love and little understanding.

Maybe Dad had an understanding with our little dog, just as I have an understanding with Sonny. One of the many superior-to-human virtues of dogs is their ability to bridge the gap between what we say and what we intended to communicate. We can express our deepest emotions to our dog, things we could not even whisper to our spouse, kids or siblings. In canine company, we are less moody, more optimistic, simpler and more honest than in our complicated human relationships, even the good ones. I don't know why or how but I do believe that our hounds calm the fears of our darkest night and complement the cravings of our soul. The tumultuous tangle and many contradictions of my faith is somehow wrapped in up the simple comforting relationship with my dog. Dumb concept, dumb dog, dumb me, and happy to be.

"God will not look you over for medals, degrees or diplomas but for scars."

ELBERT HUBBARD

# CHAPTER SEVEN
## KING OF PAIN

WE ARE OUR FATHER'S SONS. WE DON'T DO EASY. MAYBE IT IS THE HERITAGE OF 800 years of oppressive British rule in Ireland, the cataclysm of the Great Hunger or the many hardships of forced relocation and pioneer life in Canada. Or maybe we are just stubborn.

After I'd written a few young adult novels, people asked me why I didn't write a plot involving long-distance running. But it never occurred to me. What interested me about running seemed likely to bore a reading audience. In truth, nothing much interested me about running; I mostly therapeutically run from myself so as to get over myself. I also have an aversion to conversations about training regimes, nutritional supplements, projected racing times, fluid intake, frequency of bowel movements and the newest running gear that dedicated endurance athletes likely own. Still, there is something about endurance sport competition that has to do with my greatly flawed attempt at faith, so I will write a few pages.

It begins, as so many of my recollections about family do, with whimpering nostalgia. During the 1980s, I was a pretty good, though not great, distance runner. I was sponsored by a shoe company for years and could win races but was not going to be competitive at the highest level. My younger brother Mike was a better cyclist, making Canadian national teams, the world championships and the Olympics. Not bad for a young guy from a northern hockey city without cycling teams, tradition or role models for his chosen sport. On Sundays, we gathered at my mom's house for dinner with siblings, a slew of kids in tow. During the limited warm months in our part of the world, often both Mike and I had raced earlier that day in Ottawa, Montreal or possibly Toronto. And for a period of parallel years, we were in winning form in our respective sports. Information about how we fared that day was not the centre of discussion and generally not of much interest to the entire group. We'd exchange a few details at the table maybe, maybe not, but always in a low-key manner.

If we'd won difficult or highly competitive races or achieved a personal best, or if a national or provincial title was on the line or a dominant rival had been taken down, the same applied. After dinner, briefly, passing in the hallway, "How'd you do today?"

"Okay; you?"

"Yup. You win?"

"Yeah; you?"

"Second."

"Tough day?"

"Yeah. Yours?"

"Not bad."

With only a touch of facetiousness added. Our Irish Catholic upbringing taught us to get over ourselves, which, since the takeover by the self-esteem industry, is regarded as a negative. But understanding that the world does not evolve around oneself is a valuable lesson to learn early in life. It also made us better athletes. Winning a local race is not winning the Olympics. Self-satisfaction at winning small becomes the limiting factor. Not suffering from self-satisfaction is a prerequisite for maintaining the hunger and moving up to the next level.

Drive, or what endurance mules call "the hunger," matters. Endurance sports require physiological attributes and a rather brutal training regime. But toughness is an intangible quality that can separate winners from also-rans. Mike and I shared an inability to win a race in a sprint. Natural speed is a handy physiological attribute to have in your arsenal if you have selected your parents well. We were grinders who knew from experience that if a race came down to a sprint we would lose, but if it came down to toughness—that is, unrelenting, raw hunger—we could often win. It is not always possible to isolate factors, but once you know that you will not wilt under pressure, and your opponents have taken note, it gives you an edge.

Funny thing is, many people can never live up to the promise of their training and talent. Not living up to an expectation from both yourself and others can deflate and erode that all-important hunger. And racing is not necessarily the sum of its parts. The bringing together of disparate training parts on a particular day is enhanced or diminished by the intangible wild card in your head. I certainly lost races to those with greater talent, but I tended to win if it was possible to grind it out in pain. Beating a superior opponent based on the capacity to suffer was not a rare feat for either Mike or me. Mike is understated and has the calmest demeanour of the seven of us but was a world-class grinder, surprising opponents who had written him off.

Racing well consistently is harder than it looks. It isn't just that you are working hard for a long time; to win requires that in each race you exceed what you are realistically capable of doing—which is to say, people often put limits on themselves. You don't just suffer in a marathon; your life is on the line until you finish, at which moment—win, lose or draw—you put it completely behind you. If you confuse these seemingly opposite reactions, you will back off the pace when you are hurting, convince yourself that fifth place is good enough, let yourself off the hook, settle. It would be nice to be known for your talent; Mike and I settled for being known as the kings of pain.

I'm not going to describe any of my races. One of Mike's is far more interesting. I know this to be true even though I wasn't even there. My marathon training partner was in Toronto and decided to watch the big Carlsberg Lite Classic, 80 laps around the two kilometre circle surrounding Queen's Park, Toronto.

In 1983, Mike was at the beginning of his cycling career. He was young, had limited cycling experience and was a complete unknown in a sport where in any given race the top cyclists are well-known. The circular course was ideal, the crowd was big and appreciative, and the race was televised for a national program called *Wide World of Sports*.

Since it was a pre-Olympic year, some of the national teams were there, the Russians and the Americans among them. Cycling is a team sport, with riders drafting off each other throughout the long kilometres until one or a few riders can break away and challenge to take and hold the lead against the charging pack, or peloton. Even a team working in tangent rarely makes a move too early for fear of the power of the fully drafting peloton in pursuit. The conventional wisdom, backed by the reality of physics, is that you cannot win without your team.

Mike did not have a team, he did not have a proven record, and he was possibly too inexperienced to have conventional wisdom. He relied on unconventional toughness. Many a racecourse has been littered by the hubris of the overeager who fail to appreciate that the race is not won until the very end.

At the beginning of the race, Mike jumped into the lead by himself. Going against him were almost impossible odds. Going for him was not suffering the curse of overthinking. The peloton of 100 or so did not react, did not care, would easily reel him in when the time came, or, more likely, he would die a thousand deaths and come back to them like a three-year-old on a tricycle.

At this point, my friend is animated. Mike is working hard, the peloton easily gliding through the laps like a predator stalking its prey. There are no bold moves from others to work up from the peloton to where Mike, the sucker, suffers. The crowd is reacting, loves an underdog, and Mike is fully committed, but if he is caught now he will not rest in the peloton for an attempt to win later in the race. He will be finished for good.

And on it goes into the second half, still very early in a cycling race, the crowd clearly hoping for the sucker and impatient with the risk-adverse peloton, unwilling to hurt, sacrifice, take chances. The peloton knows what it is doing. The peloton often allows a breakaway group the illusion of victory until quite late in the race and then accelerates its ferocious collective engine against the wilting debris up front. There is little incentive to react since the function of the team is to set up their best sprinter for the final push to the finish line. A lone front rider—that is, alone and against the odds and the wind for 160 kilometres and three full hours—is to be ignored even if the crowd thinks otherwise.

In the final laps the crowd becomes frenzied. No one had anticipated excitement like this. The lone rider has inexplicably held on, but the peloton has woken up and begun its colossal push to the finish.

And then a funny thing happened. Mike was always an open-mouth breather, so he rode with a trademark hangdog expression. Problem was, about ten laps from the finish line, a bee flew into his open gob and stung him. Oh yeah, and he had an allergic reaction. So Mike had to finish the race oxygen deprived with throat swelling, quadriceps screaming, crowd screaming louder. He was lucky he was able to finish the race, but luck is not why he won it. Lucky, because within five minutes of finishing, with his throat swelling, he could not ride at all. Not lucky to have won, because he had the courage, tenacity and toughness to pull it off. Even with these qualities, 95 times out of 100 you lose.

The other quality he had that day was self-confidence, or possibly faith. The word *faith* may seem misplaced as applied to winning a race. The word we are supposed to use and believe in is *self*, that thing of our own making, under our own control. Maybe, but when I raced my best, I was surprised and felt that my effort had been not entirely of my own making.

Sometimes I would go out at a blistering pace to try to put some distance between myself and the sprinters and to discourage opponents. No one knows if your early suicidal pace, at least on that day, is a new level of fitness or plain old stupidity. So you go out and commit to a pace and effort that hurts early on, and if you finish this sentence with self-confidence, all the pressure is on you. But if you substitute the word *self-confidence* with the word *faith*, the pressure is no longer on you alone. Semantics. Maybe, but at the end of a race when you are suffering, when you desperately want to quit, you will cling to any psychological or—for the truly weird and dispossessed like me—spiritual edge. Desperation at the end of a race breeds humility and submission, not to the rival but to the pain, which ironically can be the difference between winning and losing.

Oddly, in later year races, rather than hope for the demise of my opponent, my mantra shifted to giving him strength to finish well and to let that strength pull me along. This does not mean I gave an inch. I would always win if I could, never settle if I could resist, my last stride always the last I could take. Win or lose, racing does provide a good metaphor for life. A race well-run is not quite a life well lived, but the ingredients of success, commitment, perseverance and upholding faith will serve you well. The problem is, in this fitness-crazed world, people are increasingly less likely to apply these qualities to life.

Self-actualizing moderns are expunging the necessity of pain and substituting a *Lululemon, "fun run," everyone is equal in all ways* mentality to the beauty and brutality of competition. The emphasis is now on the look of the outfit and the physical look of fitness rather than on the accomplishment of doing and finishing something difficult and placing yourself on the line against others and, in consideration of the clock, all others. We are not to judge, and therefore it is an unpopular notion to submit to the dispassionate judgment of a clock that ranks your effort without consideration of your feelings or self-esteem. The new mantra is that life is to be enjoyed, always, and a life well lived is the accumulation of pleasurable experiences. But a life untested is unlived, and the centre will not hold, even if one's exterior is held together by the seaweed fibres of Lululemon spandex.

For all the expectation of pleasure without end, it is only in the face of adversity that the term *life well lived* has meaning. Always the most even-tempered, and with a measure of contentedness absent from the remaining six of us, Mike became an example of a life well lived as the losses piled up. Over 25 years ago, as one of the fittest people on the planet, he experienced a temporary loss of sight, followed by numbness in one leg. Nothing alarming, but not quite right. Dismissive doctors, a number of years and opportunity lost. In February 2001, he was diagnosed with multiple sclerosis. His particular case unremitting, ironically deemed *progressive*—that word again.

Thirty years ago as an orderly on a spinal cord unit, I learned that loss of mobility was not the same experience for all people. The extent of personal loss correlated in direct proportion to the level of activity preceding injury. In training for the 1984 Olympics, Mike cycled an average of 500 miles each week. His loss extreme, his presentation to the world serene.

In this modern life, we are supposed to emote all things felt, to all people, all the time. But if everyone actually did that we would have emotional anarchy. Emoting is not in our Irish Catholic DNA. The only comment ever made about what he is up against was that he is unwilling to make his condition unpleasant for others. The Canadian MS motto is *MS affects the entire family*. No one should have to endure the entire burden himself, and though others are deeply affected by it, it is not easily shared. For all his losses, he has always been good company, which few of us can pull off under the best of circumstances.

But Mike has no faith. Not a little, not negative, not sometimes. Instead he has a deep, informed and persuasive conviction that this difficult, complex, contradictory life has no meaning and that death is final. Mike is not your average atheist—angry, defensive or determined to prove a point. I hope he is wrong more than I think so, and his arguments are compelling and at some level irrefutable.

The thing is, proclaiming or writing about faith means nothing. I struggle to have sufficient faith to get through this day to the next, to find a modicum of meaning, to keep despair at bay. Faith does not conjure up a comforting deity. A practice of faith may allow me to become somewhat aware, maybe change my life by increments (or not) and, at best, help transcend my many faults and connect to my higher self. Spirituality helps, but it is not a life well lived and can be used to cover a lifetime of weakness and hypocrisy. Mike does not believe in God but has the capacity to stoically accept the cards he is dealt, live life well and help those whom God places in his path. His interpretation of how and why people are placed in his path may differ from mine, but surely a living faith is more a function of what we do than what we say we believe, just as actually winning a race has greater value than one's self-confidence to do so.

I pray that Mike is wrong, but this is my stuff, not his. For Mike it is what it is, and it is not. That being the case, stop fretting and start living. For me, the issue of faith is complex, even as I attempt to delineate it down to either God is or isn't. I struggle, and the results are varied, subject to change and very much tied to meaning. Mike believes that there is no God, which makes the future clear, certain, simple. Apparently, I don't do simple, much as I tell you I would like to. I could stop struggling over faith about as easily as I could stop breathing on a hard run. Faith with conviction can give people comfort and serenity. I know I've seen it, even if I've rarely felt it. Atheism with conviction can make people self-righteous and angry. Not Mike; he is comfortable and has no desire to convince anyone of anything. Besides, who can argue with someone who is content and a good father, husband and brother? If my faith means anything, I should be more content, have less angst. I can only dream.

Which is what I did. I've had three dreams in my life that have left a profound impression. They have all been clear, in vivid detail, and whether phenomena or fanciful imagining, they were something markedly apart from all other dreams. I'm inside a church. It's not just any church; it's St. Francis of Assisi Catholic Church on Wellington Street in Ottawa. The church is a massive grey stone edifice, dwarfing buildings close by as the neighbourhood has grown up around it. I know this landmark well as it is close to where I grew up, but it is not our parish church, and weirdly, I had never been inside before and haven't still. Still, the church feels familiar, and I am running inside. There are no pews, and my feet do not touch the ground. This is not the usual grinding slog I expect and am used to—I am not just light on my feet, I am flying. My two older daughters, Shannon and Kristen, are watching, and I feel euphoric and literally take off, flying up to the great heights of the church ceiling. But a thought occurs to me and I quickly descend to where the girls are standing and say, "This is great! Now Mike will have to believe in God." And the dream is done.

The next day after I had the dream was a Friday, and after work I went to Mike's place for the evening, as I often do. On this particular evening Mike's wife, Jennie, and his two daughters, Jessica and Natalie, were out. The girls are accomplished singers and had concerts, but not always in an accessible venue, so Mike's attendance depended on where it was held. Since he hadn't gone, I assumed accessibility was the problem, but I didn't ask. Mike and I ordered takeout Chinese food and shot the breeze, which is as close as emotionally retentive Irish Catholic brothers of any generation come to talking. As for the dream, there was no way I was going to mention it to him. Mike is tough and amiable but is not looking for sympathy, and, most of all, he is not open to finding God. Besides, the dream struck me, vivid as it was, as too silly for words, at least words spoken to an atheist brother who is smarter than I am.

Jennie and the girls arrived home around 9 p.m. Mike went to the bathroom, and Jennie sat down. I asked how the concert went and where it was. She answered St. Francis Church. There had never been a concert there in their years of performing, they had never been to St. Francis Church before, they had not known it existed.

So what does this mean? The details of the dream do not mean that I received divine intervention. They may very well mean nothing. Even as far as coincidences go, it is easy to dismiss this as quaint and meaningless. I am split. The dream in my head is powerful, has meaning; the dream as written, silly and weak-kneed.

Further removed in time are Mike's dreams. He won't remember them, but it is not because of the passing of time. When he was about five, Mike would often sleepwalk, look you in the eye, talk to you, answer questions, even as he was locked in a terror-filled dream, searching the house, claiming he had *lost his balance*. He would not remember a thing the next day and would then proceed to have the same dream that night. Again the source of his fear was a futile search for his lost balance.

In cycling, Mike found his balance at a world-class level. Then he lost it, this time not in a dream but likely wishing it were so, with the progression of MS. But here is the miracle of, if nothing else, character. Mike made changes, great and small, with his family there every step of the way. He found a way to reconcile his life to MS in order to have a life in a way that works, and as an exemplar of a life well lived, he has found his balance.

We all lose our balance in life, and maybe the point of life exists in our frantic sleepwalking search for its recovery. Maybe those who have lost and found their balance are the waiting signposts along the rocky road pointing home. Maybe the most common story in the world is also the most profound.

If God is, miracles are. Not once in a while, but always. That being the case, we have to notice them to know they have happened. This thought leaves much for personal interpretation and advanced flakiness. But to dismiss, as we do, day by day, minute by minute, the unfolding of miracles might be to miss the most obvious, most significant and greatest of human experience in this all so short a life.

Every day I look around and think, how can all this be? How can all this beauty, these intricate moving parts and living entanglements, flourish in near perfect harmony, with repeat performances always a glance away? There are scientific explanations that contextualize, obscure and distance more than explain. They are complicated but miss that the essential thing is missing in not explaining the essence, not understanding the question, the real one behind the easy answers, the one asking, shouting why, without answer, echo or heartbeat. In skirting this question, the scientific answers strike me as simpler and more naive than the crayon drawings of a five-year-old. Actually, the drawings of a five-year-old are at least more likely to catch what is, a glimpse of essence. It can be seen, possibly understood; it cannot be explained.

Inspiration and reasons to believe come in surprising and unexpected ways. In my work, family, strangers, old friends, new ways of seeing old ways, sitting writing in a Prague café along the Voltava River on a hot fine July day. These things keep me believing something, something, and, more importantly, prevent me from sinking into the morass of modernity and settling, explaining away and sliding into the vacuous comfort of nothing.

"Surely some revelation is at hand."

W. B. YEATS, "THE SECOND COMING"

# CHAPTER EIGHT
## HOURS BETWEEN SECONDS

SHERLOCK HOLMES INGESTED OPIATES IN HIS BAKER STREET DIGS BETWEEN GIGS. HIS blood coursed and quickened to the excitement of the case but sunk into despondency and gloom whenever his genius was not taxed. The case was the addiction, the opiate the substitute for the addiction, filling the space until the next case. He needed cases or drugs so as not to wither and fade into nothingness. Sitting quietly in his front room and thinking was not a step toward becoming a saint—it was boredom; it was death. Sherlock was a very modern man.

For some reason, I was reminded of Conan Doyle's character Sherlock while thinking about the very real death of Philip Seymour Hoffman. Sadly, after 20 years of being drug free, Hoffman was found dead with a needle in his arm and over 70 packages of heroin nearby. Wealth, fame, adoring fans, he had it all; his suicide or recklessness, a mystery worthy of Sherlock Holmes. Not exactly a regular guy, but he had a regular-guy cluster of three beautiful kids, which makes the mystery inexplicable, perhaps too much even for the mind of Sherlock Holmes.

Hoffman was known for devotion to his craft. He was an actor's actor. Hoffman didn't just act; he became the role. While becoming the role, Hoffman put his life on hold, and maybe, just maybe, returning to his life—adoration, wealth, kids and all—was just too boring without acute pharmaceutical assistance. For both Sherlock and Hoffman, life without a role distant from life was not worth living.

Since we cannot fathom another's consciousness in search of why Hoffman's kids did not defeat his nemesis of boredom, we speculate. The awful irony is that the man who could not sit alone in a room and think lay quietly alone in a room and died. Of course addiction is more complicated than my simple musings. It is more than boredom, and his reckless death does not mean that Hoffman did not love his kids. But there are moments. The darkest hour strung between the longest seconds of our life have moments of clarity and simplicity in the midst of confusion and distraction. For Hoffman and many other celebrities who have succumbed to drugs in reaching for more—more excitement, stimulation, escape, ecstasy—there is still the last conscious thought after the point of no return, no longer reaching, no longer bored, just intense, distilled thinking, but what? All stimulation and distraction deflated to a few images, a flash of memory intense or mundane, the last smouldering ashes of a life. Paradise lost, home forsaken.

Perhaps the elemental thing, my dear Watson, is that all our individual passions, intrigues and distractions are merely a misunderstood archetypal desire to go home. What was Hoffman's last thought—his unattainable stash of heroin or his kid's delight on his third birthday when he unexpectedly arrived back home? Did he regret not being able to use the full 70 packages of heroin or, for all his deep-felt passions, that his life was about to come to an inglorious end? Did Hoffman exit wanting more, or, far more likely, was his a silent scream for less? Just one more simple minute without ambition or design, to breathe deeply, take in the silence and feel the exquisite, deeply satisfying boredom of life.

Of course we just don't know, and this piece is not really about Hoffman or Holmes. We divide ourselves from ourselves, chasing a multiplicity of modern distractions by which we are supposed to find ourselves. We spend a lifetime thinking, saying, that life is complicated, that there are no simple answers, that there are no answers. Maybe we are wrong.

———————

At the precise moment I was writing the preceding paragraph in a coffee shop, a friend interrupted my writing to give me a lesson in boredom—that is, the value of contemplation in a distraction-free zone. I like coffee shops. They allow public anonymity and, weirdly for all the constant distraction, a place to perform the rituals of reading and writing that remain only intentions in other places. Coffee shops remind me of sitting at my parents' linoleum kitchen table, a fly on the proverbial wall of life. But I don't go to chat, as seems to be most people's purpose. Still, I watch and listen as I silently perform my daily rituals. I'm not exactly alone in this, but we subversives remain mostly hidden, which is what we like about coffee shops.

Which is why David's full-circle lesson in boredom was oddly timed. I was reading my newspaper, holding it up in the air, just as my dad did all his life, less a habit than a defense against the intrusion of man. From behind my thin defenses, David asked if he could join me. My defenses penetrated, coupled with the fact that I like David, I pointed to the empty chair at my table.

This was not an intrusion. I'd met David 30 years earlier in grad school, and he'd lived several lives since then. He'd been a fellow marathoner and had a passion for outdoor active life, cycling from Amsterdam to Athens by himself after grad school as one of his many adventures. (Parenthetically, true adventurers are becoming less common in the age of fear and distraction. Travel and adventure have become synonymous with cruises, all-inclusive packages and last minute deals.) Our contact had been infrequent over the years, and conversation mostly centred on running, training and the like. But his life and our conversations changed, and here we were sitting, talking about Philip Seymour Hoffman, man's inability to sit and think, and boredom.

David has been tested in this life as few have ever been. With a career in full bloom, marriage and four kids, his was an intense and fulsome life. But, as the saying goes, his life was forever changed in the blink of an eye. Cancer. To say the surgery that followed was intrusive is an understatement. Thirteen months in hospital, six months in intensive care, four months on a ventilator, three months in a coma, and somehow, to the astonishment of all his many doctors and nurses, he did not die.

David does not know why he did not die as expected. But not dying does not inform one about how to live life again. After he came out of the coma, David spent long days awake on a ventilator, unable to communicate. Machines monitored all his vital signs; machines allowed him to live. And so he lay, mind separated from body, body sustained by machines, a mind free-floating, filling in inert hours with thinking. But not the distracted thinking that is the fodder of our everyday lives. This was the Pascalian challenge of sitting in a room alone and thinking, but assisted by modern medicine, it was Pascal on steroids. Cut off from people to see, from places to go, in short from everything that conspires to make hours into seconds, David's mind slowed seconds into hours and went to places most humans never go or can imagine existing.

His mind reeled, searching for something to adhere to, to provide context. He went backward through the cobwebs of a past not so much forgotten as permanently archived. So he thought, or more to the point, didn't think, until he arrived at the memories of his deep past. Memory is not objective fact. Research shows that when we uncover a memory, we figuratively unwrap it and then rewrap for future recall, but in the process it is forever changed. Subsequent recall or unwrapping results in change on each occasion. Therefore, memories frequently recalled are more changed than memory rarely accessed. So people not only have different perceptions of shared experience; their frequency of recall can create further divergence. Previously unwrapped memories recalled 50 years after the fact under conditions of extreme sensory deprivation create the perfect storm for revision and revelation.

David's mind unwrapped memories from age six, five, four, three, and perhaps earlier years, interior places inaccessible in the modern distracted world. Perhaps more impressive was the vivid and precise nature of details recalled. He remembered being four years old and searching for specific items in a trunk, a fitting metaphor for psychological searching, mining the mind. And what was he looking for?

Throughout these months of memories, his state of mind varied. He was in a coma, was semi-conscious, was heavily medicated, did not dream, but then remembered dreams long after the fact of dreaming, and always in detail, intense and real. And not waking from the unreality of a dream, how was he to know real? David says he went through a long indeterminate time remembering dreams filled with terror, always ending with him facing death. During this time, he literally fought for his life, and on three or four occasions his wife and kids were called into the hospital to say goodbye. No one is supposed to be able to buck the medical expert odds three or four times.

The death dream he remembers most vividly took the certainty of impending death farthest. Death dreams tend to be followed by the reprieve of awakening. But David did not wake, could not wake, and waited without reprieve from his firing squad. Like Saint Sebastian, he arms were tied, in this instance to a tree—a fitting metaphor for immobility—and he watched his assassins prepare. Though terrified, his final thought was not terror. In the end, he did not bargain; there was no silent scream, just acceptance; and curiously, with a wife and four kids, he reasoned he'd had a good life, which made it easier to let go.

Violent death was David's recurring dream as he lay battling a horrible cancer, suspended between life and death, with death expected to win and a wife and four kids pleading for him not to let go. Do we let go, do we willingly surrender, or do we go kicking and screaming all the way? David let go in his dreams only to come back as Lazarus in real life. The most desperate will to live is cradled in a blanket of willingness to let go. Maybe David decided he should drop home again before going home.

Waking from the firing squad was not much of a reprieve. After months on a ventilator and in a coma, David did not know how to breathe. Even our most basic reflex for air cannot be taken for granted. Measured amounts of air regularly forced into our lungs seduce us into surrendering that which we would be most resistant to letting go of in a heathy state.

Breathing was no longer natural but a deliberate skill to be mastered. Learning to breathe is difficult, not unlike being on the verge of drowning— two breaths forward, one breath back. Then inexplicably he forgot to breathe. He remembers frantic medical staff working over him while he watched their expressions and activity.

He knows he is the centre of attention but is also aware that he is not quite a part of what is going on. He knows they are trying to make him breathe, but he leaves it all to them to figure out and lies watching, thinking, slipping away. Not quite a welcoming tunnel bathed in celestial light, but an awareness of separation between the physical world while still part of it, slipping into something, perhaps peace.

Which raises the existential question to the out-of-body phenomena— are we transformed to this, our higher selves, with a profound sense of peace if the cessation of life is oblivion? Can our higher selves really be that stupid? If we were watching the obliteration of self, wouldn't the common refrain to the silent scream be "Make me breathe; don't let me die!"

As such, I am struck less by the presence of light than by the absence of darkness. Why is there a palpable willingness, even desire, to leave?

The archetypal fear of the unknown is replaced by a fearless attraction to something, not nothing.

Still, this is my bottom line, not necessarily David's, whose conclusions carry a tad more validity. It is hard to imagine someone going through more of life than David—more adversity, love, gratitude, pain, boredom. In escaping death he was reborn, though he was not necessarily born again. The miracle of his recovery has not compelled David to an absolute belief in God, and he remains an agnostic. And why should we expect anything else? David's miracle does not have to be experienced to be believed, so why expect him to have found faith more than any of us? We moderns doubt everything, every moment, except for a select few who either have a true gift of faith or adhere to the modern cult of knowing there is no God.

I suppose I wanted David to know that there is a God and to impart his wisdom to me. David said he was an agnostic before his cancer experience and remains one today. I'm not disappointed. Profound experience rarely fills us with the insight of knowing. It more often reinforces the humbling truth that we do not, cannot, know.

I asked David, "So what is the difference for you between your life before and since your ordeal?"

His answer was simple. "Before I didn't think about it much. Now I think about it all the time."

"And ...?" I followed.

"To think that all of this is nothing doesn't make much sense."

At which point I hurried off to work, thinking that I'd have to introduce David to Northrop.

---

Sherlock Holmes and Philip Seymour Hoffman lusted for the world speeded up, craving not the mind of a saint but rather the stimulated mind of themselves. Liam sought a world slowed down, particularly as his condition worsened. Constant, unrelenting voices from unfamiliar and hostile sources, not of his own making but of his own mind. Schizophrenia infects the mind like a computer virus, pervasive, invasive, intermittently shutting down systems and leaving just enough residue function for the host site to know the depth of its loss.

As both a father and a mental health professional, Neil understood at the onset of his son's diagnosis that the centre could not hold. He was in his early twenties, and he was a gifted graphic artist working in New York City, waiting for his career to be born. Liam was gregarious and audacious and had a tiger by the tail. Problem was, it turned out that the tiger was actually the "rough beast [that] slouches towards Bethlehem to be born" (W. B. Yeats, "The Second Coming").

The next decade was courage and grace in the form of a losing battle. From the life of the party in the centre of the universe to living alone in the bachelor apartment over his father's garage in the Canadian wilderness. We Canadians don't actually see living outside of a town of 2,000 as being in the wilderness, but to the rest of the world, and particularly to those of New York City pedigree, it was deepest, darkest wilderness.

In the splendid isolation of Wakefield, Quebec, 30 minutes from Canada's capital, Liam could not hold a job, had no career, was not the life of the party, had no parties to go to. Liam was not unhappy with his new digs, nor was he ungrateful for his father's devotion and continuous help. He loved his supportive father and family, but with all the love in the world, *things fall apart*. He had too much time to fill, but time was not *the* problem. Voices, impulses, forces from his mind but not *of* his mind always talking, directing, ordering, and never listening. Always noise, never quiet. Liam needed quiet, but his mind could no longer do quiet.

If he could cobble together a few bucks, Liam would leave, go away, run from the voices that never left. Once he travelled by bus from Ottawa to San Francisco, 3,000 miles away, and still the same voices. But once off the bus, Liam was on the street without love and a supportive family. Just a pathetic creature of the street. Unfamiliar cities are brutally cruel to lone wolves with severe mental illness dropping by to quell the persistence and amplification of voices. From there Liam travelled to Death Valley, California. Though it is unknown why he chose this destination, it hangs suspended, equal parts ominous prelude and thundering irony.

It is both a profound truth and a cliché that parents are only as happy as the unhappiest of their children. This does not change once children become adults and may be even more painful for the realization of the fading of the hope that otherwise sustains the task of parenting. Parenting may be the purest love—we love our children unconditionally for who they are, not for what they become—but they do not necessarily share our sentiment. If they fail in their own estimation and fall to self-loathing, they can resent our steadfastness. The hardest person to rescue is the person we love the most.

Back home, without money to travel, Liam began slipping into the forest to still the voices, with some relief. Liam loved nature and especially the blanketing quiet of a snow-covered forest, because only in cold and isolation could the voices be quieted, if only for a time. But Liam did not love his medication. The side effects were nasty, making him gain weight, feel bloated and puffy. Worse, the medication for the disease made him less himself than did the disease. Liam stopped taking all medication. Neil the mental health professional understood, respected and suffered the patient's choice; Neil the father understood, respected and suffered and suffered the death sentence of his son's choosing. *Please God, it can't be this way; it was always going to be this way.* So Neil watched as his son declined, doing what he could, whenever he could, and otherwise practiced restraint—surely the most difficult task asked of a parent—an act of pure love when the only thing left to do is nothing.

There are some people, many or perhaps most, for whom confinement is too outrageous to bear. Extreme psychiatric trauma is a prison without the possibility of parole. As the beast slouched towards Bethlehem, Liam made his plan. Just after Christmas Liam asked his dad to drop him off at the edge of Gatineau Park for some—who knows?—peaceful wintering camping, quelling of obnoxious voices, meeting the mind of God. Liam's playground, Gatineau Park, is a wilderness of 361 square kilometres on the doorstep of the Canadian capital. It is easy to disappear in the Canadian wilderness.

Liam had done this before; it was what he wanted, needed; and besides, there was no normal with which to assess his behaviour. It was cold, the beginning of a severe cold snap. Liam knew what he was doing. Most people create distractions so as not to face the disquieting questions of who am I, why am I? Liam sought solitary refuge in quiet places as solace from the disease, to remind himself that *he* was not the disease that inhabited his mind. His solitude in nature was not a silent scream but a sacred escape.

As Neil dropped his son off, Liam said that if he was not back in five days he was in trouble. He then said, "Dad, I love you," and he was gone. New Year's Eve was the fourth day. Temperatures had stayed unbearably cold, without reprieve. I happened to be at Neil's house on New Year's Eve, and during our subdued celebration, he asked if I had some time the next day. I had lots of time, and we had lots and lots of space.

It should be mentioned that Neil and I are close friends, and it is a privilege to recognize one whom God has placed, with purpose, in our path. We are brothers really, though odd siblings we make. I am my father's son, Dad being a thin rail of a man and me more of the same, exacerbated by 30 years of distance running. Neil is a big guy, equivalent to two of me strapped together. Neil got his PhD in psychology but is a philosopher at heart, astonishingly well-read and erudite, the conversationalist of choice on a desert island. Still, as the next day dawned, in contravention of all previous days together until that point, there was no conversation.

New Year's Day was impenetrable grey—dark grey skies, blowing grey snow across a bleak grey landscape. Our moods were grey but determined to pursue futility to the end. We chomped through the snow, I built for movement and Neil not so much, trying to find hard-packed paths where none existed. Often hard-packed gave way suddenly to soft snow below, more often for Neil and with worse consequences. The going was rough, and we had no idea where we were going, just why.

Hours later, our exercise in futility as exhausted as our over-exercised bodies, we handed the search over to the police, who gave it to the military, who gave it an extensive helicopter attempt, bigger, better, same result— because for all the effort, and it was extensive, in the godlike stillness of Liam's mind, he did not want to be found.

For two months, nothing. On March 1, in the midst of Neil's birthday party, he received the dreaded word. Liam's body had been found by a couple snowshoeing far off trail, far from the maddening winter crowd. In the newspaper the following day, a tiny piece, a few reported facts. Liam had been found, not in Gatineau Park but 50 kilometres away in another forest. With all the space and wilderness to get lost within Gatineau Park, why had he hitchhiked to another part of nature? One obscure fact dangled from the rest. The newspaper mentioned that the hikers had only found Liam's body because they had heard a bell through the trees in a place where bells do not ring. They followed the sound to a huge white pine tree. A tiny bell hung from a branch, blowing and ringing in the wind. The expansive pine provided beauty and the illusion of protection canopied over Liam's exposed body. Silent night and day, except for the bell.

Neil had read about the bell in the same short article but was in no frame of mind to regard it as significant. Small thing to wonder about. Of course we had talked about the certainty and pain of Liam's death for the past two months. These were not our usual competitive conversational slag session. Conversations about Liam involved few words with gaps of silence, poignant for what remained unsaid. The inarticulate speech of the heart is just that, even for those who are competitively verbose.

I asked Neil what he thought about the bell in the short perfunctory piece announcing the discovery of Liam's body. Neil asked what significance it could have. I said it was curious because in Christianity a bell has significance. As well, I couldn't help but relate it to Zuzu hearing the bell on the Christmas tree in *It's a Wonderful Life*, precociously declaring, "Every time a bell rings an angel gets his wings." At the end of this Frank Capra classic, clumsy Clarence Odbody has earned his wings and become a full-bodied guardian angel.

Neil's expression went blank. He did not immediately respond. He said that Liam's body had been found in a forest called L'Ange Gardien, or "Guardian Angel." Inarticulate heartbeats. And silence.

When do we need our guardian angel? For passage through our longest, darkest, loneliest and possibly holiest night. This is how time is slowed, hours between seconds; this is how mortals become saints, contemplating the mind of God. Even Christ passed the night in the Gethsemane garden in terrible loneliness and near despair. The symbolism of a guardian angel would not have been lost on Liam—a deliberate final act, a sacred scream, and the beautiful, incongruent piercing of a bell.

Liam's last purchase on this earth was not life-sustaining food or drink or provision of any kind. Liam went into the Buckingham Giant Tiger store and purchased a lock and key and length of chain. He then found his place in nature under the colossal pine tree and lay down in his cathedral. His spot was chosen carefully, away from trails, the possibility of people, but not so secluded that he could not later be found. His spot, his hallowed ground, was just far enough away to be the loneliest place in the world and just close enough to the trail to allow a tiny bell to be heard, in time.

This act, achieving the mind of a saint, took time, and at some point, he must have lain down, no doubt looking upward into a swaying tangle of pine branches and sky beyond, and committed to the silence, slowing time, with

157

deep frosty breaths, punctuated by the single click of a lock. Now chained to the tree, Liam gripped the key and threw it and his life irrevocably away, the key deep into the snow, and Liam deep into the next life.

For us creatures of distraction, and without the affliction and wisdom of his disease, it is impossible to know what went through Liam's mind. I never met Liam, but I have a single image from one of Neil's photos. Liam and his brother Shawn, together with their dad, Neil, frozen in time, in frozen rural Saskatchewan, all young, animated, happy, and at home in the holy moment.

I think Liam's life and death are a miracle. But there is another miracle that I am closer to, and perhaps closer to knowing. In 1960, when Neil was 10, his father, who also had schizophrenia, committed suicide. For a year Neil only knew that his father had died. He remembers an acute sense of abandonment. Ten is a very tender age to learn that life is about pain and loss and death. A year later, Neil learned that father had died at his own hand. So Liam's suicide was not only every parent's nightmare but Neil's longest held and deepest fear.

The good news is, there is more. All Neil's relationships, his professional life, and his pursuit of God are defined by the moment of learning that his dad had committed suicide. Neil describes his outward expression upon receiving the news as shrugging his shoulders and saying, "Let's not let this ruin our day"—surely a monumental moment in human history for its pathos and tenderness—no words, no experience, no defenses, no experience to know how to process pain, too painful to admit meaning or feeling.

Later in life Neil became a devout Buddhist, and he is among the very select few who *know*, have that rare palpable, undeniable, inscrutable living faith, unlike poor saps such as yours truly. I am not talking about his encyclopedic mind for information that he struts out daily, proud as a peacock. I mean he knows that thing for which all other things matter not—that God is real, that there is something, and yes, something better, beyond the tragic trifecta of pain and loss and death. And sad as the passing of Liam's life was and is, Neil knows that his son is the happy boy in the Saskatchewan photo and not the corpse found under the pine tree. He feels the reality of Liam's presence daily, and not in the vague, conjured way of wishful thinking. Over 50 years later the "let's not let this ruin our day" response of a child continues to inform Neil's every thought and action. It is *the* defining moment, the psychic wound that becomes the kernel of faith that leads to spiritual wisdom that underlies the compulsion to act, in this case to alleviate the pain of mental illness. But we're fairly competitive in conversation, so I'm pretty sure I'll never tell Neil that I have these thoughts.

There are an astonishing number of ways we can wreak havoc on the world, on those we hate, on those we love, especially those we love, and on ourselves, navigating the common tragedy that is the reality of this life. Still, the older I get, the more I have come to the view that, on balance, we humans meander through the maze of life rather well, given that for all of us it doesn't end well. We know this always, and yet enlightened consciousness or the tiny buried truth inherited from the archetypal memory of our trailing clouds of glory keeps nibbling from the fringes, reminding us that all is not as it seems, nothing is as it seems, and a vale of hope lies beyond this vale of tears.

"The point of philosophy is to start with something so simple as not to seem worth stating, and to end with something so paradoxical that no one will believe it."

BERTRAND RUSSELL

# CHAPTER NINE
## FAITH FROM THE ASHES

MOST OF US, MOST OF THE TIME, EXIST ON AUTOPILOT, CRUISING THROUGH LIFE ONE Netflix episode at a time. We get the full season but may be missing the fullness of life. The fullness of life does not preclude pain and hardship. Which raises a question: how does one actually pull a phoenix from the ashes of life?

There was another priest, another family friend, but unlike Father Crampton, Father Bob Bedard did not make house calls. He was too busy. Except for that one time he came to Mom's house to baptize my daughter, Shannon. This thought occurred to me while sitting across from Shannon, her daughter Pearl cradled in her arms as she tried to multi-task eating pizza while tending to a rambunctious two-year-old. Father Bob had baptized Shannon as a favour to my mom, who revered him, for which there is a history.

Father Bob was both principal and teacher at the rival Catholic high school across town from my own. On October 27, 1975, at 2:20 in the afternoon, two of my brothers were at St. Pius X when the world changed forever—this being a time before mass school shootings became tragically, if not commonplace, something that happens with disturbing frequency.

Robert Poulin, an 18-year-old student, walked into Father Bob's class with a shotgun and fired four times, killing one student immediately, injuring seven others, with another dying soon after, before exiting the classroom for the corridor to empty the last shot into his own head.

The horror continued. Earlier in the day Robert Poulin had raped and murdered a 17-year-old girl with whom he had some limited contact because she felt sorry for him. How he was able to convince her to come into his basement is unknown, but he had likely planned to sexually assault her ever since he had met her a couple years before. Robert had a crush on Kim Rabot, and she had been to his family's house for dinner on at least one occasion. She was not interested in a relationship, but—uncharacteristically generous for a teenager—she perhaps sensed his need for a friend and his deep loneliness and was kind enough to extend herself. (I am writing this chapter the week that extreme loner Alex Minassian drove a rented van down Yonge Street in Toronto, murdering 10 people and injuring 14. He, like Robert Poulin before the term was coined, is a self-described "incel" or involuntarily celibate— both intensely frustrated, resentful men, in the hell of complete self-delusion and self-imposed isolation.)

Suicide is difficult to fathom. Still, we can understand that the pain of living can be greater to bear than a desperation-induced belief in liberation from suffering. But the rage and resentment in an 18-year-old intent upon a scorched earth policy of taking others into the abyss is incomprehensible and cannot be explained by psychological labels. Psychological labels allow us to categorize behaviour and feign understanding; understanding how personal pathology metastasizes into evil takes us beyond the limits of psychology. It is the nightmarish silent scream where the convulsing question *why* is never answered.

Robert Poulin handcuffed Kim, his friend, possibly his only friend in the world, raped her and stabbed her 14 times, and went upstairs into the family domain, where he calmly ate a sandwich his mother had prepared earlier and watched a TV show before setting the family home on fire and travelling to Father Bob's classroom. There are many ways one could interpret this murder, but it is hard not to conclude that Kim Rabot was murdered as a consequence of her compassion. It would be easy to further conclude that distance, suspicion and self-interest should displace compassion in the violent and dangerous world in which we live.

Robert Poulin had been Father Bob's student. Robert had chosen to murder *his* students in *his* classroom. Whatever else was going on in Robert's life, Father Bob had had the opportunity to teach, to connect, to extend help to his troubled student, and he had failed. What happened to Father Bob's students in his classroom was his responsibility. It was the most spectacular, unforgivable failure in the world.

Not my assessment, but very possibly Father Bob's. After the murders, he struggled. It was not something he talked about in public. Faith likely suspended, with the prospect of being extinguished. Motive for mass murder incomprehensible; cessation of faith after mass murder comprehensible. Father Bob was, after all, only human.

Many years ago Mom gave me a sense of Father Bob's struggle as she understood it, based on limited information, speculation—not sure, though the whole scenario falls within the category of life tragedies that one never gets over. Still, not getting over an experience in life, what that experience means and how one lives with it, is perhaps the point of life. One is deeply moved by tragedy, and its corrosive effect can certainly diminish faith. Movement is active, not passive, and the question remains, when moved, how and in what direction does one move? What one does with the compulsion to move is the difference between death and renewal, for which the mythological metamorphosis of the phoenix is symbolic. If there is no God, if when confronted by tragedy we conclude that life is simply inevitable capitulation to brute forces, the application of self-interest—even ruthless self-interest—is all that matters. But if there is a God, then to be moved requires moving in another direction. And being deeply moved means we must move deeply. Living life to the fullest is not achieved with half measures.

Responsibility requires that we respond to every situation. Capitulation is irresponsible. The irony of the modern nihilistic world is that the easy route, the irresponsible way, condemns us to despair of death, even in the bloom of youth and in perfect health. We can feel great sympathy for people who despair, but it is still an abnegation of responsibility. Victor Frankl, Holocaust survivor: "Everything can be taken from a man but one thing: the last of human freedoms—to choose one's attitude in any given set of circumstances, to choose one's own way. If there is a meaning in life at all, then there must be a meaning in suffering. Suffering is an ineradicable part of life, even as fate and death."

Through prayer Father Bob chose life. And in choosing life, he came to understand that he was chosen. He'd only prayed mechanically for years until he prayed for the gift of prayer. Nothing happened. We sometimes experience mini disillusionments, asking, not receiving, followed by apathy, self-congratulations for trying or else possibility petulance for what is clearly not our fault. But Father Bob was a creature of persistence. As a 19-year-old student he fixated on a gospel question: *What does it profit a man to gain the whole world and suffer the loss of his own immortal soul?* Young Bob Bedard's future was decided in his response. "I think I'd like to spend my life making that question as clear as possible." His spiritual persistence paid off. Though his prayer for the gift of prayer initially was not answered, he woke up one morning with a burning desire to pray that never left him. The mechanical obligation to pray was gone, replaced by a feverish desire that he describes as his watershed moment.

The ripples from his watershed moment eventually affected thousands, and the concentric waves continue outward to this day. In 1974—a year before the shooting—he went to his first prayer meeting out of curiosity because of people who claimed to have had "charismatic renewal" of their faith. At the end of the meeting he said, "It'll be a frosty Friday before I set foot in one of those meetings again"—a quote he later described as his "famous last words." At the time his bishop in a letter warned Catholics against the movement because it was too emotional. My emotionally retentive dad had the same reaction, his expression mimicking someone who had eaten a bad clam whenever my mom talked about her new religious discovery. If I thought about it at all during that time, I ranked talk of charismatic prayer closer to bad clam than religious discovery. Speaking in tongues or any religious phenomenon, particularly demonstrative claims, rubbed me the wrong way and were immediately dismissed as fake, with material-world-centric fervour. My dad, who doubted, though he never spoke of doubt, and I, who double-doubted, which is to say dismissed spirituality in advance of knowing truth, believed that if anything was to be believed, it had to be in a certain low-key dispassionate way. That is, we non-emoting Irish fellas figured we had God figured out, *if* he existed, and that was a big if. It didn't come into focus for decades that if God is, everything at every second is subject to the one fact that God is, that nothing can exist independent of that one fact, and that the fact of God is far beyond what we can conceive in space, time or distance, however wise or smart we ever become. In retrospect, projecting doubt and placing restrictions on humans in the thrall of experiencing the presence of God may have been ill-advised. I was my father's son.

Father Bob was also a low- to non-emoting level-headed guy's guy who was never going to make claims, practice histrionics, or jump up and down for attention. Like my dad and me, he wasn't about to exit his predictable frosty Friday and enter the unknown of the crazy charismatics. But in 1975—the year of the shooting—things changed, everything changed, and to Father Bob's— literally—ever-lasting credit, change was only possible because he was open to all possibilities of God. Whatever happened, however the trajectory of his faith from frosty Friday to fully embracing the phenomena of transcendent possibility, Father Bob makes the central point that belief, conversion, awaking, is not a consequence of individual will, is not achieved without help in the form of direct intervention from the Holy Spirit. "Grace produces the renewal. It's a spiritual awaking, which means you become aware of things you believed but never really experienced. The grace can move belief into experience, and that's what makes the difference in people's lives."

For years, my mom hosted a regular charismatic prayer group meeting at her house. I would try to sneak past the living room where they were gathered, where they prayed and talked, not so much in tongues but certainly in raptures. I would move stealthily past the group, trying to remain unnoticed, and they, intent upon their raptures, seemed oblivious to me, until one of them, usually Mom, looked up and welcomed me, as if I needed an invitation to either their meeting or the family house. A few social niceties done, I escaped what I judged to be a group that was a bit weird but in retrospect were seriously nice people in the thrall of grace moving belief into experience. It is amazing how much more you see when you open your eyes to the reality that all that can be seen cannot be seen by the naked eye; further, what must be seen is both beyond vision and right before our eyes, always.

In 1975, the year of transformation, the year Father Bob had an awakening to the power of prayer, he coached the St. Pius X boys high school basketball team to a eastern Ontario championship. This was the down-to-earth priest-guy that young guys identified with. He was old school in terms of respect and responsibility and drew people to him by way of humble example. And though he was a teacher and religious figure who emphasized taking responsibility, he didn't take himself too seriously. As a very human jocular jock with a compelling non-didactic message, as a cool and calm guy who spoke little but meant what he said when he spoke, young men listened to him and were drawn in. I never heard a word of disparagement about Father Bob, and for a high school teacher and principal to be universally respected is rather remarkable, and may be a world's first.

The world groans under the weight of empty virtue signaling; it is easy, it is lazy, it does not require action, it signals no action will be taken, it represents a flattening of societal drive to make actual change. Father Bob's understated ways belied a burning ambition to experience God and allow opportunity for others to experience the same. In 1984, he was appointed pastor of St. Mary's by Archbishop Plourde and was mandated to implement a vision for parish renewal based on his, by now, extensive experience and leadership in the charismatic renewal. Knowing that he needed renewal of his faith, of his commitment to the priesthood, that all people of faith need renewal, and that the need for renewal never changes, Father Bob took the appointment with a minor caveat that had major repercussions. In taking on the role of pastor, Father Bob requested, required actually, that he be free to give himself *permission* to do whatever he needed to do to accomplish actual renewal. The word *permission* does not suggest radical change, but in fact, radical change is exactly what Father Bob required he always be open to. With permission to be open to permission, Father Bob prayed to be God's instrument for whatever was required to accomplish renewal.

When Father Bob began at St. Mary's church its attendance and spiritual renewal were in severe decline, but Father Bob changed it into the most revitalized church in Ottawa. This would be an observation my mom made many times, which I ignored every time. Mom was one of Father Bob's most passionate and loyal adherents, and with loyalty being one of her many endearing traits, she had a potential conflict. She was also loyal to her much less vibrant home church of Our Lady of Fatima, so she resolved her conflict by attending both regularly. She and my dad went daily to Fatima for the conventional somber Catholic mass, and Mom attended St. Mary's for the impassioned, no holds barred, charismatic experience. Mom didn't regard her double duty as duty at all; it was what she did and who she was. We, her progeny, didn't understand it, and increasingly people cannot understand such devotion. Abnegation of self in the age of the selfie is rather incomprehensible, but for all my cynicism at that time I can still recall the electricity of the passion she experienced. We, that is mostly I, forgot then that there is much more to the world and in this life than surface perception and that the triggers for transformative experience are not possible in the pursuit of self-interest. The irony of the realization of self is that it requires going far, far, outside of self. The selfie captures the moment and loses connection to eternity.

In 1985, Father Bob gave himself permission to create the Companions of the Cross, whose purpose was to provide communal support and reinforcement of faith. In 1990, he resigned as spiritual leader of St. Mary's in order to work full time on Companions of the Cross. In 1992, Father Bob teamed up with Father Roger Vandenakker to host a television ministry called *Food for Life*, broadcast across Canada and into part of the United States. Unlike Father Crampton's foray into television in the 1960s, Father Bob's approach was humble, a role he performed without desire for the show to become about his personality. Ironically, by seeking and giving himself permission to find spiritual renewal and absolutely without intending it, Father Bob became an unlikely star.

The shots Robert Poulin fired on that sad October afternoon in 1975 continue their trajectory, but in a manner contrary to their malevolent intention. Sickening resentment coupled with isolation caused murder; being compassionate as well as feeling responsible for murder brought Father Bob to the abyss of despair, and despair defeats all. But that didn't happen. Out of the ashes, out of the experience of murder, Father Bob created a vast community of people committed to each other and to giving themselves permission to experience God.

The fulfillment of Father Bob's spiritual vocation is the end of the story of Robert Poulin, though it is never quite over. For most people the Robert Poulin story exists in the sensational details of October 27, 1975, which ends with his last shot. In an exclusive physical world paradigm, that is the logical end of that and every story. Whether out of fear or a perverse aspect of our fundamental nature, humans tend to be drawn to, have more interest in, evil, psychopathy and vice than goodness and virtue. We also find it easier to believe that humans can be pure evil than purely good. Books and movies about virtue are almost never made; whereas vice is what most movies and many books are obsessed with. Again, I present Netflix as my witness. After the sex scandals of the past several decades within the Catholic Church, there exists a terrible assumption that the word *priest* is synonymous with sexual deviance. Simple facts are, some priests committed terrible crimes and must be punished; most did not. The first fact does not impinge upon the second, though this logic is easily lost. For the majority of priests who would never commit such acts, the cloud of guilt by association must have been and continue to be difficult.

Goodness cannot compete with the Hollywood version of life because it does not preen for the camera, does not promote itself, prefers to remain anonymous. Father Bob's selflessness is such that his life was literally invested in the lives of others, where there was no separation between what happened to self and to people who mattered, and as a final testament to his virtue, everyone mattered. As long as people suffer, as long as people struggle with faith, Father Bob's mission continues.

I remember sitting across from Father Bob one day in the change room of the gym. These were my early days of long distance running when I struggled with the mental toughness required to run long and hard and in discomfort, without faltering. Even in my cynical days I was drawn to him, but being unmoved by his mission at that time, I didn't know what to say. He asked about my mom, we exchanged succinct comments about sports, and the moment passed. As I got older, even as my physical abilities diminished, I didn't falter in distance races, was able hold it together and finish consistently well, and really beyond what age and training should have yielded. Some call that mental toughness, which is not misplaced but not quite accurate either. Closer to the truth would be the word *faith*—that is, an emerging sense of connection outside of self that allows for a parallel dispersion of pain outside of self (i.e., offering up suffering in communion with all who suffer together in this race at this moment). So, psychological game playing or spiritual revelation, take your pick, but either way it worked, and though I didn't know it at the time, and I would have been surprised to have it revealed, much of the reason for coming to the realization of how to win races without the ability to do so was sitting across from me, hardly speaking, no agenda other than gentle caring camaraderie, each measured word food for thought, thought for life. Since that time I've regretted not asking him for his thoughts about faith when I had the chance. But, of course, it doesn't matter that I didn't ask, whatever his explicit words might have been. The message had been sent; I just didn't get it for a few more decades. Youth is wasted on the young—well, until we grow older, think back, and examine the ashes for the possibility of renewed life.

# CHAPTER TEN
## TED TALKS

I HAVE A STRONG IMPRESSION OF TED FROM AN EARLY AGE. HE SWEEPS INTO TOWN and protects us. Ted the protector. He was a first cousin who treated us more as brothers and sisters than we treated each other. His arrivals and departures were full of flair, adding a bit of drama to our small, predictable lives.

He'd run away at age 16 and joined the navy, just like his dad, Ernie, and Uncle Tom and Uncle Leonard had done as teenagers. The difference was that his dad and uncles had enlisted to escape from the Depression to the war. Ted was rumoured to have joined to escape his dad for reasons unknown, and he gravitated towards my parents.

So when Ted got leave from the navy, he always came to see us. He was older than us, older than my oldest brother by five years, so that fact alone gave him status. He knew each of us, never confused our names, never treated us as a group, never talked down when he talked, which was most of the time. He constantly told stories, he retold jokes, he made each of us feel as if we were individuals and not just part of a group. He often said that together the McCloskeys would rule the world. I believed Ted, I believed his stories, but I didn't believe that the McCloskeys would rule the world.

But Ted was more than talk. Everyone talks about bullying today, but bullying was far more rampant then and not talked about at all. There was little means of recourse. You didn't go to your teacher or parents about bullying. For better or for worse, kids had to work it out for themselves, and that often meant taking or giving a bloody nose. In today's world, sensitivity is valued above all else, but toughness, both physical and mental, had its place, and really still does.

When Ted arrived in town in his impressive navy and white uniform, the first order of business was to clear house. Any bullies, any threats to the McCloskeys, were called out and had five seconds to either submit or take a beating. Ted's meticulous and clean uniform rarely took more than a dusting, and he never took credit for just doing what a decent older brother does when he comes home.

It's strange how small, trivial events can deflate or bolster us. I remember Ted arriving and suggesting that we all head to Jimmy's Restaurant on Wellington Street. Jimmy's was an authentic 1940s classic—big booths with a jukebox, 10 cents for one song, 25 cents for three—and the food, setting and rates never seemed to change, until it was all gone. Easy to get nostalgic for neighbourhood greasy spoons, the place to go for bacon and eggs, coffee and a smoke before Starbucks infected the planet.

*Side note*: In the mid-1990s the Avenue Restaurant in the Glebe neighbourhood of Ottawa went out of business after about 50 years of success. For $1.99 you got a great breakfast and a bottomless cup of coffee. There was a distinctive atmosphere, with original booths, decor, plates, and nice people whom you knew and who knew you. In comes a restaurant called Zaks, complete renovation, to give the restaurant—you guessed it—a retro look, complete with booths, decor, the works, all new, all fake. A new, young crowd moves in and literally eats it up, never having noticed the authentic restaurant they had passed their whole lives. And for the privilege of eating retro, the cheapest breakfast was $5.99. Soon after the grand opening, Zak's went out of business. Maybe if we didn't treat things as museum pieces before they were gone, we wouldn't lose them. Nostalgia before death, I say.

Ted's *we* in my older brothers' minds did not include me. They were old enough to have one foot in the adult world, where they wanted to be, and Ted was clearly an adult. I was too young, too small, and had both feet clearly anchored in childhood. But Ted said I should be among the *we* going to Jimmy's Restaurant, and I thought it the luckiest day of my life.

But there was a problem. We were specifically going for Jimmy's signature French fries with gravy, cost 25 cents. My older brothers each had 25 cents, but I had nothing. This was ample reason for exclusion, but when one of my brothers made this point of the obvious, Ted swatted it away and said he would pay. I am still filled with gratitude for that moment. And it's funny that in my adult inability to accept sequential time as the absolute arbiter, I don't fully accept that the past is past. I don't think that impulse for gratitude is misplaced 50 years after the fact. Somehow, the past is never quite done.

I have no idea what the three older guys talked about at the table as we whittled down our respective mountain of animal fat and carbohydrates. I don't know what music was played on Jimmy's much used jukebox. I just remember being part of something going on, something that mattered. I never said a word, and I loved every minute.

Ted was never around for long, but he always came back to see my parents and their brood when he had a chance. It didn't matter how much time passed between visits, you could always pick up with Ted where you left off. This fact never changed, even in later years as the time between visits was not months but years.

Ted loved my parents, especially my mom. My mom responded to him nicely, and my dad listened to Ted, sometimes by the hour, but I, watching, learned that adults don't always show what they really feel. Ted told stories and had an endless repertoire of jokes, but my dad wasn't much of a talker, wasn't much of a listener, wasn't much of a joker. Dad tolerated Ted, much like he tolerated his own brother Ernie, because he had to, because they were family. Poor Ted; Dad was most comfortable in silence behind his paper.

After being away for most of my teen years and into my twenties, Ted returned to Ottawa. Much time had passed, and he now had a family. Ted had married a career naval officer, and together with their three children they settled into Ottawa, just as he always said he would do.

Ted and his family became regular visitors to my mom's house. My dad had passed away in 1980, and Mom enjoyed the odd visit from Ted's odd little company. Without a car, they would take the bus everywhere, often spending more hours waiting and travelling than visiting. They never seemed to mind. They seemed happy.

The first crack in the foundation of their happy little world was their casual mention that they had given back their adopted daughter. How do you give back a child? And who do you give her to? My emotionally retentive Irish Catholic family were never much for probing people's private lives, so the answer to these questions remained a mystery. But something was wrong.

Ted worked for the Department of Veteran Affairs. The Canadian government decided in its wisdom to decentralize federal government departments, costing untold millions, and Ted's department was to be reassembled in Charlottetown, P.E.I. So Ted and family moved out east, and all was quiet in that sleepy provincial town. Until all hell broke loose.

Before they could get to know the Charlottetown community, the Charlottetown community got to know them. Ted's wife went to the police and filed charges against Ted, claiming that he had sexually molested a minor. A sensational charge in a town like Charlottetown means complete exposure and scrutiny. In a heartbeat, Ted lost his family and his career and was awaiting trial.

Sometime between the breaking of the story and the trial, Ted came up to Ottawa, and I asked him directly, what the hell happened? He first claimed innocence but then proceeded to implicate himself with a convoluted tale of sexual impropriety, at the very least, and more likely gross indecency. Mostly, he deflected attention from past actions in his resolve to spare the victim from having to testify at the coming trial. He would plead guilty, regardless of the consequences. Knowing Ted, it was possible to believe that he could convince himself that he was doing this for noble reasons. Still, offering himself up as a martyr did not make sense for an innocent man.

Ted pleaded guilty, was convicted and universally condemned, and began his life as a social pariah. I wasn't sure what to make of the whole thing, what to make of Ted, but I knew that from then on, life would chew him up as never before. Though my childhood image of Ted as the conquering hero ridding the world of bullies took a serious hit, I've remained suspended between his terrible actions and what else I knew about him. I used to wonder if preserving my neutrality was a weakness or a moral flaw. I suspect that much of the reason for Ted's long absences was to spare us from having to deal with lingering moral ambiguity about him.

Ted's life became torturous, so he mostly disappeared for some years. His infrequent contact came mostly through my mom or Aunt Isobell, neither of whom played the condemnation game. They simply left judgment to the appropriate source and gave limited comfort during infrequent forlorn telephone calls from a lost soul. Ted always feigned optimism, his facade always punctuated by a string of jokes, but between punchlines, Mom and Isobell read his loneliness, desperation and failure. Ted was a walking and talking death march in advance of the fact.

And then he was saved. I think it is likely that he would have committed suicide early on, if not for the fact that he remained a Catholic. But there is no doubt that he spent considerable time perched on the precipice, undecided, perhaps moments away from the fall—until he fell in love. In a psychiatric ward, somewhere in the Maritimes, Ted met the love of his life. They exited the psychiatric ward and married, and once again, he had a reason to live happily ever after. Ted really was that kind of guy. No matter what life delivered, in all its raw brutality, he could believe that his life would get better, his wife would get better, and the McCloskeys would rule. He was always unrealistic, spectacularly naive, and his belief in eventual redemption and deliverance cost him dearly.

The problem—one of the many problems—was that his new wife, the love of his life, was never going to get better. Though saved by Ted—at least in his mind—she could not save herself, so she killed herself. She had been sexually abused when she was young, so the painfully complex relationship between victim and victimizer could not have been helped by Ted and was quite possibly exacerbated by the same. Her unfathomable psychic wound could not be healed, and her response was to go destructively inward. Ted did everything he could to convince her to choose life, but his love, or desperation, never could have been enough. Ted could not sweep in and clean out the bullies in her mind, and the grand plan for redemption was not to be.

Ted had never completely disappeared before. But for a couple of years no one heard from Ted. We worried, but only passively and distantly. No one would have been surprised if Ted chose to follow his wife to the grave.

Finally, contact. It would be disingenuous to say that anyone was sitting on the edge of their seat obsessing about Ted. In fact, most people didn't care what happened to Ted, and he knew it. Though Ted's exile was of his choosing, he craved contact with our family, and I didn't want to deprive him of his last crumbs in this life.

We all walk by people living on the street. We think we see them, but we don't. We see destitution, we smell failure, and whether we stand, chat and drop some coins or hold our nose and hurry on by, we note the separation between us and them. But seeing someone in a casket does not tell you who they were in life; it simply confirms that they are dead. Witnessing the last vestiges of humanity looking up at you from the gutter does not impart who the human being is or what path led to these tragic final moments. If, as a priest friend said, the holiest place on earth is where there has just been a birth or a death, we need to pay more attention to people on the precipice between death and rebirth. There is deep mystery here beneath the surface as we sidestep whomever God has placed in our path. If we hesitate, if we scratch the surface, our vague unease becomes shame, for it is not separation we feel but recognition.

We see addiction and mental illness and assume predictability in the gutter. But the stories and people are more complicated than where we conveniently place them. People become isolated, displaced, and lone souls tend not to do very well. After a while, the few people you meet are other lone souls who tend to recoil with recognition without feigning connection. Life is very hard once one believes the inevitability of loneliness on a planet of seven billion people.

Ted ended up at the Monks of Morin, in Monastery, New Brunswick. As far as names go, it is quite perfect. I dropped by once out of curiosity on a drive to the Cabot Trail. Monastery is not far from the highway, but I was surprised that it is essentially just one building looming among the trees in splendid isolation. Imposing, beautiful, incongruent to the natural surroundings. I sat in the car and just waited for a few minutes without knowing why, since I knew Ted was not there at that time. The place seemed empty, though there were some signs of human habitation. I took a last look at the gothic structure, inhaled organic pungent smells and inhaled again, the smell of loneliness.

Ted, whose primary urge in life was to tell stories and jokes, told us something about life at Monastery. Nothing disparaging, full of routine, funny and odd. Ted described his fellows as fostering co-operation but creating distance, or at least not encouraging familiarity of any kind. He said people ended up at Monastery to escape a past life—not criminal past, but something that was off limits, for which there would be no discussion. Ted was escaping his past, now a criminal conviction, but as someone who needed to talk constantly, he was a poor candidate for self-imposed isolation. His perfunctory work in the kitchen, nodding to people in the hallways and not talking, would have been hard for him. Ted and his fellows were of course free to go but had no place to go to, a prison of their own making.

Ted conceded that a few people were there for contemplation and prayer, but that was the exception. He was among those for whom life and routine were a quasi-permanent penance. Whatever life was like at Monastery, it was, depending on your view, refreshingly or disturbingly out of step with modernity. I like to think there are still a few Monasterys out there, untouched by globalization, technology, Miley Cyrus or Lululemon. For all his talk, we never did get a clear picture of life at Monastery, and I doubt his sporadic trailer matched the feature film. Ted certainly withheld secrets, but mostly no one wanted to hear his inner narrative.

After a few years of fleeting greetings from Monastery, on a cold day in February Ted called to say he was in Ottawa. Someone from Monastery had been driving to Ottawa, so he came along for the 1,400 or so kilometre ride. My older brother Pat was living with us at the time, and the three of us agreed to meet the next day. He had a place to stay, for which I felt relief. I have three daughters and was glad the issue of accommodation did not come up. He likely was too.

The three of us met for pizza, and Ted abruptly announced that he was heading back to Monastery. Pat and I were puzzled, but there was no reason that the talkative Ted could articulate. It may have been as simple as the shoemaker in *A Tale of Two Cities*, and he needed to place himself back in his cell.

We were in the middle of a cold snap, which in our part of the world is cold indeed. Ted was planning to hitchhike, which meant he was completely broke. He earned room and board and cigarette money working in the kitchen at Monastery, but it was not a regular paying job. I gave Ted bus fare and a few bucks to sustain life and limb, but the next night I received a call from the Montreal police. Hitchhiking, Ted got stuck on a Montreal highway in the middle of the city, in the middle of the winter, in the middle of the night. The police wanted me to verify that Ted was who he said he was. Ted didn't carry—probably no longer had—identification. He had become a persona non grata. It took him three days to get out of Montreal, eight days to Monastery. I never asked him why he didn't take the bus. It probably had to do with choosing between bus fare and cigarettes. I just wish I'd coughed up a bit more so that Ted could cough in comfort.

Nothing. Then another call in summer, and Ted is back. I was stunned but shouldn't have been when he casually mentioned that he was staying at the men's mission. I picked him up and took him home. We ate lunch and walked in the park behind my house. We walked and talked for a long time—that is Ted talked, joked and smoked, and I walked, choked and listened. I still marvel that under any circumstance, under any cloud, he could unravel a new repertoire of jokes. Always one reminding him of another, until distracted back to reality. I realized on this last walk in the park that jokes were simply Ted's armour. Of all his hundreds of jokes, I only remember one, and perhaps it is fitting that it is both badly dated and just plain bad: "Hear about that new Newfie rock band? They're called Boy George and the Agriculture Club." Sorry, but if I have to explain it, you're too young. I saw a news clip and photo recently about Boy George. Oldest boy on the planet.

Ted always had a McCloskey tale or two that I enjoyed. His repertoire from McCloskey mythology was almost as infinite as his comedic material. How do you know a guy for over 40 years, talk about the same subject, and continue to be surprised? I learned lots about our family from Ted over the years, some of it probably even true.

This story was very likely true and filled in a few gaps in our spotty family history. Dad and Uncle Tom, his older brother by 18 months, had been close growing up and had enlisted in the navy the same week, but after the war they became estranged. That is, Tom exited the scene, and his name was never mentioned by any of his siblings again. Odd, but in our Irish Catholic emotionally retentive low-on-communication world, these omissions commonly hung in full view to unseeing eyes. In 1956, Tom turned up dead in Montreal, age 36, supposedly from heart failure, although it is more likely that he died from causes related to alcoholism, and he may have been living on the street. In the decades afterwards, it had seemed strange to us that neither he nor his story ever became known to us.

As mentioned, Ted could cough up the story when you least expected it. It seems that after the war Tom was rumoured to have been convicted of burglary and given a five-year prison sentence in St. John's, Newfoundland. Ted may have told me his source for the story, but I don't remember who it was. Being older than us, he had family sources that fed him stories from before our time.

Ted continued talking, but his narrative became muted in my mind. I had stopped listening and was thinking. So that was it. Dad wasn't swatting me with the Persuader for stealing five dollars all those years ago; he was expressing his disappointment with his brother; he was expressing his fear that I would become like Tom if I wasn't properly punished for stealing. This was not the answer to a lifetime of turmoil; in fact, I had hardly thought about the incident over the years. Still, this tale reinforced my belief that the past is still stretching its tentacles far into the illusion of our limitless future. A tentacle from Uncle's Tom's sad life had reached me, with comforting clarity.

Though Ted's talk was a constant barrage of nothing in particular, this one time he had something particular he wanted to say. He took his time and began to tell me about his wife. He told me details about her, their limited time together, the life they had hoped to have, her death, but he could not say the word *suicide,* and close as he likely had been to suicide himself, he probably did not understand it in her, or maybe he did. Inconsolable grief, all the same. He let it pour out and came close to feeling sorry for himself but didn't have it in him. People who feel worthless do not tend to indulge in self-pity. His loss was intense, his bitterness at believing there was still something left for him in this world, more so.

I was conflicted; he made it easy. I had a full house; he didn't mind the mission. Really. I felt ashamed, but didn't, was not close to, insisting. Still, I hated to think that the guy who used to sweep into town in his navy uniform to slay the dragons would be at the mission slaying his demons. I called a cousin, ironically Uncle Tom's daughter, and she was glad to have him. Sharon and Ted spent a nice week together, and Ted was spared the mission, and I was spared the guilt.

We had reached an unspoken agreement. Ted would not stay overnight with us, but he was always welcome to visit. It was an important but tenuous family connection. Life had become complex, but we shared a need to be connected to family, and we shared a pathetic nostalgic sensibility. Ted pleaded for connection on our last walk in the park, which was no walk in the park. Life had been tough, but he was going to get his act together, make the move from Monastery to Ottawa; he was going to re-establish his few remaining family connections, such as they were, at least with the McCloskeys. He was going to stay in touch with me, would not disappear, and I would look for work for him. Things would work out. After all, together the McCloskeys could rule the world. This from my cousin who was residing at the mission and heading back to the isolation of Monastery, God love him, without a hint of irony.

A couple of months passed. No updates from Ted on the pending move. When he did call, Ted was greatly diminished. He was in hospital in Moncton. Troubling symptoms, significant weight loss and fatigue, and exploratory surgery the next day. Hmm, I thought, and I went about my business. A few days later, weaker still, Ted cheerfully recited the surgeon's assessment—cancer, terminal, esophagus and stomach, no intervention possible. He was sewn back up and prescribed palliative care.

So Ted was dying, alone. Sad, but no surprise, really. Tragic and commonplace. We agreed to talk, not once in a while but often. I disingenuously assured him that he was not alone, knowing full well that he was and had been desperately alone for years. He was a drowning man clinging to a rock, knowing that both the centre and his hold on the centre could not hold. Still, he wanted some connection, and that was good.

And we did talk regularly after that. Ted continued to joke, he continued to tell some McCloskey stories of dubious truth, but he also wanted to say some things, perhaps to make up for the non-emoting years at Monastery. We talked about life, death, the hope of afterlife. He did not make a deathbed confession about his sexual conviction; I was not his confessor, after all. He was fatalistic, courageous and comforted by the belief that he would soon be reunited with the wife he could not save.

At this time, I was in my usual state of work and commitment overdrive—a lifelong habit of taking on more than anyone can reasonably handle and then sticking with the plan. As Ted worsened and weakened I worried that he was about to die alone, so I asked if he wanted me to come to see him. To my surprise, and some relief, he declined. I knew he'd say it was too much trouble, but it was more than that; he meant no. He said he didn't want me to see him in the state he was in. He's gone from a robust 220 pounds to a lithe concentration-camp 110 as the cancer feasted upon his carcass. We joked that maybe he wasn't sick, he was just running too much, and that I could now kick sand in his face. He assured me that he was not going to be alone. He had had a surprise visit from friends who recently relocated to Moncton, who promised and did come by often. Until he died.

About two weeks later. The news delivered from a member of the nursing staff. Thirty seconds and done. Mostly sadness, a small part relief. No more hour-long from jocular to philosophical to spiritual conversations. No more heartfelt "I love you" that Ted had signed off with at every call, always a bit embarrassing to this Irish Catholic emotionally retentive male. No chance that the McCloskeys were ever going to rule the world.

I've since pondered long and hard about what to make of Ted's strange, contradictory life. I mean by way of understanding, not judgment. I did not judge the omission of his conviction during our many talks as moral deficiency. But I wanted to understand if this act preyed upon his mind. Ailments of the digestive tract are often associated with repressed emotion. Given the enormity and consequences of his conviction and the fact of his stomach and esophagus cancer, it is possible that Ted's repression literally consumed him. It was also in his character to talk, to emote, to make plans for ruling the world. It was not in his character to repress. He would not have wanted to see himself staring back from a mirror at 100 pounds. Ted must have known that the act was reprehensible, and it remains unknown if he faced that fact every hour of his later life or not at all. I believe the former, and I believe he judged stomach cancer to be a fitting punishment that he could live with and die from. God love him, Ted was not much one for irony.

During our many fireside chats, Ted seemed serene and ready to go. He had once hoped to save his wife and protect her from the ravages of her own mind. Somehow he still regarded himself as a protector, albeit one who had failed. And this is where the human justification system becomes both insidious and complex. Despite his one-time convoluted explanation of his sexual crime that had to do with his failed attempt at protecting his victim, he remained not perpetrator but protector. Ted pleaded for redemption but could not fully face what he had done, could not ask for forgiveness, could not forgive himself. Ted always wanted to be useful. When he came into town, if there were no bullies to manhandle, he helped you move or lay rug or within five minutes had lined up what needed to get done and had started doing it. But he was no longer useful; he could no longer protect; time to move on.

I've often thought about Ted since he died, especially with all the attention on the subject of bullying. Awareness campaigns are a daily fixation, especially in schools. I recently saw a photo of several hundred kids in a school gym, each wearing a pink anti-homophobia, anti-bulling T-shirt.

I suppose the idea is to take the bullying and homophobia out of the boy and create a taste for pink while engineering a gender-neutral world. But the cookie-cutter approach to human relations, not to mention the laying of blame on the pink backs of boys, is flawed. Boys aren't doing so well in school these days, a claim for which there is mounting empirical evidence. Part of the reason may be that they don't see themselves in it.

Is there a better way? Maybe we could all progress from passive awareness to active inclusion, including those we don't normally consider. Teachers, try this. Take your big oversized, sports-crazed obnoxious male lug—you know, the one prone to bullying and making pejorative comments about that skinny gay kid. Resist the temptation to dress them both in pink; they are not the same, and wishing won't make it so and may be a formula for creating resentment in the one and encouraging a sense of victimhood in the other. Tell your lug that he has an important role to play; appeal to his higher self; and tell him that the skinny kid needs someone to look out for him because he has been bullied before for simply being who he is. Tell him he doesn't have to wear pink, though he can if he wants to. Here is what may happen: your resident lug's chest will swell, he will not wear pink, you will surprise him, which teachers don't do often enough, and there will be no more bullying or homophobic comments; but if—and it is unlikely—there is some interaction between students once the lug is in place, let them work it out. Which, of course, parents and teachers are no longer willing to do, no longer trusting that kids are capable of doing it, but in fact it is precisely what they can and must do.

Ted put himself on the line and protected us from neighbourhood bullies all those years ago. Everything that happened after—what he did, who he became—does not change this fact. Equally true, the case against him is not mitigated or forgiven by his earlier protective actions. Still, for all his role as protector, he couldn't protect us from the neighbourhood bullies once he left town.

There was a boy who used to pick on me. I would passively take it, hoping he would see that I wasn't going to get mad; I pathetically wanted him to understand that I was a nice kid. The truth is, I was afraid, and my behaviour guaranteed that he was never going to let up. Until I had had enough—that is, the aggravation of putting up with bullying became greater than the fear that sustained it. I switched from deer in the headlights to flailing fists, and it was soon over, without a hint of possibility of it ever returning. I know the many objections to this simple little tale, but I maintain that bullying is fuelled, not lessened, by the notion that universal pink, not individual resolve, is the only solution.

True, there are better ways to resolve conflict without resorting to violence, and fistfights certainly don't solve the growing and disturbing problem of cyber-bullying. But the point is, kids have to learn to stand up, not physically but actively confront bullying for themselves rather than passively defer to adults to solve this and other problems involving adversity. They don't have to do it alone; we must help them, but even when one is completely blameless, even if one did nothing to provoke bullying, there exists the imperative to take responsibility and do something. Bullying comes in many pervasive forms, and difficult as it is to take responsibility, our considered, measured— and with time—confident response to any and all situations in life is where our integrity and character ultimately reside.

Ted was a convicted sexual offender for which it is unlikely amends were ever made. He had a naive, unrealistic version of life—basically that everything will work out; wishing will make it so. Still, misplaced as it was, my decades-in-the-works takeaway was not all negative. In the end, I've never been able to figure out where to put Ted's influence on me, and chances are I never will. But strangely, or maybe I'm just strange, knowing Ted somehow does not diminish my modicum of faith. I am able to place all imponderables into a category of plausible deniability by shrugging my shoulders and concluding that faith and mystery are intrinsically linked. It may be as simple as the fact that looking at any life close up and personal provides some reason to believe. Or maybe even simpler. It may be that he bought me a plate of French fries and gravy at Jimmy's Restaurant when I was hungry, in all senses of the word.

"Whence come I? I come from my childhood, I come from childhood as from a homeland."

ANTOINE DE SAINT-EXUPÉRY

# CHAPTER ELEVEN
## LITTLE MOOSE

I WROTE THE FOLLOWING, WHICH WAS PUBLISHED IN THE *GLOBE AND MAIL*, ON THE occasion of my Aunt Isobell's passing.

## LIVES LIVED
## ISOBELL MCCLOSKEY

*Nun, family historian. Born Feb. 23, 1917, in Ottawa. Died Aug. 10, 2005, in Peterborough, Ontario, of natural causes, aged 88.*

Early recollections of my Aunt Isobell are shrouded with fear. Sister Saint John, as she was called until the mid-1960s, seemed to mysteriously appear and disappear in her severe and sweeping habit, a holy if unsmiling apparition. Being young, none of us seven nieces and nephews knew who Sister Isobell McCloskey really was then.

My Aunt Isobell was accomplished and self-effacing. It was by accident that we discovered that she was a pioneer and innovator in the field of medical records. She was precise and methodical, and so we should not have been surprised to learn that when she retired, a national award was established in her honour. But it is as our family historian that I will most fondly remember my aunt. For Aunt Isobell, history lay beyond the recitation of dry facts, and she loved to tell and retell our family stories.

My favourite story happened in 1959. Aunt Isobell had been in the convent for 16 years, but she had never been allowed to spend Christmas at home, and her mother had become very ill. Mother Superior, in her wisdom, and without being asked, broke the convent rule and gave permission for my aunt to go home. My Aunt Isobell's expression was pure joy whenever she recited the delight she shared with her mother upon learning they would be together three whole days that special Christmas. They stayed up all night, talking, eating treats and drinking tea. My aunt was always careful to say how grateful she remained her whole life for that time with her mother, especially because when she returned to the convent she learned that her mother had died peacefully in her sleep.

My Aunt Isobell had come from a traditional world where siblings, parents, and even distant cousins remained in contact with each other their whole lives. Aunt Isobell didn't resist change. In working her magic to reconnect people, she simply and anonymously brought the best from her generation into the present. As a result, our warm memories and her unique legacy are secure.

We eventually did come to understand that she was the invisible link between many in our extended and dispersed modern family. Cousins and even siblings who had not seen each other for 10, 20 or even 30 years knew the basic storyline of one another through my Aunt Isobell. In some cases the connection that she maintained between people, long after they had given up, resulted in reconciliation.

My Aunt Isobell lived her life in the community of sisters at the beautiful Mount St. Joseph in Peterborough. These nuns broke all stereotypes, and I came to believe that their sense of community might just hold the prescription for a long and happy life. Ironically, I learned at my aunt's funeral that the convent was to be sold, with a small modern facility to be built on the grounds to house and care for the remaining nuns.

My aunt remained aware and intelligent in her final weeks, even as she shrank to the size of a child. She loved an outing to a restaurant most of all, and as I left that last time, we exchanged words about where we would go once she was able to put on some weight and get strong. We both knew that the outing would never be, but the next best thing to a good conversation with people you want to be near to is to pretend and intend for it to happen.

From somewhere in the great unknown my aunt is wide-eyed with anticipation as she continues to keep our family history and, inexplicably, make connections between members of our scattered family.

---

Throwing the story of a nun into a book about faith seems a predictable formula for reciting Catholic dogma. But it wasn't like that, at all. Aunt Isobell and I didn't do dogma, she even less inclined than I, and for that matter, rarely were faith and religion discussed. Very occasionally she put up with and answered a searching question from me and then changed the subject. She had other interests.

The Irish—at least the Ottawa Valley version that I know—tend not to show their warmth easily. A propensity towards emotional retentiveness, the old formal nun's habit, infrequent visits, and you have the makings of a distance relationship, prone to conjured stereotypes and misunderstandings. Also, in the 1960s, talk of closeness in relationships among practicing Catholics had to do with a vague notion of closeness to God. Simple truth is, we hadn't known Aunt Isobell, and she had no way to get to know us.

During those early years, the singular feature I remember about our aunt, or the spectre we called Sister Saint John, was our incessant jokes about her indifferent health. Every time her name came up, it seemed to us mischievous little troublemakers, she had had another surgery. There wasn't much truth to this, but making corny jokes was how we amused ourselves before technology splintered our attention in a thousand directions. Anyway, we joked that maybe she should have a zipper put in for easy ongoing access. Not funny, but in our defense, this was before we knew her as a human being. She wouldn't have minded.

It wasn't just the habit and lifestyle that set Aunt Isobell apart from our other aunts and uncles. Mom's family had cleared out after the war, living an exotic and mysterious life in California. On Dad's side, Aunt Mary and Uncle Ernie regularly dropped in, and with them both being incessant chatterers and Dad *so* not, their visits were a portrait of incongruence. Aunt Mary was very sweet to all of us but caused Dad to whistle through clenched teeth as he listened. Aunt Isobell talked but did not chatter, and Dad listened without clenched teeth, his hands folded behind his head, as relaxed as his stiff, angst-ridden body every got. She was a talker, but she didn't demand that Dad respond or give feedback or approval. She was the only "talker" he really listened to without looking like he wanted to hide behind his paper. Dad respected her intelligence and common sense, and I liked her stories.

Listening but not talking at the kitchen table, I learned from both Aunt Isobell and Cousin Ted that well-worn familiar family stories did not always end the same way. Since we never learned anything about Dad's family from Dad, we were always hungry for Aunt Isobell's detailed narratives. All kids think the family that surrounds them is pretty dull. With the exciting O'Neill side likely hanging out with Hollywood movie stars, and without context from Dad for what in the world being a McCloskey meant, we thought we lived with the dullest, most square family in the world. Truth is, we just didn't have any idea who we were.

Aunt Isobell was a master storyteller, even if each scene was loaded with superfluous detail. It was a point of pride, perhaps even minor vanity, that her fine mind could instantly and accurately recite names, dates and events with impressive recall and narrative flair. Like all good storytellers, she didn't embellish so much as polish commonplace facts into little sparkling vignettes.

A listener could not help but be swept along by Aunt Isabell's enthusiasm as she told the story of the McCloskey siblings meeting in Halifax during the war. The long train ride with her sister Mary that she savoured every second of; the excitement of wartime Halifax swarming with sailors on leave; the reunion of the two sisters with their three dashing navy brothers; and the sense of urgency and purpose as they stuffed as much as life had to offer into three action-packed days. The often-travelled story of the serendipitous moment when Mother Superior granted that one-time exception to the rule, allowing Aunt Isobell to visit and share cherished moments with her mother just before she died. The terrible tragedy of the twin boys who drowned at Wolfe Lake, and the inconsolable mother—a distant cousin whose connection even Aunt Isobell was unsure of—who never forgave herself for a moment of inattention. And most of all, the many and varied stories of family gatherings, arrangements made, distances travelled and the fulsome cast of characters divined from her voracious, fertile mind.

All of her stories had a common theme: authentic, ongoing, lively connection, and her narrative stressed, without ever saying so, our collective reason for being. I am nostalgic for Aunt Isobell's storytelling, but more than that I wish young people today could hear and understand her. Facebook-reared young people from one-child families who don't know any of their first, second or third cousins don't have the social context to understand what they are missing, that they are missing.

The world of the extended family has been utterly lost, and with it much that matters is no more. Social media and social causes cannot replicate this loss and do not represent connection but rather may be reasons why authentic connection is becoming harder to achieve. Even the notion of common values has been swept away as archaic rubbish, with *common* sacrificed on the altar of diversity. Somehow, the acceptance of difference has come to mean repudiation of similar, or common, but these concepts are not mutually exclusive. Separateness, or the full realization of one's perceived human rights, is the answer to what matters in this life. Convent life, contemplation and prayer are archaic relics of the oppressive past.

The problem is, schools and the media eat this stuff up. Kids served buzzwords like *equity*, *social justice* and *multiculturalism* are told that previous assumptions and traditional common values are the reasons for the ills of the world. Still, if logically conceived and stripped of ideological signalling, inclusion is a worthy, even essential human value. I just wish kids were taught to celebrate Martin Luther King's version of a diverse and inclusive world in which external features no longer determine how we think and who we are capable of becoming. The primacy of the individual reaching for his or her transcendent higher self in community with others is not achieved in a groupthink environment. Beneath all our differences is what is real, but it takes faith to find it, and not colour or age to define it.

For all the variety of choice that is supposed to set this generation apart, there is a huge and disturbing social expectation to conform to the proper ideological cause. Unfortunately, young people cannot help but slip into the resultant vacuum characterized by the phrase *If you don't believe in something, you'll soon believe in anything.*

The reaction against former common values is so strong and reactionary that parents, teachers and kids often reject something without even considering the possibility that it might hold value. Christianity and especially Catholicism are surely the easiest targets these days, with other established religions next in line. But when you ask those who reject religion most vehemently, "If not that, what else?" they tend to be stumped. For the first time in history it is acceptable to reject religious belief for belief in nothing. If not religious instruction, context and meaning of any kind, what do kids have beyond the vacuum? We are witnessing a mental health crisis among young people today, who were reared to have faith in self, to believe in the illusion of endless choice in a consumer world, for whom answers to the fundamental questions are fraudulently presented as lifestyle choices. A belief system based on the primacy of self without commitment and connection to things outside self leads to huge generational anxiety. This is the white elephant in the room: no context, nothing to believe in, infinite choice that is no choice at all, and the pungent, disturbing smell of fear.

Compare this to convent life—no, this is not a recruitment drive, and yes, they are Catholic. After we visited Aunt Isobell a few times and faced a three-hour drive each way, she asked if we would like to stay overnight. Interesting, but not something we had ever thought about. After Cara and I stayed overnight, we were forced to drop all stereotypes. For example, the most striking feature of convent life is not its religiosity. The grey nuns of Mount St. Joseph have a long and truly illustrious history of service in hospitals, other orders in education. It is no exaggeration to say, though it is a long forgotten fact, that our education and hospital systems owe much of their development to the commitment of religious orders. Choice is fine to a point, after which commitment is necessary for both personal and spiritual development, and I am not talking about nuns here, since they worked out this truism a couple of hundred years ago.

But even their commitment to good and necessary work is not the most striking feature of convent life. It is the sense of community that is palpable as one visits for any length of time. One cannot help but notice the way they interact, their relaxed ways, the absence of anxiety, and the undeniable fact of their longevity. They don't marry and they don't have kids, and yet we know that married people generally outlive divorced people, and people with kids outlive people without kids. But what if you completely withdraw from the circle of romantic relationships, breakups, hanging your shingle between failed romances, meeting new romantic interests, endless disappointments and possibilities? What if you are spared the stress of relationships that end badly, of working towards a career in a world that can eliminate it before you even graduate, of having to pay off a student loan for the degree that will not get you the career? I don't know, but nuns seem to outlive us all.

It is true that nuns surrender much of their autonomy. But young people today suffer from an endless unfulfilled array of possibilities, that is, the illusion of infinite choice. Still, there will likely not be any convent revival in this or any lifetime. Convent life is dying, and with it a way to connect to a sense of home that is sorely needed today.

In retrospect I suspect that part of the reason Aunt Isobell and I did not talk much about faith is that she had her doubts. As a nun for 65 years, it was perhaps a bit late to indulge in a discussion about whether or not God exists. I doubt she ever spent much time wringing her hands over the choice of her vocation, but of course I don't know, and much as I got to know her, there was much she did not divulge. A convent is a fascinatingly contradictory place, where connection is palpable and nuns remain refreshingly inscrutable. Never a dull moment, silent corridors notwithstanding.

Aunt Isobell and I shared my dad's healthy skepticism. People confuse skepticism with cynicism or, worse, a lack of faith in the latest ideological cause. But real faith does not exist in devotion to feel-good causes without personal conviction. Skeptics will continue to doubt but at least understand that a living faith requires constant scrutiny, that faith does not live without vigilance and examination. Unquestioning faith is most likely a portrait in complacency. People who doubt or whose faith is shaken do not lack for faith. Flip side, people whose faith is never questioned do not necessarily have much to sustain it. The crass commercial exercising mantra "No pain, no gain" may have more relevant and direct application to our spiritual endeavours.

I found it interesting that Mother Teresa questioned her faith and may have doubted the existence of God. Predictably, people reacted to this revelation, or all too human utterance, as if it was a scandal. Christopher Hitchens used this as a pretext to denigrate her life's work, as if Mother Teresa's doubts eliminated the comfort she gave to the dying poor. The real question is, how could a thinking, feeling person work for a lifetime with the stench and decay of certain and immediate death and not question faith? Even Jesus briefly succumbed to doubt and despair—"My God, my God, why have you forsaken me?" (Matthew 27:46, NRSVCE)—and he had advance knowledge of the outcome, which we poor mortals do not. What mattered was that while Mother Teresa doubted, she never let up on her work, the true measure of a human being.

This is what we saw at the convent, under the habit, so to speak. The sisters could be petty or impatient, were flawed and had doubts, but rather than go inward they placed their faith in work with people. Mother Teresa and the sisters of Mount St. Joseph, among others, understood that for all the doubt one might—or perhaps must—have, faith is a discipline. The easiest thing to do, as increasingly practiced by trendy atheists, is to first abandon faith and then rail against it, just to ensure it never comes back. Atheists practice not a negative faith but a negation of faith, which makes sense as the natural consequence of a secular, death denying modern world. People need to believe, even if in their desperation, they will park their belief in nothing. My parents, Aunt Isobell and their generation realized that practice and ritual kept you leaning in the right direction, kept you somewhat grounded and gave you a modicum of hope in a world otherwise devoid of meaning and purpose. They did their best, did not debate or nitpick the finer points of belief, and practiced the discipline of prayer.

Aunt Isobell's physical demise started with skin cancer. She had to apply strong cream to her nose that badly burned her habit-white skin. She was conflicted. Not about death—no point thinking about that—she was conflicted because she didn't want to be seen looking as she did, but she also didn't want to miss out on a visit. A tiny vanity maybe, which is a good sign in the elderly. I was pleased when she informed me that the general moratorium on visitors did not apply to me.

I knew the first moment I saw her that this visit would be the last. Her perky, affable ways were unchanged. She was full of good humour and obviously was glad to see me. Even her scabbed-up nose, the source of her vanity, was not that bad. But she was terribly shrunken, as if on the verge of collapsing in on herself at any moment. Which she immediately acknowledged, which reminded her of a story, which was funny, which reminded me again just how bloody tough and resilient these old Irish Catholic dolls were, with a nod to Mom and Kaye and the like.

Sure, she was shrinking, but when she was a child she was considered big for her age, especially compared to her older sister, Mary, whose height was never beyond 4'10". As a consequence, Isobell's childhood name had been *Moose*. As Moose told the story, I noticed that her paper-thin ultra-delicate white skin was folded and wrinkled in ways not seen before. Moose was folding in upon herself, becoming a black hole, or perhaps, given her complexion, a white hole. The black humour of her story was given a darker edge with the knowledge that Isobell was now barely bigger than the recently departed Mary, sister, friend and lifelong rival. Whatever else was at issue in their many-decades-long tussle, Isobell always had the advantage of height. Now with the prospect of shrinking to Mary's size, Isobell probably decided it was time to go.

Just as Ted had done a couple weeks earlier. It is strange how Ted and Isobell, unlike in every way except for their fidelity to family history, were always linked during their lives. They died of cancer within a few weeks of each other after a lifetime of precarious, mostly unbroken, contact. Aunt Isobell was the only person for whom contact with Ted was fairly constant. Ted revered her—they had common stories, she listened, she didn't judge, and she didn't fit anyone's stereotype of a nun, didn't fit any stereotype. Enduring relationships between convicted sex offenders and elderly nuns are probably not so common. To her everlasting credit, she remained constant and did not avoid or banish Ted. She must have understood that her steadfastness was tantamount to throwing a drowning man a lifejacket. To me she did allow that she was not necessarily thrilled at her role, but there is no doubt in my mind that she saved Ted's life on more than one occasion.

We had a good chat. She was weak, her voice a raspy whisper, but she remained animated. We talked about my parents, as we always did, especially my father, her favourite brother. We shared not only family history but a deep nostalgia, and she was determined in her way to impart to me, who was determined to receive, what parts could be passed along from a time and with a people I never knew. Even as an 88-year-old wisp of a human being, she continued to astonish me with old facts—new facts 50, 60, or 70 years old, brought to life again anew. Appearance vanity down; memory vanity up, to the very end.

I hadn't meant it to, but something came up about my dad, his back accident, how his life had changed. Aunt Isobell shook her head and pursed her lips, recited once again the image of Dad at home just after surgery, sitting on the edge of his bed each morning, clutching the metal railing of his bed, not unlike the metal railing of the ship that stole his youth, waiting and praying for the pain and spasms to subside to allow him to endure another day.

And then I just said it. The pain, the intense, relentless pain, had been the reason Dad had drank alcohol; Dad had been self-medicating, you know, for the pain. It had been the only subject that we had not, could not, talk about, until now. Aunt Isobell looked at me with intelligent, watery, pale-blue eyes. "Yes, yes, that was it, for the pain, and who could blame him?" She could live with this; it made sense and was true. It was a pleasant, amicable way for us to finally put spoken closure on that issue as we worked towards putting unspoken closure on our relationship.

She reached for a thick envelope. She had written extensive, meticulous cursive notes on our family tree and history, mostly drawn from memory, she let me know, the rest from notes decades old. The passing of the notes was casual, understated, matter of fact, but we both knew, though would not say, that the timing was because this was our last time. It was not Mom and Kaye's goodbye, not nearly so sad, not nearly so unexpected. They had faced the moment—were wired to own up to and face all hardship presented in this life—painfully, reluctantly and, for all their years of intimacy, awkwardly. Aunt Isobell and I never expected to have become close, and so closure was bittersweet, sad to end but pleased to have pulled it off. Still, there is something elemental about the final breaking of the circle of an enduring relationship that sticks in your craw. If it is over, why does it replay and repeat and compete for the present moment so often? Is it over?

The extensive notes, the legacy gift itself, do not have much application, is pretty much a list of names, dates, births, deaths and the like. Much as I may try to make it so, it does not live, cannot jump from the page and give me something to connect with or even feign interest in about our extended family. I have no doubt that these were people I would have loved to have met, to have known and learned from, but as I read the notes, I could not conjure up anything except bewilderment and inertia. Still, it was a fitting and appreciated gift, and who knows, it might speak to me someday. The gift was generous. She needed to give it to someone, and I was pleased that I was the one. Maybe once she reads this account, she'll find a way to breathe life into her notes and then make me see it too.

Interesting thing is, when we were kids Aunt Isobell was the holy unsmiling spectre, more adultlike than any of the severe adults in our orbit. But as I got to know her as an adult in her great old age, she was not what we had made her out to be; she had softened, become funny, decades stripped off, until she was left in front of me, small, vulnerable, laughing, looking for reasons to continue having fun, to keep our little party going.

I wasn't present at her birth—"trailing clouds of glory do we come"—but came to rest at the threshold of her death, the holiest place soon to be. I felt the power of her passing and have a hunch that to trailing clouds of glory she did return. Still do.

---

The following article was published in the *Ottawa Citizen* in February 2011.

## A LAMENT FOR PRAYERS UNSAID

I grew up a doubter, serving mass at the cloistered convent on Richmond Road in Ottawa. I remember being filled with trepidation walking to Les Soeurs de la Visitation on cold dark mornings, the echo of my boots crunching on snow still on my mind as I entered the warm, dark silence of the cloister. I remember the surreal feeling of serving mass as shadowy figures glided behind screens further obscuring the cloisters, just in case the dark room and traditional habit didn't fully do the trick. I was both terrified and vaguely aware that deep mystery resided in that place.

But that convent life is now gone; the grounds and the stone building—surely the most impressive piece of architecture in Ottawa—are to be developed into, what else, condos. The only mystery may be what the fixtures and kitchen cabinetry choices will be.

The spacious convent gardens held another mystery. We knew of it, but no one had actually seen the garden, and not being visible, behind a high concrete wall, only increased its sense of intrigue. What we did know is that for many cloisters this garden was their only exposure to the world outside the stone building for months, years, a lifetime. The new plan for the grounds features a tug of war between developers and the neighbourhood, and it is a mystery whether the gardens will be parcelled up or sport another full-fledged condo tower.

A few years ago I stopped by the convent and asked if it would ever be possible to see the garden. I was told that I had just missed an opportunity, as the convent had celebrated its 75th anniversary and briefly had opened its gardens to the public. When, I asked, might there be another opportunity?

Why, for the 100th anniversary, I was told, straight-faced and without a trace of irony. Time in the convent was not measured in minutes.

My Aunt Isobell was a nun for 65 years, mostly with the Sisters of St. Joseph of Peterborough. Before she died in 2005, my wife and I visited her regularly, often staying overnight in one of the many empty rooms. Visiting my aunt was not an act of charity. And her community of sisters did not fit any stereotype about uber-pious heaven-obsessed nuns. They were without exception feisty, engaged and engaging, keenly aware of current affairs, and diverse in their opinions, and yet their opinions were singularly well-informed. They did not talk much religion, liked their modest creature comforts, had careers in the community—in fact, the order since its beginning had served in and administered community hospitals. In the expression of their vocation they were worldly, in the best sense of the word. Perhaps most curious, whether from living a selfless life or simply not having to capitulate to marriage, convent communal life absolutely held the secret to longevity.

My aunt died at 88. She outlived her six siblings by several decades, and yet she had had health problems in middle life that should have done her in many years earlier. After her funeral I sat at a table with four of her fellow sisters. We talked about Isobell's 65 years in the convent, and I commented on just what a bloody long time that was. But once again I was to learn that nuns do not share my perspective about time. It turns out that two of my table companions were 98 years old and had entered the Sisters of St. Joseph convent in the same year; and in two years, when each turned 100, they were going to celebrate their 75th jubilee together. How can you not like the word *jubilee*? The other two sisters were over 90 years old and had 70 years in the bank as nuns. So Aunt Isobell was actually the kid and had died tragically young (wish I'd known that for the eulogy). My companions could have all passed for women in their early 70s. As our reminiscing ended, one of the sisters mentioned that the spectacularly beautiful, pathetically empty convent building was to be soon sold and that a small functional convalescent facility was to be built next door, to care for the last remaining nuns as they exited this mortal coil.

Last May, the Ottawa Independent Writers asked me to give a three-day writing workshop at the convent in Pembroke. The large convent and grounds are mainly empty now and so are available for such functions. Though not as dark as the cloistered convent of my childhood memory, the Pembroke convent had vast, ominous empty wings, and being both superstitious and high strung, I had to investigate. The dim lighting could not extinguish the luminous impression staring back at me from the hundreds of photos of convent life through the decades along corridor walls. There had been real and vibrant life here, and if ever a place was haunted, this was it. I liked that thought.

A few weeks ago, the *Ottawa Citizen* featured an article on the closing and sale of the Sisters of Sacred Heart, an Oblate order on Main Street. Given that the nuns are dying out and not being replaced, the Oblate and the sisters hired an architect to develop a community design plan. The plan envisions building 1,300 housing units in townhouses and apartment blocks. And there is nothing fundamentally wrong with this plan; people need housing, and downtown intensification makes sense.

Still, this piece is a lament. It is a lament for an ancient way of life that is disappearing in the blink of an eye. But more to the point, it is a lament for what most people, especially young people, will never know is missing. I grew up in an Irish Catholic family, one of seven kids—another lament for another day. My mother had a bracelet with seven charms, one for each of her children, and, the days of the week equalling the number of her brood, we had an assigned day when she would pray for each of us exclusively. Being a middle child, my day was Wednesday. I don't remember Wednesdays ever being special or lucky, but now that no one is praying for me, something seems to be missing.

When I was young I asked my mom why we need cloistered nuns. I was and remain fascinated by those who seek to remove themselves from the world for the greater cause, but I couldn't figure what theirs might be. She answered that they chose not to be of this world in order to pray for it. And she added that the world badly needs people, especially these devoted people, praying for it. If that were true in the 1960s, it must be even truer today.

There are stories about the power of prayer. I don't know if they are true, even a little bit, but I do have a deep, palpable feeling that our collective shift away from religion and into ideological causes is not the answer to what ails the world. Can we really have devolved to the point where obsession with all things "green," as an example, or brandishing our own personal form of social justice, or joining PETA trumps trying to figure out why the heck we are here on this earth in this bloody form for this brief—in nuns' thinking—period of time? No, I don't know, haven't any answers, just a gut feeling that spiritually we have lost our way. Are we a soul encased in a physical body, or are we just a collection of cells soon to become compost? If the latter, being buried in compost bins instead of coffins might make our death more meaningful in a green sort of way. No afterlife, but no after-waste either.

No one prays for me on Wednesdays anymore. Not that I deserve it, but that is not the point—or perhaps, the fact that I am unworthy but someone still prayed for me for most of my life is the very point. Maybe the passing of convent life doesn't matter; gardens and superb architecture are just physical things, after all. But there really was more to it than that.

With each passing day it seems that there are fewer people praying for the world and more people meddling in it. I lament the passing of convent life. I lament the devotion, the separateness from the world and its various causes and temptations, the understated examples of these lives well lived, the mystery and the fact that perhaps no one is left in our corner anymore. Most of all, I lament that when the light is finally extinguished few will notice the dimming of our green, troubled world.

"All happy families resemble each other; each unhappy family is unhappy in its own way."

LEO TOLSTOY, *ANNA KARENINA*, OPENING SENTENCE

# CHAPTER TWELVE
## FAMILY, THE ONE THAT MATTERS

HAPPY FAMILIES ARE HOME; UNHAPPY FAMILIES ARE A REMINDER THAT WE ARE NOT there.

It is true that my nostalgia can lend itself to an idealized version of the past. I remember with fondness people, events and occasions that were unremarkable by any objective measure. Still, a life is only unremarkable if there is no one to remark. It was and is home, and you will never be home unless you know you are there when you are there.

Our family was far, far from ideal. Your family will never fit an ideal, and will only be home to the extent that you fit into it and appreciate it for what it is, not for what you would have it be. Fortunately, for us, large families were very good at quelling voices of dissent and democracy. We learned to have respect and came to understand humility and that it was up to us, and only us, to make our mark out there in the world. The family was not for displays of individuality but where you laid down self for the collective good, or because Dad said so. We all had personal secrets, ambitions, and palpable drive to be something outside the family. We knew each other best, and not at all. Unhappy families are unhappy in their own way but have in common individuals who fail to get over themselves.

Both the McCloskey and O'Neill sides of my Irish Catholic family ended up in Canada out of desperation. They did not thumb through travel brochures from their cozy Irish cottage, legs up in front of a peat fire, sipping Irish whiskey, thinking about possibilities. An innocuous shift in crop conditions led to a cataclysmic end to the world as they knew it. There had been dry rot and curl potato crop failures before; the potato was considered an unreliable crop. Still, it had the capacity to bounce back. Even in 1845, the year from which Ireland would never recover, as late as July 23rd *Freeman's Journal* said that "the poor man's property, the potato crop, was never before so large and at the same time so abundant." Then it came time to dig up the abundant potatoes, and to everyone's astonishment, much of the crop was ruined. Nobody could have predicted in October 1845 that this disaster was only the beginning of much worse to come. Life was and is that precariously balanced. *But for the grace of God* is the everyday reality of our existence. Though we take it for granted, life on earth has always been and remains spectacularly unlikely.

It is absolutely no exaggeration to say that during and after the potato famine of 1845–49 Ireland was the poorest, most ravaged and hopeless country in the world. Repeated crop failures from the potato blight infection in Europe hit Ireland hardest because of its complete dependency on the lowly potato. Dirt-poor Irish peasants did not have the means to recover, diversify or draw upon provisions put away for a rainy day. The only provision for a rainy day in Ireland was rain. When pestilence visited the Irish peasant, it poured misfortune in biblical proportions, with the potato famine and the resultant diaspora throughout the globe destined to become the defining moment of Irish history.

There is no hard evidence to suggest that the death of one million, mostly Irish peasants, was deliberate genocide. It was rather from neglect and indifference by their British rulers and absent landlords, which to someone displaced from his land and starving to death is splitting hairs. Death was everywhere and means of escape limited, and even for those who managed it, leaving was almost as bad as staying and starving. For untold tens of thousands, the result was the same—painful death, inglorious end.

Of the million peasants stampeding to leave Ireland, few could afford the cost of passage to Australia or the most sought after location, the United States. Keeping in mind that the United States was a better, preferred destination, it is worth reciting a comment made by a prominent black leader watching the "coffin ships" unload at Ellis Island, this before emancipation: "At least we're not as badly off as the Irish."

For those with little or no fare, their fate was sealed; there was no choice. They sailed for Canada. Anyone who could move gathered their kin and boarded the coffin ships, infamous for their inhuman crowding, horrific conditions and prevalence of death. Survivors of the famine pitched across the Atlantic for six long weeks, suffering only boredom, motion sickness and overcrowding if they were lucky. For the rest, dysentery, typhoid and death were a daily reality, and even with land finally in sight, the coffin ships lay anchor within sight of Grosse Isle near Quebec City and waited. And waited, with their sick and bored and dying.

For those who survived the famine, for those who survived the coffin ships, for those who survived the wait for quarantine—often taking weeks—there was still quarantine itself, where again death was a constant, banal occurrence. And if the famine, sailing and quarantine had not been enough, survivors now had to forge a new life in a barren cold country as pioneers, for which they were completely unprepared. Still, having escaped Ireland—where at the height of the famine, the average life expectancy of an Irish male was 19 years—they persisted, settled, suffered, and slowly, painfully thrived. The formidable challenges facing those who made it this far was the good news.

It was in the immediate wake of the *great hunger*—a figure of speech later used to describe the indescribable by the world's most literate people—that my family came to call Canada home. We never knew any of this growing up, but it is worth knowing, and it explains a lot. How little or much my parents knew of their own history remains a mystery. What is clear is that the famine and great waves of emigration profoundly shaped Irish history. Just before the potato famine, the population of Ireland was approximately 8.5 million, the highest in Ireland's history. Today Ireland has just over 6 million, or not much more than the approximately 5.5 million inhabitants recorded for the distant year of 1800. Ireland was overcrowded and overcultivated when the famine occurred, with the death of one million people and emigration of another million, or loss of about 20 percent of the population, the final historic tally of carnage. And yet, as they made their mark in the world, most notably in the United States, Canada and Australia, they were known for having *the luck of the Irish*.

Though the potato famine is somewhat known, few would think of the Irish as ever being oppressed or separate from mainstream society in their English-speaking Christian-emigrant countries. This view is exacerbated by our progressive view of history, which insists on regarding the past through the lens of contemporary (piecemeal and unshared) values and assumptions. There can be no understanding of history without considering the values and struggles of the time in question. In writing this lament it is my contention that the future-oriented progressive view of the world makes us blind to the actual values and facts of history. Those who peopled the past and what actually happened were not the products of our critical judgment. They were not simple and wrong; we are not complex and right. The modern lens as portal to understanding of the past is simply bias, or worse, wilful ignorance, not history. These, my people, were not of the majority, did not enjoy white privilege, and did not have social acceptance, understanding or support of any kind because of their status or plight. They were dirty Irish, under-class, outcasts, but they were alive. As a group, they were close-knit, clannish, likely did not speak English, were of the Catholic minority in a British Protestant colony, and as such were resented and unwelcome. In Quebec City, Montreal, Ottawa and Toronto, to name a few, there was hostility and fear against the low-level half-human disease-ridden Irish who had been dumped into their fair cities without food or work or prospects of any kind. Shop windows had "NINA" signs prominently placed: No Irish Need Apply.

So it really was an interesting moment around 1970 when my dad picked up the old, discarded McCloskey Road sign at the foot of the new shiny metal job, metres away from the old McCloskey farmstead. I remember first hearing about the McCloskey farmstead with excitement and bewilderment, thinking, *We had a farmstead? We had a past?* Inexplicably, we learned there had been about ten Irish families that had broken or been broken by the land, built houses and farmed here. The *here* is a beautiful wooded area high in the Gatineau Hills, about a 15-minute drive from Parliament in Ottawa. But in the second half of the nineteenth century it would have been one of the most isolated places on earth. And spectacularly unfarmable.

Well, apparently they didn't starve, so not quite true, but it is a wonder that they applied years of back-breaking labour to this horribly rocky, acidic, root-entangled soil barely able to yield a scant anemic crop. They endured for some decades, until someone must have espied the fertile Ottawa Valley below and said, "There's got to be a better way." Then inexplicably they left, or else it is inexplicable that they had stayed so long. When exactly they left, no one knows, likely by 1920, with the trees and roots soon cancelling their labour and their existence, except for the telltale stone fences, the last remnant of their Spartan existence. A terrible beauty of crumbling fieldstone still borders my great-grandparents' land and continues as a testament wherever the Irish broke their backs trying to turn forest and rock into field and food.

Dad must have known something of the McCloskey origin, but what else did he know? We have names and dates on a family tree, but who were these people? What were their lives? How did they relate to the other families, to each other in the family? Did people get along? Were there *characters* among the tribe? Was their isolation splendid or horrible? Were there secret affairs, broken hearts, longing or fear for whatever was out there? Did secrets last long? Did they have music? Did they have fun? This would be an interesting little world to step into, but the point is, they wouldn't likely have allowed a strange stranger in, even if he claimed to have a clan name and had the inbred look of the family up the road.

Growing up, we knew many other large Irish Catholic families. Our families were not special, and our common individual experience was that we kids were anything but special. This concept may be difficult to accept in the self-esteem era, but it was generally accepted that anyone who made a comment, gesture, or, Lord knows, hint of putting himself on a pedestal should be slapped down as being an egotistical braggart whose comeuppance was to be mercilessly delivered. For your own good, you understand.

Families, especially the one you are born into, are hard to write about. You do not write about your family as a detached sociologist. They represent a world of good, a world of pain; they are, among many other things, a labyrinth of possibilities and differing opinions, sometimes widely divergent views, on what was assumed to be shared experience. The experience of family is never a straight line and always a mixed blessing at best. I feel very fortunate to have come from a big family, and I do lament their passing, for all their various blemishes, warts and quirks, with progressive modernity pulsating, pressing, primed to strike and drive a killing spike through their vulnerable heart.

When we grew up we felt sorry for the kids from those small, insignificant clans of only three or four, and there was even rumour of a family with only one child, whose mother had been told by her doctor that another pregnancy would kill her. Poor kid, forever *oreo-ed* between his parents, anyone's parents, I thought at the time. A big family not only afforded time away from parents; it gave a certain distinction or identity—granted, liability for some—that branded you in the neighbourhood, school and parish. It was a better-or-worse thing. As the only one of seven kids who did not skip a grade, and as the runt of the litter among five boys, comparisons to siblings did not do me any favours. Still, I say better than worse, on balance.

Kids in big families have to learn how to share—everything. Shared values are only possible among people who learn to share. In our crowded house, there were our few scant personal possessions, but they didn't matter. What mattered were the family items, like the TV and record player and radio. We didn't think about it then, but these items brought us together, made us share, and contributed to a sense of home. Sports equipment, bikes, clothes, and toys were passed out of the older hands into the younger's eager grasp, if anything useful was left of the leftovers. Not good, not bad, just the way it was.

It never really occurred to us that because of our expanding and fulsome slice of humanity, the slice of what we got just got less. For instance, when we had ice cream. A one pint container, such as I've polished off by myself in seconds, and then some, standing with the fridge door open after a run. Back then, one pint was a special treat for everyone—always Neapolitan, meaning tri-coloured: strawberry, vanilla and chocolate. There were seven kids in our tribe, six before the last and latest, plus our parents. So as a minimum, the one pint of ice cream was cut into eight slices. Try it. Not easy to do, and, quickly now, before it melts, hold it up and see the light shining through the thin Spartan film. Almost like stained glass in a church, but lasting a whole lot less long. So much of life is better for what you don't know. It was a special treat, much appreciated, and it never occurred to us that ice cream might come in a larger quantity. Not that we would have asked for it in front of Dad.

That's right, folks, they don't make families like that anymore. This is literally true, and you won't be surprised if I think something has been lost that cannot be replaced. It isn't for lack of trying on the part of parents, and sometimes the amount of trying by parents who outnumber their progeny is the problem. The modern experience of family—once involving a large number of siblings and a cluster of other adults, including aunts, uncles, grandparents, and likely various and many cousins—tends to be more narrowly focused on the one-on-one or two-on-one parent-child relationship. Parental involvement is fine to a point, and it is true that our parents perhaps erred on the side of too little involvement, but we all know that the best relationships in our life work to the extent that they balance involvement with relief from each other. Kids of all ages need that relief as much as any of us, and given that their task is to ultimately find their own way, I would argue they need it more.

It isn't only Christian fundamentalists who have noticed that the family is under assault. This statement is not reactionary; it is not against social changes, court rulings, inclusion or diversity. And it isn't just large families that are disappearing. We are under-breeding ourselves out of existence with dangerously low and dropping birthrates in the Western world. The pattern is somewhat spotty, with Europe and Japan having the lowest rates, then Canada, and only the United States holding its own, producing above the requisite 2.1 children per family required to replicate the population. In fact, no country has ever recovered from a fertility rate of 1.9, and Spain's fertility rate, among the lowest in Europe, is currently at 1.3. This rate guarantees the end of the family in Spain, the end of Spain in Spain, though hot-blooded Spaniards seem remarkably stoic in the face of certain extinction. Immigration can help balance low birthrates but cannot make up for an entire declining population in any country.

Many will rhetorically respond, who cares? Well, if there is any part of this life worth preserving, including democracy, capitalism, and Western civilization, we might want to give pause. Again, who cares? Good riddance; let's move on from the Bible, Mozart, Shakespeare, mouldy old cathedrals and the like. But if the self-loathing of hard-won accomplishments of the West ever fully comes to fruition, the good news for the good-riddance folks is that the barbaric uncivilized world from which we painfully emerged is possible to achieve again. Western economies and political and cultural institutions are in crisis, languishing in a spiritual entropy, fraught with complacency, cynicism and ever-expanding interest group accommodation. Those wishing Western ways away are realizing their heart's desire.

I am not suggesting that the way forward is for women to replicate my mom's euchre table, where, dropping by one evening, I calculated that the assemblage of six widows had an average of six kids each, with their average being about average for the time. For all my nostalgia, those families are no longer realistic. Besides, parents today could never let go of the first long enough to get to the next.

And there is something else. Much as parents today try hard to be good parents, we no longer have enough faith to have many children. We are afraid of not having money to provide the best, we could not live with the limited parental time each child would receive, and we would be ever anxious about their protection from any and all perceived threats. Mostly, we do not have faith that it would work out without our deliberate efforts at controlling the outcome.

The world is changing. In Europe, Muslims still have large families and will dramatically shift demographic trends in the coming years. In 2016, the medium age of Muslims in Europe was fully 13 years younger than the medium age of Europeans, at 30.4 versus 43.8 years. Also, Muslim women have an average 2.6 children versus 1.6 for non-Muslim, so non-Muslim population replication is not possible. By mid-century and in consideration of migrant trends, the Muslim population of Europe is expected to rise from 4.9 percent to 14 percent, or from approximately 26 to 75 million. This figure assumes that migration patterns will continue, which is reasonable since most of the recent migrants came from desperate situations, whether due to war or lack of economic opportunity. Meanwhile, Europe is the only region in the world where total population is expected to decline by 2050. A population vacuum by the European majority, if only nominally Christian, population will inevitably be filled by people more committed to perpetuating a continuance of family. The fact is, atheism correlates to low birthrates, non-Muslim Europeans are increasingly becoming atheists, and Muslim families are not *taking* Europe as such; rather, non-Muslim Europeans are *giving* it away. My argument is not intended to assign blame in any direction but rather to expose the historical nature of unintended consequence, which generally has much to do with denial. Human populations always seek higher ground with regard to opportunity for their families, and populations with cohesive family values do it better than those without. Religion and family are the anchors that until recently have ensured that inevitable change occurs with stable social parameters. Relative to its historical progression, Europe is in free fall, and perhaps the only shared value left is that values no longer are shared. Seismic change is inevitable, accelerating, and of Europeans' own making.

In China, the one-child policy has resulted in over 400 million reported sponsored abortions since 1971, which means that the unofficial number is much higher, certainly higher than the combined populations of the United States and Canada. But the real kicker is a related outcome that the venerable leaders may not have thought of when they enacted the one-child policy. In 1975, just 27 percent of children were singletons, but by 1983 it was 91 percent. With a population of 1.3 billion and with a preference for male children a constant, the number of eligible Chinese males who will never find a female partner will be in the tens of millions. Think about the cauldron of conflict, strife and testosterone brewing here—a generation of millions of Chinese males with unrequited lust, no experience or balancing influence from women, no family or future to civilize and commit to—an absolutely toxic formula for fomenting revolution. The one-child policy was supposed to control China's population and make it prosperous, and it has worked. Population growth has been significantly slowed down, though with a disproportionate percentage of mini male holders of family fortune, often called "little emperors" for their pampered, entitled behaviour. Still, behaviour is not their biggest problem. The much bigger and unacknowledged problem is that once a country takes down the scaffolding of the family, it takes down the civilization that supported it. The 2015 decision to change from a one- to a two-child policy will not undo the seismic consequences to the family and the economy that are percolating on the horizon.

To mention the word *abortion* is to be labelled a religious fanatic. We seem so intent upon getting what we want today that we often miss the fact that we don't want what we've got. Consider this: in Russia today, 75 percent of all pregnancies end in abortion. Seems odd, since birth control is readily available. But Russia today is in such a state of decay about the family that abortion *is* birth control. This is beyond laziness and indicative of complete societal decline. The Visigoth barbarians clamoured from without, and Rome corrupted from within, with the latter being the actual story of civilization's inevitable decline. Civilizations can withstand huge outside pressures for long periods of time, but when they lose faith in themselves and forsake the values that made them great, they can disappear in a historical heartbeat.

So civilizations can decline and disappear over, what, sex? In China, not getting enough; in Russia, too much. Maybe, but the real issue is the extent to which a civilization safeguards or relinquishes a workable version of the family. Sex seems to be a strangely accurate barometer of family values. I grew up at a time that was at the crossroads between sexual repression and sexual revolution. Being Irish and Catholic with uncool traditional parents, my experience was far more on the repression side, which I regretted then but have rethought in later years. This is more variation on *be careful what you wish for*, which as a theme related to faith cannot be overstated.

In a Catholic high school in the 1970s, not much happened. And because sex happened rarely, or incompletely, or not at all, it became a lifetime obsession. Make something subversive, and watch it grow. Sex, or even the possibility, only happened as a consequence of a developing relationship called *going out*, all but absent today, and hooking up was something your grandmother did to a rug in front of the TV. Several dates in, a French kiss or, height of excitement, copping a feel was a memorable experience, and not just an unfinished means to an incomplete end. The experiences in our little suburban Catholic high school must have been what inspired the French philosopher when he coined the phrase "the height of sexual passion is the flight up the stairs to the room." We were square, limited and naive, and, thankfully, have never lost our hunger.

Things are different today. One would have to conclude that young people are no longer square, limited and naive. They are cool, likely have experienced real sex years before we ever did, and are very well-informed. Still, from reading and various sources over the years, another picture emerges. Young people are not having great sex; their many, often cyber, relationships are limited in a cyber, non-human way; most of all, they are not happy, and they don't know why.

We inhabit a more permissive world today, and young people are not oppressed by restrictions. Hooking up replaces dating, porn replaces anticipation, and familiarity with every act and body type replaces curiosity. The contrived and demeaning world of porn is a commodified multibillion dollar industry, available to everyone with access to the internet in a second, every second, and makes sex, ironically and inevitably, less interesting. Seems a disingenuous comment with untold billions pouring in, but the audience is dead. Sex is dead.

Sex is what people passively watch because they can, but the image on the TV does not translate into the act in the bed or even flight up the stairs to the room. Otherwise put, communication between the person hooked on porn and the person looking for a relationship is lost in translation. Young people increasingly say that they are not particularly enjoying what limited sex they are having—and this in a guilt-free, permissive age. Young women report that young men are just not that interested. Further, young women feel that they can't compete. This doesn't make sense, unless you consider the disturbing fact that the competition is not coming from that other attractive woman. The ultra-exciting, up-the-ante world of porn is the reason why young men present as flat, passive personalities to the real, all too human women standing before them.

I remember walking the halls of my high school with an internal dialogue from my head to my head, trying to talk my penis into not erecting, an embarrassing situation in front of girls who had excited me for simply being. If young women are to be believed, and there really is no reason to doubt them, young guys, part of the sexual ennui revolution, are non-pursuing, specific-act oriented, nothing less will do, passive semi-placid duds, unwilling to even take the flight up the stairs, let alone know, care or wonder what to do once they get there. This phenomenon does not have the makings of a robust future for the family.

This is not a diatribe against young people. It was the boomers who gave it all away. My parents demanded respect. We wanted our kids to like us, and therefore we made the Machiavellian choice—which is that you can be liked or respected, but not both. So we shortchanged our kids because we were unwilling to do the hard work, which is harder to do when you are closer to your kids than we were to our parents, but that is an excuse, not a reason. I'm reminded of Al Pacino in *Scent of a Woman*, after he has blinded himself by pulling the pin on a grenade while drunk. In a moment of insight and despair, he says, "I always knew what the right thing to do was. I just didn't do it."

So what's all the fuss? Well, young people are not doing well today on the mental health front. Magazines across North America have recently run cover articles on the mental health tsunami that threatens young people who have grown up with the greatest affluence that the world has ever seen, the most parental involvement the world has ever seen, and the greatest freedom and choice, ditto, that the world has ever seen. This picture does not make sense.

Hara Estroff Marano, the former editor of *Psychology Today*, went on assignment to investigate a disturbing increase in suicides at American universities. The assignment was so big that she wrote a book, entitled *A Nation of Wimps: The High Cost of Invasive Parenting*. Her thesis contention is that today's parents do not parent. Parents have one child (this is not a Chinese policy, by the way), two maximum, and he is less a child to be parented than a project to be managed. Further, Estroff Marano says hell is paved with good intentions of parents desperately wanting to shield their projects from adversity, and consequently the little embryonic projects do not develop resilience—that ingredient necessary to adulthood, which allows us to cope, survive and even thrive. Without resiliency, kids are forever dependent on their parents—the ones who put them in this state of affairs with all their caring.

I recently gave a workshop on mental health to a group of teachers and asked if they had any insight into why the mental health profile has worsened for young people. Common responses to this question might typically be bullying, homophobia, technology and the like. Only one teacher put up her hand on this occasion. She simply said, "A lack of spirituality in their lives."

I wasn't expecting this. But I had to agree that this unorthodox, much maligned answer likely pinpoints a major contributing factor. If, in the modern world, we are increasingly tending towards the path of least spiritual resistance, our prospects for good mental health are not good. Mark Muldoon said in "The Addicted Pilgrim," "The path to better mental health, and therefore, to better spiritual depth will call upon all of our physical, mental and spiritual resources, which at moments will drain us and bring us to our knees in submission—so deep is our resistance to the unconditionality of a Living God."

There are more fallen Christians than there are fallen soldiers in all wars. Well, tough call, but lapsed Christians often identify with the religious values from which they fell far more than they tend to admit. Fortunately for us, fallen does not mean forsaken, and Christianity is singular among religions in its emphasis on forgiveness and redemption. For most people with any grounding in any religion—regardless of how often or far they fall—it informs their values, inspires conscience (regrettably a concept much out of favour) and forms the basis for feeling guilt and making amends when they have done wrong. This most detestable state, guilt, allows for forgiveness—of ourselves and others—saying sorry works wonders, and the gift of redemption, once we have done the right and difficult thing. In other words, a religious upbringing provides context—to be rejected or embraced as informed adults, but context nonetheless—which many children today sadly and completely lack. Without parental guidance that sets limits, religious instruction that provides context, and siblings that teach the necessity of sharing, young people cannot help but drift in the vacuous waters of unfulfilled, never to be fulfilled, modern spiritual ennui.

I am not saying that you have to grow up in a big family in order to foster healthy relationships. I think the advantages of growing up in a big family outweigh the disadvantages, but it is a moot point since no one is having one anymore. For us aging boomers, there is an obvious advantage to having siblings around as the clock counts down, and, weirdly, as people enter retirement they sometimes get acquainted, for the first time, with that barely known brother or sister who left home 40 years earlier to make his or her mark in the world.

But there is a downside. In comparing notes with other dinosaurs from the last of the large families, there seems to be a common theme. Many families seem to have at least one sibling who is estranged from the herd, and, strangely, discernible reasons don't seem to come into it. That is, with the passing of time most family members tend to pull together, since whatever the conflicts were, they have long since passed. Still, there are individual holdouts who cannot compromise self for the good of family cohesion, instead giving way to a narrative of perpetual grievance. You won't see it listed in the DSM-5 psychiatric diagnostic handbook, but I contend that these people's identities, impulses and personalities are commonly shaped by their habitual need to create and sustain grievance. In our family, we have a couple of estranged parts, holders of grievance, withholders of affection.

It is true that we all have an early psychic wound of varying degrees as we figure out who we are and where we fit into the world. The vessel for that learning experience is the family, and it is often the dumping ground for a sense of inadequacy from those who never quite figure it out, at least according to their expectations. Sad fact is, expectations can be deadly. I love the wisdom of this anonymous quote: "All psychological pain is derived from being unable to reconcile the world as it is with what you would have it be." This truism does not jive well with the essential fact of life in a big family:

in the rough and tumble of jostling bodies, limited resources and competing agendas, factions and personalities, no one entirely gets what he or she wants and possibly deserves. Fostering co-operation, compromise and sharing is a source of psychological resilience for most and reason for grievance for a few lone souls who never did get over themselves.

Siblings not seen for years can remain in a permanent state of being blamed for errant comments or perceived slights made years or, more sadly, decades earlier. Grievance, that perpetual state of feeling the wronged party, takes on a life of its own. Of course the others, not understanding a grievance that cannot be named and therefore cannot be addressed, habitually attempt to reach out, extend, forgive, but basically exist on the defensive, which is the source of power for the aggrieved sibling's passive aggressive stance. Muldoon said on the antidote to grievance, "We begin to tell the story of our lives based on an unconditional foundation of divine compassion instead of a story of victimization and scarcity on the endless preoccupation and search for our core wounds."

God love 'em, we would like them, for their own sake, to get over themselves. The door is not closed, but at some point in our family we have simply stepped away from the control drama and let them go. They don't know this and are continuing to withhold contact, affection and who they might have become to the rest of us. Poor things. Life is devastatingly and spectacularly short. We wish them well.

The truth seems to be that sometimes you have to let go of family in order to have a family. I used to believe that you never give up on siblings, but you have to adjust to what is and let go of what you would have had it be. There is always an interesting moment for a large family of adult siblings talking about the past at the dinner table. You mention a memory, all seven siblings give their perspective, and you are left wondering what family the other six came from. Neither nostalgia nor grievance are particularly objective. Still, if nostalgia's fault is that it conjures a better world than might have been, grievance makes sure that everyone understands it never was.

If the family once held up civilization, we are having trouble holding a family dinner these days. I may be nostalgic for the large traditional family, but I don't kid myself that it is ever coming back. Still, the question lingers: if not the traditional family, what else? Much of my argument for faith is based on fostering a sense of wonder and embracing the mystery that is our everyday existence. We flatten, deconstruct and reject today, creating these unholy vacuums that lead to that self-filling, oft-repeated prophesy, "If you don't believe in something, you'll believe in anything."

Self-confidence, self-reliance, belief in self can be positive traits, and modern living choices reflect increasing emphasis on individual autonomy. In 2016, the most common living arrangement—over couple, family, and multiple family arrangements—is living alone, at 28.2 percent in Canada, and highest in the Western world, Sweden at 39.2 and Germany at 41.4 percent. These percentages are up from single digit figures in the 1950s.

Living alone denotes one's choice at a given moment in time, but perhaps more indication of choosing self as an emerging value exists in a growing trend, from a September 8th, 2018, full page profile entitled, "Saying 'I do' to You," in the Life by Design section of the paper. The article provides the logical conclusion to the deconstruction of marriage and family with the kitschy lifestyle choice of self-marriage. It is not enough to opt to be single, or to be reconciled to being single, or even to be open to being other than single if that path becomes a possibility in the future. The self-marriage movement is about making a public commitment in declaring one's fidelity to self for now and all time during a marriage ceremony. "It makes sense that people are hungering for a different type of ritual, says Sasha Cagen, the California-based self-married author of Quirkyalone, a manifesto of sorts for people who prefer being single." Or from Dominique Youkhehpaz, another Californian, self-marriage minister and counsellor, whose expanded business helps "women plan wedding ceremonies (including a 10-week preparatory course starting at US $200)." I am not disparaging single life, or suggesting that people need to find their soul mate in order to be complete. But surely this ritualized public declaration is commitment to step over whomever God places in our path in a faux sense of ultimate individual choice, control and virtue. Far beyond the Hollywood version of romance is the very real possibility—or even certainty for those who are truly open to the phenomenology of intimacy—for deep human relationships, that taken together become our family.

I may be missing something, but lying awake at night, we, all our individual selves, and maybe even Richard Dawkins knows that the mystery and wonder of the world that we have witnessed this and every day are not of our own making or understanding, and certainly not of our own control. Without people who constitute family, we do not have context, relevancy or meaning for this wild, astonishing and terrifying ride. Stripped bare, at our waking to self at night, we know the ride is not about any one of us, but may well be about all of us.

Thing is, we need a family, we need to find our way home. For all my nostalgia, the good news for people from families, large and small, is that your family, the one that matters, is less what you are born into than it is the connections you make and the deep, meaningful relationships you develop throughout your life.

I have a hard time believing that the screen-time-created technology-assisted friendships of young people today will allow for relationships that matter and will endure. And there is evidence to support my contention, despite my Luddite tendencies. Many studies have shown that increased screen time correlates to an increased sense of isolation. Also disturbing is data taken from the General Social Survey of American, which gauges values and lifestyle choices. Researchers Howard Gardner and Katie Davis in *The App Generation* cite findings related to the number of close interpersonal relationships Americans report over a 20-year span, from 1985 to 2004. Incredibly, in 1985 the number of close discussion partners was 2.94, whereas in 2004 that figure had fallen to 2.08, or by nearly one-third. Surely the rarified number of people we can bare our souls to is more important than the number of friends one has on Facebook for whom intimate details are merely too much information. The proliferation of social media at present and into the foreseeable future has the potential for disturbing consequences to the family we create or are born into.

If we are surrendering quality for quantity in our relationships as we move from old-fashioned human connection to ever more clever strains of social media, what might the implications be? Though a direct empirical link to social media is not definite, there is considerable evidence that young people are suffering from a lessening of that all-important ingredient for connection: empathy. An analysis of 72 studies done between 1979 and 2009 by the University of Michigan concluded that American college students are indeed becoming less empathetic. In the age of endless ideological feel-good social causes, this is a not a good sign. Absence may make the heart grow fonder, but distance does not make the heart grow softer. Distance—that is, the hallmark of relationships through social media—allows people the option of complete emotional detachment, a friendship that is the empathetic equivalent of passing someone living on the street, noting the details of their plight and feeling nothing.

A study commissioned by Microsoft—not known for their Luddite tendencies—found that people's attention span has fallen from an average of twelve seconds to eight since 2000, with personal technology devices cited as the likely culprit. As a point of comparison, our eight-second and likely falling status compares unfavourably to goldfish, whose attention span is a robust nine seconds. I will concede that social media can connect people in a multiplicity of ways that would not otherwise be possible. I am not disparaging technology and social media per se, except insofar as the virtual world substitutes for authentic and meaningful relationships, of which we really have very few in our lives. For some people authenticity and intimacy through social media may be possible. I don't get it but am prepared, am actively hoping, to be wrong.

It is possible that the emptiness that is the secular world will inspire a hunger for meaning. And maybe without a slew of siblings to take for granted, young people will value those whom they include in their family by choice. As for the dwindling of faith and faith-based teaching, maybe it will become like sex was for us in the 1970s. Okay, bit of a stretch, but the point of comparison is that the denial of spirituality today, much like the repression of sex then, makes it interesting precisely because of its subversive nature. My hope for young people today is that they are hungry enough for authenticity to conduct a thorough investigation into what is missing in their lives. With a flight up the stairs to the room of faith and a little help from their close friends, they might find their way home, and we'll all be waiting.

"Science is not only compatible with spirituality; it is a profound source of spirituality."

CARL SAGAN

# CHAPTER THIRTEEN
## IT IS OR ISN'T

I AM SITTING IN FRONT OF THE MAGNIFICENT VOTIVE CHURCH AT THE REGINA HOTEL café, Rooseveltplatz, Vienna, Austria, at 6 p.m. on a warm July evening. The sky is an undisturbed whole, shockingly blue, the temperature perfect, Austrian beer more so. The bells begin to ring, pure sound, seemingly more clear for the clear skies in all directions. I feel a wave of—what else— nostalgia, for bells are no longer heard at home. Church bells, the calling to ritual, celebration and obligation for over a thousand years in the Christian world, have gone silent mostly, but not here. It is a perfect moment.

I've been pleasantly surprised by how open and accessible the great churches of Europe are. In Canada, this is not the case. Churches rarely seem to be open outside the posted times for mass. The idea of just dropping by a church to pray or stay for a while has quietly slipped into the past. For some the past is but a passing thought; for most it never happened.

The European churches are not only accessible; their architecture, history and sense of grandeur are superior to almost anything in North America. Sitting at the Regina, sipping coffee in the morning and beer in the afternoon, my eyes can barely comprehend the scale and wonder of the edifice rising before me. The outside has ornate spirals and splendid flying buttresses, the perfect medieval answer to form and function. My eyes scan the intricate stone detailing again and again, breathtaking and overwhelming, and with a little imagination the white stonework gives a strange impression of primitive dinosaur bones, angelically carved.

This church and all churches, the purpose of architecture, were once conceived and executed for a single purpose: the glorification of God. Easy to forget this fact looking at the architecture of box stores and condos today. Inside, the architectural expression of the Votive is even more focused and impressive. Whether standing, sitting, or kneeling, legions of tourists notwithstanding, there is an unspoken consensus, oddly shared by people of faith or not, that the overall effect and mood is inspiring. Everything is intensely detailed visual harmony—stained glass, wood and stone carvings, artwork, icons, fantastically high ceiling, the effect greater than the sum of its parts. For all the intricacy and intention that went into an edifice whose aesthetic complexities defy comprehension, a simple feeling seems to pervade most people who visit. It just is.

There was once great faith here. The conceiving, building, attending and attending to this church is of another time. We cannot do this anymore; something has been lost. The church was once the anchor of the world in which it was centred. But for all its beauty, it seems hopelessly out of place now. It has been preserved, has remained the same, but all around it the world has changed. People crowd in, are impressed by what they see, but it is more oddity than awe-inspiring. And it occurs to me that for all the crowds, nobody goes to church in Europe anymore. The percentage of people who identify as both believing and actively practicing religion in Europe is approximately 7 percent, in Canada 14 percent, and in the US 20 percent. Some, and only some, of the Catholic churches still have Sunday mass. I attended mass at the equally magnificent St. Stephen's Cathedral in Vienna with a dozen or so other lonely souls. A couple of hours later, the tourists flocked in by the thousands to gawk and wonder for their requisite five minutes.

While I can barely take my eyes off the side of Votive Church from the Regina café, I could hardly force myself to take in the front view. The church is being renovated, as most of the ancient churches seem to be, and without parishioners, and given the scale and complexity of the building, one wonders, who pays?

Which is why the front of the Votive is covered by an expansive billboard, perhaps 35 high by 100 feet across. As a nod to modernity, in predictable fashion, the billboards are a paid advertisement for Coca-Cola. It occurs to me that the churches of Europe, for all their magnificence, truly are dinosaur bones, or maybe the bones of the saints, relics of the past. Coca-Cola is a perfect metaphor for resurrection, the new living business model giving the old dead medieval bones another life, or perhaps living death. For these stylish Europeans, perhaps it's not a question of whether God is or isn't, but, as Nietzsche prophesied, God was and is no more. Even as a provocative atheist philosopher, Nietzsche did not mean that God had actually died but that our pre-Enlightenment idea of God had died. The primacy of physical world thinking was taking hold, and faith was becoming openly disparaged. Of faith, Nietzsche dismissively once said it is simply *not wanting to know what is true*. I feel the same way about atheists. Nietzsche's despair is an easy and perhaps even natural state, born of this vale of tears that is this life in the raw exterior physical world where most of us live, most of the time. Still, there is reason to believe God is, but for all the distraction of despair we are not listening, we are not seeing. We of the modern age gaze inward to ourselves, and worse, we like what we see.

Do most people struggle with the elemental question of is or isn't? It doesn't seem likely. Most people seem to live for, but not in, the moment, a perpetual escape from an examined life. I'm not making much of a case for faith, I guess. Even as I've argued that we have to move from complacency and to actively confront the question of whether God is or isn't, my weak-kneed ambiguity likely seeps through every page. My only defense is that I have been struggling with the question my whole life.

I realize that faith is not simply nostalgia steeped in hope. Wishing it were so is not an examined life. But my nostalgia, attempts at faith, have echoes of memory infused with mystery, which does carry an element of a reverence I cannot describe. Throughout our adult lives, we not only become distant from the trailing clouds of glory into which we are born; we spend our years actively repressing the idea of home even as we desire it with all our being. We are funny little creatures.

I used to worry endlessly about searching without finding. But faith cannot be outcome-driven. The search is the thing, and we can only pray for insight as we continue to search. I am woefully ignorant of the Bible. I seem to have yet another affliction. Growing up, whenever there were gospel readings in church, my mind would automatically wander. Still, there was a passage that has always impressed me for the way it turns orthodoxy and people's expectations on their heads. A woman comes to Jesus with an alabaster jar of very expensive perfume, which she pours on his feet. No, this scene does not anticipate spa life or put women down. It is a spontaneous act of generosity, and interestingly, Jesus responds from the desire realm, agreeing to the treatment, which if nothing else shows he is human. His disciples are indignant; they have an idea of Jesus, and in this regard he does not fit. They want to know how he can partake of the indulgence of expensive perfume when the money would be better spent on the poor. How can this champion of the poor not surrender all excessive spending and worldly possessions to those who need it most? How could their original virtue signalling be wrong?

But Jesus was not some Hollywood celebrity trying to impress the public with public virtue signalling. Which parenthetically reminds me of what Russell Crowe said about celebrities who virtue signal their public causes: They should just write a check and shut the f— up.

Jesus taught by words and example and, unlike many celebrities, never confused the message with himself. For all the angst and struggle of a life well lived, maybe the purpose is not to simply suffer through it. Jesus ignored his disciples' expectations and answered, "You always have the poor with you, but you will not always have me" (Matthew 26:11, NRSVCE). Incredible. No, this is not capitulation to complacency, an act of hedonism or a weak moment. This is pure insight. Yes, we need to do what we can to alleviate poverty. Still, if it is true that the poor will always be with us—and everyone knows that it will be so—maybe the purpose of life should not be premised on social causes, social justice or social engineering. Maybe the purpose of life is not to endlessly correct but to watch, listen and observe, to look deeply into what is and not be distracted by what everyone else says it should be. Maybe we are here to connect—whether or not the lavishing of perfume is involved—to look for faith as we can, with the application of persistence and humility, without obsessing about finding the answer or appearing to be virtually spiritual. Maybe our continuous and pathetic churning on the hamster wheel of faith-finding has merit, and our refusal to give up the struggle is the embodiment of our living faith. It is just possible that my nostalgia, your nostalgia, is more than dead shadows to be finally buried but represents our search fuelled by echoes of love, reminding us that the past is not past, the present will always be present and the future is simply finding our way home.

I really am a hopeless nostalgic, whimpering and pining for the past, consumed by a sense of loss, little encouraged by the great unfolding amnesia-obsessed, technologically driven future. Out of step, tragically unhip, and a poor excuse for a human being on the question of faith. Mostly.

Though nostalgia is a longing and possibly idealized version of the past—one on which even siblings often fundamentally disagree—faith anticipates our future, the one that is still to come, the one during which we are likely to be a bit vulnerable, because we'll be dead. I say so with a hint of facetiousness because atheists often frame the debate between belief and non-belief as one of lifestyle. A kind of intellectual exercise, theoretical and nuanced, in which one listens, considers, draws up a pro-con list, makes a decision, and it's done. But if there is anything to faith, it is urgent and immediate, and the examination of its application to our lives requires passionate pursuit.

Faith is not a deathbed confession followed by redemption, heaven and eternal relief, "Whew, sure dodged a bullet there!" A belief in the eternal does not begin when we happen to get to it. Faith—attempting, doubting, failing, holding, and wondering—is actually a timeworn problem that we as spirits in a body are tasked to solve. We are not likely to solve the mystery—it is not a whodunit, after all—but we have to investigate, however long it takes, for as long as we have, until we are physical no more.

Much as I chide myself for being a sentimental fool, my nostalgic obsession with the past isn't ultimately about time. It is about our version of ourselves in relationship with others, and our eternal quest to go home. The hunger for home, the actual version of nostalgia I have been searching for, is both divinely inspired and our most fundamental window into the divine. When we look back, places, events and smells trigger memory, but what we are really accessing is how well we have loved and been loved. This is the point upon which nostalgia and faith are one. The nostalgia or melancholy of the romantic poets such as John Keats can serve to disconnect and celebrate the gloom of secular death, is the antithesis of faith, and of course anticipates the modern nihilistic world in which we gloomily reside.

Better the concept of that other romantic poet, William Wordsworth, that "but trailing clouds of glory do we come," an acknowledgement of immortality for all the pain of life and inevitability of death. Whether we have great early memories of home or none whatsoever, we share a deep, archetypal need to find our way back, or our way forward to a place at some level we have always known exists. It is our deepest human urge, and ultimately all our relationships, ambitions, sorrows, addictions, passions, fears and inspirations are about going home. We are born with the notion, which is the magic that defines childhood; we live with it, but for most of us not well; and we die reaching for what we know but cannot describe. It is the archetypal story of *Citizen Kane*, with Orson Wells playing William Randolph Hearst, unsatisfied with his worldly possessions and perpetually in search for Rosebud, a childhood toy, his fundamental connection to, and metaphor for, home.

For anyone thinking that this notion of home is overstated, turn to the obituaries of any newspaper, anytime. Look at the photos, read the summary of a life from those who grieve. The face staring back haunts us, will not go away, even as we turn the page. Look at the photos of the recently deceased, and then the other beside it, as she lived 50 years earlier, starting out, hopeful and searching, before marriage, children, grandchildren, looking for love and searching for a home.

Today, heartbreaking and hopeful. Leonard, January 21, 1951–October 19, 1973. So many years ago, so much loved still, still unreconciled to meaningless loss. A good-looking boy, younger than his years, an image still burning bright. "Time takes away the edge of grief. But memory turns back every leaf. We ponder what might have been." We don't forget; we move on from grief, always a metaphoric candle burning in perpetuity on the windowsill, waiting for what might have been to become what will be when we arrive home.

And Paul, May 9, 1980–October 22, 2002. Handsome, smiling, looking the camera full in the eye, this moment stretching out his whole life. We don't pose for our memorial photo. "Time may wipe out many things, but never the memory of the happy days when we were all together. Missing you every day, Paul." This is the elemental instinct for home. This is Edvard Munch's silent scream, not horror but connection, for the resolution of grief, for permanent home.

And inexplicably this: A few weeks later, the twenty-fifth anniversary of the death of, first, a young husband and a beloved father, January 12, 1989, and then the unspeakable, the death of a son and brother, same family, one month later, February, 15, 1989. "You gave us so much love and so much joy!" Twenty years ago, my wife Cara taught with Kathy, she being the wife to Peter and mother to Shawn, whose 25th anniversary of sudden death had arrived. Back then Cara admired Kathy's courage and determination to embrace life with a smile after the tragic, bizarre and unrelated deaths of her husband and son just weeks apart. To be able to continue living, to resist being pulled to the grave after the tragic death of our anchors in life, is only possible with faith. It is a truism that to truly live in advance of the inevitable fact of death requires that we accept death, and its equally inevitable passage back to life. The memorial from the paper expresses the truth of love, pain and joy undiminished by 25 years, undiminished by time, for all time.

After Kathy retired, she and Cara lost touch. Kathy and I met just once, about 20 years before, Cara and I recall on the same day the memorial is in the paper, as I put on my running shoes for my daily angst treatment. Then a strange sighting as I run, and I puzzle and deny until back home. Sitting, sweating, laboured breathing, pulling off running shoes, a question for Cara: "Near Brantwood park … a nice small stucco house on the corner, a middle-aged woman with red hair, she putting out the garbage, me a blur, the only way I know how to run … is it possible, *could this be your friend Kathy's house?"*

Yes, but how could you know?

Coincidence, I guess.

Once when I was grieving I talked to a priest. He had spent years working at a children's hospital, had faced the death of a child with families on many occasions. He asked if I had been with Mom when she had died. I had not. Towards the end, we siblings had tag-teamed to cover the 24-hour vigil, and she had died at night under Mike's watch. I never told Mike, but I was grateful that he had been there, had witnessed and could describe her last moments. For whatever reasons, I had been afraid, and Mike was not. I reminded myself that the holiest place on earth is where there has just been a birth or a death and that we should pay particular attention to these moments. I understood this but was afraid of it. Still, perhaps a gift, even if wrapped in bittersweetness. The trailing clouds of glory and our return home, the gift that that rips our heart out, seen only as such through faith.

Our exquisitely simple hunger for home is made impossibly complex by the way we live our distracted lives. Faced with death, most people naturally tend toward a common human response, even if they couldn't find it in their lives. A few, sadly, feel unloved, or unlovable, beyond redemption, or, worse, want to be right about their lifelong resistance to life after death. Seems to be taking righteousness a tad too far. People like Christopher Hitchens, good writer and brave guy, who was among those who maintain a sense of hubris unto death and was determined to face his obliteration without cracking. God love him, but it is defiance in the face of desperate fear. Still, most people gravitate towards loved ones, even if they have not loved well or feel unworthy of love. The instinct for home is just too strong to maintain a Hitchens-like defiance. Maybe capitulation is not weakness but, rather, closer to C. S. Lewis's final surrender: "I gave in, and admitted that God was God."

There is nothing original in what I am saying. The driving force for the archetypal longing to go home is love. Love is relationship; the ones we have and with faith will continue; the desire is for more, deeper, more complete, and everlasting. Elemental to all the great religions, though none so much as Christianity. Not the dogma and politics of religion as practiced by some— many, actually—but as in the Christ within us all. The simple exquisite truth of this is often reduced to a meaningless mocking cliché, far removed from reality.

One of the big lies perpetuated since the advent of the "me" generation of the 1960s is the horrible notion that what we think influences and creates truth—as if we determine truth rather than find it. For what it is worth, everything I think, everything I have written, every impulse towards faith comes wrapped in a blanket of doubt. But doubt is now my friend, because for all its power to make me insecure, at least I know I am alive. I doubt therefore I am ... not complacent. The best bumper sticker I ever saw was "Don't believe everything you think."

So nostalgia and faith are aligned, converging on a bittersweet, all-too-human longing for connection. All our regrets and fears, past and present, are about our need to go home and be together. Seems so natural, so logical, so right, so why do we complicate beauty and simplicity with angst and fear? Which is to ask, why are we human? Maybe best to accept that we are a heap of flaws, destined to never get it quite right, but that our best efforts are continuing to make efforts. Maybe life is process, however flawed, always trying to get there without even knowing where *there* is, with a little help from our friends.

People trying to shake an addiction tend to be discouraged by repeated failed attempts, until they realize that success is mostly a matter of not quitting attempts at quitting. Maybe it is the same for faith. Faith requires attention, training, effort and repeated failure, which is really just inevitable doubt, which is not failure at all. A little doubt, negative faith, all part of the process towards spiritual resiliency.

Success in life, education and career, in particular, is often ascribed to the very bright or truly lucky. But research shows that the greatest predictor of success is actually persistence. Personal spiritual resiliency is a direct result of gritty personal persistence. I am lazy. We are lazy. We want salvation without effort, certainty without contradiction, faith without doubt. Most of us want to forget. We are not home and cannot quell our need to go home; we have consciousness and cannot forget death.

Consciousness is our great gift but does not always feel that way. We live in fear, with the awareness of our demise, with consciousness a palpable reminder, the ticking clock edging towards our doom. Too often our great gift is associated with fear and denial without any compensating acknowledgement of the singularity of its existence, its existence compelling proof that we are more than of the physical world.

We have a voice inside our head that will not be quieted; we talk, talk, talk, but to whom? We talk inside our heads all day long—all night too; we call it thinking and think nothing more of it. But maybe, just maybe, we are not alone; maybe, our curse of consciousness is not a curse at all.

The conversation inside our head is less a monologue than a conversation. Point, counterpoint; argument, rebuttal. We are our lonely selves, and then there is *the other*. The other often expresses itself as conscience, an ally much out of favour in the modern world. Conscience limits our wants and desires, and in the age of unrestrained self-expression, this is regarded as a serious impediment.

But if the voice inside our head is something else, not just being ourselves times two, why does it exist? Maybe we have company, someone other than me, myself, and I. Maybe faith is present, and the *other* so easily dismissed is our immediate connection to divinity. It is a radical thought, and as I write these words, *the other* in my head doubts and thinks it silly, but writes nonetheless.

The best description I ever heard for consciousness is that maybe it is the universe watching itself. Maybe the universe is conscious of all things.

Still, I'd like to refine this description. Maybe consciousness is God talking to himself, or God talking to us, or us talking to God.

I remember years ago being in the company of a professor whose specialty was the human brain. I know nothing so asked innocently about the difference between the mind and the brain. He responded with a question: "What difference can there be?" I continued, without confidence, "Well, there is the functional brain, and then there is that part of us that goes beyond mere functional thinking—you know, consciousness." He looked at me without expression and responded from the functional brain, no doubt, "There is no difference."

I have no expertise with the brain, or anything else for that matter, but I know that experts often cannot see the forest for the trees, or the essence for the esoteric. I may know little, but I know the expert was wrong. Consciousness is more, far more, than simply the function of grey matter. Experts who categorically throw out the significance of consciousness, who regard it as containable and explainable, within the exclusive realm of science and the physical world, need to be able to explain the essence of Mozart's music, make-up sex, laughing, Michelangelo's *Pietà*, a parent's response to their baby's cry, Shakespeare, birth, a brush with death, looking into a loved one's eyes, a solution, desire, death, inspiration, false dawn, mist on a lake, a first kiss, the flight up the stairs to the room, church bells, memory, love, faith, home. Experts need to explain the inexplicable from my list, your list, even if equal parts cliché and profound ingredients of life that cannot be explained or explained away as mere components of the physical world. But experts pass on this exercise. It is not their area of expertise.

Even if we accept that consciousness is God talking to us, the objection remains that he (must be male) doesn't listen. This is, of course, the problem of pain and loss. Perhaps it's also the most compelling reason to deny God, challenge faith, and accounts for the justification for collective ennui, to live in the mind-numbing amnesia-driven force of modernity. Even for accepting souls, it is extremely difficult to come up with a thought or word about the inevitability of pain and loss in life that makes much sense or gives lasting satisfaction. Still, we accept all the blessings, good things that come our way, as a matter of course, even though we have no idea whence they came; but pain and loss throw us, every time. The miracle of life—duh, whatever; the inevitability of death—a personal affront. This view is understandable but not particularly logical.

What if the coming freight train of inevitable pain and loss for all humanity has meaning? Maybe our own sad facts, all parts, including their ending, can be reframed as the story of our lives that we must live so that we live. Before we throw away the concept as too self-serving and radical, it might be worth considering the singular nature of our existence. There is an increasingly common modern view that other and more advanced forms of life exist, likely in fantastical abundance, throughout the vastness of the universe. And if that is not enough, the concept of multiverse existence is taking hold, to both confound and dazzle with possibilities. True, very recent discoveries from the Hubbell spacecraft have forced us to recalibrate. There could be not billions but trillions of planets in the universe. So if trillions of planets, why not trillions of universes?

Proponents of the multiverse theory use a perverted notion of probability to argue that life on earth is no big deal and the chances are infinitesimally small of bigger, better life not existing elsewhere in the universe. Though Lawrence Krauss may say so (*A Universe from Nothing*), many other scientists have refuted and laymen, including Rogers and Hammerstein, know that *nothing comes from nothing, nothing ever could.*

Even if probability in the absence of proof is an argument, how about probability with proof? Life on earth—that life could ever congeal and thrive on earth—was and is extremely unlikely and, really, one might say impossible if not for the fact of life on earth. The anthropic principle says that the universe must be compatible with the conscious life that observes it. The principal is backed up by over 100 tangible, literally life-giving anthropic components that gave rise to and sustain life on earth, such as earth's exact distance from the sun, just the right temperature on the thin, fragile band surrounding the earth for us to be able to breath, etc. Same for the design of the world at the micro level with the composition of protons, neutrons and molecules. The information contained in the DNA of a single cell amoeba would fill dozens of encyclopedias. The common facts of life that we are immersed in every miraculous day are far more fantastical than any science fiction or multiverse speculation, which, even if true, doesn't change anything. The modern view takes for granted that these highly improbably components— which make our physical existence possible—come together with repeat performances throughout the multiverse, because—*don't you know*—nature just does that sort of thing, on its own for no particular reason. Time plus the misapplication of probability towards a multiverse theorem equals the certainty of life in ever more interesting and advanced forms. Look around at the beauty and complexity everywhere and conclude no intention required; just randomness and chaos behaving in fantastical patterns in the big picture over time. *Not.*

This fantastical assumption about laws and life simply coming into being has metastasized into popular culture as something to accept but never question. But I'll take the statistically more logical yet unproven and unpopular maverick view (I am my father's son) that human life is singular, we are alone in the universe, and we are here for a purpose. I say this knowing that to many moderns, my belief in the singularity of human life is proof of a great human conceit and, worse, evidence of being deplorably uncool.

Perhaps I know nothing and am being illogical. Logically thinking expert scientists know how foolish my views are. So it should be no surprise that 41 percent of US scientists reject supernatural beliefs or the notion of any higher power. Furthermore, 45 percent of scientists reject God, and that figure climbs to 72 percent for the accomplished members of the National Academy of Sciences. No surprise that the logical experts take the day.

But it is a surprise. If logic is the currency of science, why do we only have *only* 41 percent of scientists and 72 percent of the upper echelon who have ruled out the illogical belief in the existence of God? Because illogical as I am, that does logically mean that 59 percent of scientists and 28 percent of the top dogs are open to the possibility or even, subversive as it must be, belief in God. Maybe science and logic don't have all the answers, and there is room for the inclusion of other currency.

Reminds me of a chance—well, my perspective does question the notion of arbitrary chance, but I digress—meeting a few years ago. I was invited to a donor dinner thrown by a university in the great hall of the Canadian Museum of Civilization. I was seated beside Dr. Richard Teuscher, whose family had made a significant donation in the form of a scholarship for students with disabilities, to commemorate their son John. The parents were too distraught to attend, but their son Richard, John's older brother, was at the dinner to represent the family. Sadly, John, who had worked through adversity in dealing with his learning disability, was diagnosed with lymphoma and died just one year after graduation. A heartbreaking *life should never be* scenario.

We sat together in the great hall, feigning small talk that neither of us was much good at it. I learned he was a particle physicist from the University of Toronto and researcher at CERN, the European Organization for Nuclear Research, home for the world's largest and most powerful particle accelerator, extending for 17 miles beneath the France–Switzerland border. I had driven from Toronto the previous day and had listened to a book by Stephen Hawkins, *The Universe in a Nutshell*. I understood little of the concepts but just enough to ask a few borderline idiotic questions. Small talk over, we had a great conversation. Richard was patient, knowledgeable and deliberate and seemed to come from a distinctly unprofessorial place, less expert than informed enthusiast. So with my discretion filter suppressed by wine, I blurted out something like "I hope you don't mind, but your answers about the universe and science seem, well, open to the existence of God."

Discussions about the existence of God with those who fancy themselves intellectually superior tend not to go well. Experts chafe at subjects larger than themselves for which definitive proof may be lacking, for which expertise is irrelevant. But the existence of God is not an erroneous, theoretical debate; it is perhaps the central problem that we are all required to work out.

Richard laughed and then turned serious. He said that of course his brother's death had shaken him, and he could not help but examine his life and its meaning. But more important, his discipline of study made him confront the question of God's existence often from a scientific point of view, and he had concluded that science and God were not incompatible. So yes, he said he was open to belief in God, but only within the laws of science. Which uncovers an interesting divide on the question of God. Too often those of faith characterize God as above and beyond the confines of science; too often scientists use their allegiance to science as reason that God does not exist. But even with a superficial look at the universe—or superficial understanding, in my case—what jumps out is that known science itself is fantastical and weird as hell, let alone the truly weird stuff that we are only at the very periphery of discovering. All true scientists know that much is unknown, much more unknowable.

Most scientists don't like the word *unknowable*. The function of science is to discover until we know all. But there are limits. Try getting your head around the fact that there are trillions of stars and planets. Think about the passing of millions of years between the emitting of light from a star and the moment of it being seen by the human eye. Contemplate an expanding universe over 13 billion light years wide and then the filterless little boy in me still plaguing me with *But what is on the other side once you get to the end?*

So is a miracle the manipulation of time and matter in fantastical ways that would challenge the best and most technological advanced Hollywood special effects studio, or is it waking from the dream of our everyday lives and seeing the world differently? The idea of the common miracle is not new. Same for the much-maligned concept of intelligent design, most often dismissed as Christian propaganda instead of examined for evidence of God's design in science. For all that science can do, it can't explain fundamentally most of the everyday phenomena of our world, of our lives. Science can construct a label and find a reasonable explanation for what and when, but less often how and never why. And science will not catch up, achieve mastery, explain the unexplainable. Which is not a knock on science.

For example, science cannot actually explain why a flower is beautiful. There is no scientific reason; it defies reason. A heart surgeon can tell you how the heart works but cannot answer why it beats. There is no known mechanism to fundamentally answer this question. At the molecular level atoms are 99.999 percent space and have no mass, and yet we knock on wood, claiming the world to be entirely physical with our flawed human logic.

Theoretical physicists Peter Higgs and Francois Englert shared the Nobel Prize in physics for independently coming up with a theory about how the building blocks of the universe form the mass of everything around us. The theory is that a subatomic particle called the Higgs boson, or God particle, in layman terms, forms all things around us, provides the cohesion for matter to exist among atoms that otherwise have no matter. The theory was proven at CERN, the world's biggest atom smasher in Geneva, the same facility where Dr. Richard Teuscher does his research. Some people see the CERN results as proof that science rules, and with empirical evidence in hand, they feel emboldened to say it is no God particle; it is not God. But I think this is a great example of the coexistence between science and spirituality that is confounded by people who want to reduce everything to what can be empirically explained. Why can't the subatomic particle be both the Higgs boson and the God particle? Why must there be a demarcation between science and God? Why does the breathtaking harmony of the universe conflict with the notion of God? Given the absence of why or how, just who keeps everything in working order? There are reasonable explanations for the harmony of the universe; the harmony of the universe defies reason.

One of the frustrating things about having a debate about the existence of God with someone with a modicum of knowledge about science, which I clearly do not have, is that they have a tendency to bombard you with explanations about the laws of physics, the properties of atoms and chemical compounds, the Big Bang theory and the like. In other words, there is a perfectly logical explanation for everything, and ignorance of science is mostly why people herd towards the delusion of God. Dr. Teuscher, with advanced knowledge of science, did not do this, because knowing much, he is nakedly aware of knowing little. So I prostrate myself in deference to all with knowledge of science great and small but press on and ask, from where did all matter come with its properties that then became ordered by laws of physics? Who gave chemicals their makeup? Who wound up the universe so that it could bang? And given the unlikeness and complexity of these phenomena, why? Discussion of this nature often ends with science types noting the complexity of science and that you can't possibly understand. True enough.

Still, why is complexity exclusively the domain of science? The notion that God works in mysterious ways likely has some complexity too. I love the God particle concept—now a proven phenomenon—precisely because it takes a fundamental building block of the universe and provides an answer that is equally suspended between rational scientific and mysterious Godlike. The cohesion of matter that we have all taken for granted, except for a few theoretical physicists, has a scientific basis, as do all phenomena in the universe, but somewhere in the subatomic world of the Higgs boson is God's fingerprint. Sure, dissect and study it and all to death, but don't forget to step back and give credit where credit is due.

No one can explain the power of prayer, though we know that the collective intention of a group of people can influence outcome. There is quantum weirdness, which is that observed particles behave differently than unobserved ones. And quantum entanglement, which is that related particles react in similar or opposite ways even when separated by great distances. Physics, once a particularly secular science, has had a number of prominent scientists declare that what they see cannot be explained by science. This is not simply saying that we will know everything once we get to it but acknowledges that another power has to be.

Everything in the world has gone digital. People have thrown out their old vinyl records and cassette tapes, and video stores that rose up like a tropic storm went extinct like dinosaurs, all within a decade or so. People are sometimes nostalgic for the old technologies, especially vinyl records, for their authenticity mostly, but it is hard to fault the quality of images and sounds from digital recordings. Think about it: the most exquisite, dense and colourful image ever captured, or the most perfect operatic note ever sung, is reproduced in digital format. We take for granted that this perfection, which defies understanding for its beauty and mystery, can be seen or heard whenever we want. And what is digital but a series of zeros and ones, arranged in patterns that constitute a computer code that is delivered as said beauty and mystery? This is the simple fact of science. Science can explain how it is done but cannot not explain how it is possible. The facts, easy; the essence, unfathomable. We live a life where we can literally be surrounded by the most beautiful sounds and images of our perpetual choosing because of an arrangement of zeros and ones, and we accept this as nothing out of the ordinary. Sitting comfortably and compatibly behind the science lies a greater truth, miracles great and small.

And then there is the exquisitely absurdly, unlikely reality of life on earth. The convergence of near impossible factors, working in harmony to produce conditions for a multiplicity of living cells to thrive and layer and flourish into ever new intricate changing patterns, such that water life crawls onto the land, land life flies into the air, and human life sits under stars thinking back to when starlight began and forward to life's transformation beyond the physical world, and why. All in good time.

Consciousness evolves, is a creature of science and God, is a thing apart, in harmony without contradiction. As such, it should be our beacon for us all to bridge the gap between science and God, between the physical and spiritual world. But rather than using consciousness as the world's most powerful telescope, searching into the vastness of the universe, we most often regard it as a microscope, looking inward, focusing small, thinking that what it sees is what there is, all there is, so that the minutiae and trivial details of our life become our truth, and the expansive reality of consciousness is denied.

We live small lives, mostly to keep from thinking about the overwhelming questions, to keep from having to live what we dimly suspect might be true. It makes sense on some level to participate in the world on a small level as a means of achieving normalcy. But living in a small world in order to survive and thrive doesn't mean it is small; it is simply the facade we all agree to adopt in order to be able to cope. It is our collective conspiracy of plausible deniability, and as long as we all agree to sign on to the fiction, we don't have to be burdened by the issue of plausibility.

Coping is good, living in the moment is peaceful, and denial, well, perhaps neither good nor bad but not necessarily a formula for an authentic life of discovery. Suspending our disbelief so we can cope is living life as if watching a movie: entertaining, scary at times, always in our control, and easy to turn off if we don't like it. Relegating the world to a compilation of what our immediate senses tell us, trying to derive happiness from the fulfillment of wants and desires, denying death and the inherent life that matters, are the modern world's equivalent to driving a spike through the heart of a vampire. Faith has been killed off or is dying in many aspects of modern life, and for those who still yearn for faith—that is, fidelity to a connection with people, a mystical inner life with a notion of returning home to God—what was commonplace and conventional a mere generation ago has become subversive and radical.

And it's no wonder. The modern world does not encourage a spiritual life, even if people, among them atheists, often talk about being spiritual. Perhaps this is why the claim typically is qualified with "But I won't have anything to do with religion." Okay, I ask, how does that look? "Well, I paddle down a river, and you can never paddle the same river twice, and that's spiritual." I am not going to say that paddling a river is not spiritual, but I submit that an authentic life requires more than passive commentary on your favourite activity. People are attached to the idea of themselves as mysterious and interesting, and adopting a faux spiritual chic persona has that certain *je ne sais quoi*.

In my feeble brain, lighting and keeping the embers of a spiritual life alive require more than what we think, feel, can control or are attached to. Authentic spiritually, which is what we submit to rather than control, will be wherever the hell the stumbling search leads, and as such, we don't know in advance where it will lead. And that is precisely the point. If it is not uncomfortable much of the time, it ain't happening.

There is much to be said for contemplation, silence and meditation, though I seem fairly incapable of these practices and their subsequent virtues. The perspective of dispassionate distance is important, but spiritual connection ultimately requires human connection. Whatever roll of the dice we are given and however much gratitude or grievance we bring to the equation, we will see and feel great pain in others, if we are fortunate enough to care. The irony of connection—that is our salvation—is that it is also painful. The saying that we are only as happy as the unhappiest of our children finally extends to whomever God places in our path, eventually including strangers far removed from our familiar, well-worn path. The pain and necessity of spiritual connection intensifies as we translate the intention to become our higher selves into action. Much, much easier to take on a very public secular cause and feel good about ourselves, even as we remain unaffected, our higher selves unrecognizable even, or especially, to ourselves.

We can't be immobilized by the pain of the world, but, equally so, we can't pretend that our wants and desires have to be satisfied before we become spiritual. It seems to me that we have to suspend our preconditions, admit we don't know the way forward, be open to mystery and have a deep sense that there is more to life than the surface most of us balance on, most of the time. No one is going to make the deathbed confession "I wish I'd consumed more!" I suspect many people feel a gnawing hollowness living in a world without an overt outlet for faith. We feel displaced from ourselves without knowing why. Waking up and shaking off our deep collective slumber of the past few decades with a little mystery, discomfort and curiosity may be a good place to begin seeking an authentic life.

Looking back at my parents' life and the boomer generation that displaced these Depression and Second World War graduates, I think there exists a discernible spiritual demarcation line. Economic prosperity, rock and roll, drugs and the advent of the "me" generation were all regarded as great leaps forward towards the liberation of people from the oppression of religion, country and meaningless institutions—in short, subservience to the man. When John F. Kennedy famously said, "Ask not what your country can do for you—ask what you can do for your country," he was the last Western leader who could get away with placing fidelity to country above self. Leaders still pay lip service to this notion, but progressive thinking has taken hold with corresponding individual ennui and spiritual devolution.

With the erosion of the family and indoctrination in schools, kids conform to ideological causes in the guise of morality rather than being allowed to explore and develop personal and shared values. We educate kids today to compete for caring causes rather than to critically look at an issue and dispassionately consider the correct course of action. Ideological causes, which are notorious for subverting individual scrutiny, assume that thinking is done by those who know best and care most. If personal values come into it, they compete with the social conformity model, and the expectation today in classrooms and in polite company is that there will be no discussion or critical thought or debate when the buzzwords are *social justice, animal rights, inclusion, all things green, multiculturalism, diversity* and the like. People tend to nod their heads in silent assent to a complacent collective agenda without having much faith in what they are agreeing to.

A theme in my life, and hopefully reflected in these pages, is my belief that faith and complacency are antithetical. Complacency today is so prevalent as to be hardly noticed, which is to accept and live life in mind-numbing fear of death, which is, I guess, the desired effect. When people or, worse, classrooms and whole schools are roped into adopting causes they know and care nothing about, they may feel temporarily good about themselves for participating, but without personal commitment, faith dies. The fact is, causes are not supposed to be about the self-esteem of the people adopting them. Faith is difficult because it requires the deliberate and passionate repudiation of the demystified world and the unexamined life. Faith requires distance between what you know and the common perspective of modernity.

The numbness or ennui of modern life is understandable, to a point. Facing our obligation to those God places in our path, placing limits or even denying wants and desires, confronting or in rare instances even embracing the reality of death, all take great effort and may be difficult to face, especially without a modicum of faith. Much easier to participate in the common fiction that the world as we see it is all there is, that the height of human expression is to be satisfied by others, that death is for everyone else, or, worse, that the demise of everyone we have ever loved is easy to accept because it has no meaning. My dad, the maverick—who secretly doubted without crediting himself for practicing healthy skepticism, which is the hallmark of faith—is always on my mind as I confront the clever atheists.

But Dad was not clever. That is, in a supposedly dispassionate argument about something, Dad never mistook himself for the something. Northrop Frye, the world's greatest intellect, was not clever. His moment of humility and insight while simultaneously realizing the failure of intellect and the vulnerability of self did not make him clever. That his faith was negative, subject to perpetual doubt, does not cheapen or lesson the power of his revelation. Angels did not appear, the darkened sky did not split open, but to this perpetually doubting sinner, the admission of negative faith is all the more compelling for its simplicity and doubt, especially from a lifetime academic unprepared for unacademic life. Fifty years as the world's greatest intellect did nothing for his soul; 50 years as an ordained minister did nothing for his spirit; 50 years as a husband did nothing for his appreciation of his soulmate—until he lost her, and nothing was ever the same again. The world's greatest intellect subject to the world's simplest lesson, a lesson in humility: value what you have because you will lose it; don't value what you have, and you will lose your soul. But he did learn to appreciate the enormity of his loss, all the more so because he came to believe that her essence was beyond the physical world, and as such it became his reason to believe. Blessed be the unclever, for they shall inherit their home.

Richard Dawkins is clever. Dawkins knows what cannot be known, that God does not exist, and he has millions of adherents to prove it. His main target is Christianity, with the utter destruction of all religion and faith thrown in for good measure. More than anyone else, Richard Dawkins represents the face of the new religion, elevating himself to a pope-like figure for atheism. He would not enjoy the irony of this comparison. (Sidebar: Two atheists go door to door handing out pamphlets. A man opens the door, takes the offered pamphlet, looks at it and says, "But these pages are blank!" One of the atheists answers, "That's because we don't believe in anything.")

As a clever man, Dawkins likely regards himself as someone who does not suffer fools, or unclever people, like Northrop Frye and my dad. You can hear the irritation in his voice, as I did recently in an interview. Though unequivocal and supremely confident in his views, on this day Dawkins was being seriously challenged by an interviewer who was unimpressed by his logic and wisdom and insisted that in the absence of definitive proof, God and an afterlife *could* exist. Dawkins had had enough. Abandoning his reasoned, controlled style, he responded with tantrum-like sharpness, "Well if there is an afterlife, it is nothing like people could ever imagine!" Exactly, and thank you, Mr. Dawkins. Mystery is by definition that which people cannot imagine, what cannot be known, and this is what religion actually says, and what unclever people of faith believe. Dawkins cannot get over himself, cannot get over having to be the one who knows, whereas people of faith yearn for it to exist and don't sweat the details of what *it* is.

The shockingly simple thing is this: it doesn't actually matter what Dawkins or any one of us thinks. Thinking will not make it so. It either is or isn't. Our job in life is not to try to influence outcome, unless we are seriously into pursuing fool's errands. Maybe in our unclever state of unknowing, we are supposed to suspend ourselves and listen, look, laugh, contemplate, consider, love, reconsider, hope, forgive, ask, and sit alone in a room. Maybe revelation is as simple as looking into the eyes of a loved one you've seen a thousand times and seeing them for the first time. Maybe, the point of relationships and life is seeing and being seen for who we are.

This changes, well, precisely everything. If it *isn't*, then we need to drown ourselves in sex, drugs and alcohol just to make it to the next day, a day closer to fast-charging annihilation. If it *is*, everything is meaningful, and we might want to give some active consideration as to how we are doing. Are we driven by curiosity, passion, and connection or are we creatures of resentment, anger and attachment? We are uncomfortable with the notion of judgment today, but we will be judged by the harshest critic: ourselves.

So how is it that people don't seem haunted by the question, is there God or not? Life or oblivion aren't just mildly differing endings. Maybe it is because in modern life, a third option has emerged. Increasingly, there seems to be a view that our musings on the existence of God are misplaced. Dwelling on the thorny question of is or isn't is too complicated, restrictive and painful. A New Age paradigm shifts spirituality from God to progressive human development. Funny use of the word *progressive* these days. Much is made of things progressive, always with an assumption that the coupling of the word with any cause or event means it is good, and its absence means it is old and out of step, unpopular, not chic—in short, bad. But this is based on a shaky assumption that history progresses, that is, always upward, higher, stronger, faster, better.

Parenthetically, I wrote the last paragraph sitting in the old section of Innsbruck, Austria. Looking up, I see an impressive 500-year-old stone archway, a majestic belfry tower, with incredibly detailed and ornate plaster on the corners and around the windows and weathered wooden flower baskets. All of the ancient and exquisite architecture is centred in a cobblestoned square, where people have gathered for hundreds of years and are still drawn. We have never built cities like this in North America; they no longer build cities like this in Europe. There are reasons, economics mostly, but the fact is, we lost the capacity, will and skill to pull it off decades ago. Looking upward and around, sipping on good Austrian beer, I cannot help but think, something has been lost, something profound, hardly noticed, never acknowledged, but lost, utterly lost.

If the past is to be relinquished for the great unfolding progressive future, is it any wonder that there is a progressive answer to the dilemma *it is or isn't?* The progressive view holds that humans are on the ascendancy and with time will solve the thorny questions of death and meaning. Spirituality is what you make it—a river, yoga, a Pilates workout, a forest, protesting against people who wear furs, whatever one fancies at the smorgasbord of social causes and virtue-signalling. No religion, no spirituality as relates to God, no hunger for home, just me, myself and ever so progressive I.

Increasingly confronted with progressive arguments I occasionally ask, is self enough? And sadly, people more often than not answer yes. My reaction is a profound mixture of bewilderment and gratitude. Bewilderment because in my perpetual state of nerves, nostalgia, sin and angst, I can barely imagine my humanity, let alone my sense of divinity. Gratitude because in my pathetic and flawed quest for faith, third-option atheists validate my assumptions about the delusions of man. We live our lives, in the full knowledge of death, as if we will live forever, or worse, with the third option that death can be averted by a belief system that insulates against the curse of consciousness with the comforting cool moss of a forest floor. I am grateful because standing in the great St. Stephen's Cathedral days ago in Vienna, filled with doubts about faith as I always am, at least I know that on balance I am not deluded into thinking that this world, this life and the purpose of it is about me. If the exercise of searching for faith is only to be and stay outside of self, that is something.

Being outside of self, there is meaning in others. Being with and about others, there is meaning in relationships. Being concerned with relationships, there is meaning in love. Being concerned with love, we can contemplate, believe and have faith in going home.

"Every happening, great and small, is a parable whereby God speaks to us, and the art of life is to get the message."

MALCOLM MUGGERIDGE

# CHAPTER FOURTEEN
## GOING HOME

DAY BY DAY, MINUTE BY MINUTE, THERE ARE THINGS GREAT AND SMALL THAT CAN and will shake faith to the core, if you are lucky enough to have a core. I'm sitting in a Prague café, notebook open, the opening sentence of this section bared to the world, when a large splat erupts, and a mass of green bird crap covers the entire page. Waitresses in white linen scurry with fresh towels, apologizing for my besmirched writing book and soiled shirt. Two stories up, the offending pigeon sits unapologetically, unimpressed and with the stoic demeanour of one who might create another volcano if the movement moves him. What does crap on my notebook say about my faith-writing pretensions? I find myself briefly hoping that things don't happen for a reason. But the moment and the crap session pass, from both the bird and my soiled pages.

Back to the terminal problem of pain and suffering that I am compelled to suffer through that will not satisfy adherents of the wholly material world. We suffer, those we love suffer, everyone suffers, some horribly, unevenly, seemingly without purpose or pattern. Then, in all manner, we die and are forever dead. A tough gig to argue for faith. And it is so much easier to argue against faith from the material mindset. There is logic to the faith argument, but it is perhaps less compelling than the absence-of-proof condemnation from atheists. Advantage atheists, unless the thought of complete annihilation is disturbing, in which case faith has life.

Modernity's seductive cultivation of the ego has overpromised and underdelivered. Fifty years after the advent of the "me" generation, with the primacy of self and the continuing machinations of the self-esteem industry intact, the world is far more attuned to the voice of atheists than to the meek whimper of faith adherents of any stripe. Advantage atheists.

Of course there is that little detail about the state of the world. With unprecedented affluence, choice and freedom in a guilt-free world, people are unhappy. Young people, surely humanity's canary in the mineshaft, are unhappy and suffering mental stress and illness as never before.

Never. Not during the Depression, not during the Great Wars, not while struggling with deprivations and hardships of immigrant and refugee resettlement. In recent years, anxiety has displaced depression as the number-one mental health concern. One rather compelling example: in 2016, the American Health Association found that 62 percent of undergraduates reported "overwhelming anxiety," up from 50 percent in 2011. This lower 2011 figure is actually disturbingly high, compared to indicators in the recent past. This picture does not add up based on material world indicators of what should make us happy. People are unhappy and disconnected despite having everything at their disposal, because of a pervasive hollow ache that will not go away. Not deprivations, not restrictions, just a deep sense that something is, for all that there is, lacking. I feel, therefore I am unhappy. Advantage faith, unless seriously dedicated to material world pain.

It is disturbing to behold the myriad of distractions that flood into the wake of what once was the domain of God, religion and spirituality. Sadly, the vacuum is not full yet. The absence of God leaves a big hole, and the secular distractions are many, varied, can be quite seductive and sophisticated but are distractions nonetheless. On this day in Prague I pondered an article that says it all: "Inside the Cult of Lululemon." Despite the look of adoration in the eyes of adherents as they talk about the super spiritual qualities of their clothes, Lululemon is a business, with a highly successful business plan, revenues going from 40.7 million in 2004 to 1.37 billion in 2012. The article has a photo of 1,000 people on the beach doing yoga and warrior poses, with compliment-ary yoga mats from Lululemon and shopping bags adorned with "Have you woken up two days in a row uninspired? Change your life!" Then a comment on the bag from a Lulu representative: "That is super inspirational to people. It inspires the way they live their life. It's about being healthy and living a great life." From Laura Klauberg, V.P. of global brand and community, the bottom line: "It's the clothes, but it's more than the clothes. It's a *lifestyle brand,* and the clothes are the catalyst to changing people's lives."

The great religions have always cultivated art, architecture, music, garments and icons that reflect historical and cultural contributions and provide context for individual expression and, yes, sometimes oppression. But never has the message been that the icons are the objects of our homage. Art and architecture have never been more than a means to an end, that end being God. There are those, many actually, for whom spirituality is a lifestyle brand and, worse, who are able to sustain the illusion throughout their lives.

For anyone with any religious foundation, it is easy to dismiss Lululemon and other lifestyle brand pretenders as an unlikely "catalyst to changing people's lives." But sadly, the majority of young people do not have context with which to judge religious conviction, and we should not underestimate people's profound need for their spiritual vessel to be filled. If distracted from the hunger for home by the "super inspirational," people will pour their heart and soul into something, anything, until their disillusionment leads to another distraction. People will take the *super inspirational* path well-travelled when life is good and they are able to exercise the illusion of control, but real spiritual transformation requires the twin virtues of humility and surrender in the face of inevitable pain and strife.

Of course not all people reared in the Lululemon lifestyle paradigm confuse their desire for lifestyle with their need for spirituality. There is nothing intrinsically wrong with tight workout clothes with seaweed fibres, yoga or warrior poses. Still, attempting to extract spiritual meaning from clever branding is worrying. When the Lulu super inspirational reign of power is over, the next lifestyle choice will feel and end the same. If we have everything and we feel emptier than ever, maybe, just maybe, the answer is not about me and my many distractions.

Ultimately, faith is not an argument; it is a feeling. It is not a frivolous feeling; rather it is a kind of disturbance, deep-seated and unsettling. This is not a concession to feeling, and I think the logic of faith arguments are stronger than argument of non-consequence from the nihilistic majority. The world, the universe, the collision of seemingly arbitrary matter in unimaginable proportions into precise laws and the singularity of life are not just atoms doing their thing over time; the spiritual hunger that we feel, are privileged among species to experience and to know in our gut, is not just so much subjective noise. Our observation of and incessant wonder at beauty are not misplaced. Beauty comes from somewhere, does not appear from nowhere. Still, as I write this I am not comfortable concluding that the bottom line for deciding *it is or isn't* is a feeling. Ouch. I've argued against the unbridled capitulation to feeling, as indicative of what is wrong with much in the material world. By feeling I don't mean emoting, reacting, or fulfilling appetites. Authentic feelings about faith are forged over time, likely with some pain, or at least some discomfort, wrestling though the vicissitudes and contradictions of an examined life.

Sifting through all the complexities, worldly debris and ocean of possibility of modern life, we are left with a choice. Well, we can always defer choice and choose to anesthetize ourselves with distractions, addictions, frivolity and stupefying numbness, wilfully choosing the unexamined life that is close to death, the annihilated life from which few return.

But for the rest of us, God either is or isn't. When Dawkins quipped, "Well, if there is an afterlife, it won't be anything you can imagine," he inadvertently opened the possibility of unlimited possibilities. What can't be imagined cannot logically be denied. Sorry, Richard, your argument weakened at the moment feeling stirred and anger crept in. Though we cannot easily escape what we feel, our feelings are not necessarily the immediate consequence of our wants and desires. Feelings of substance are the result of lifetime ponderings with the application of curiosity, consciousness and logic, leading to the potential for elevating the existence of God into a self-evident truth. It is the feeling of conviction to the core, rather than the common use of the word to denote being ping-ponged between feeling good and bad in the absence of a core.

I think God is, and because God is, miracles are the hourly, daily, mainstream of our existence. I also think that the world as it exists to most people doesn't make sense. Such thoughts pervade my consciousness, my dreams and occasionally my logic. If nothing makes sense, then anything makes no less sense.

Some years ago I was talking to a friend. She was not a close friend; it was not a memorable moment. Then she started talking about her mother, who had recently died. Her mother had suffered for weeks with advanced cancer, with pain a constant, unrelenting force. Then my friend said something that resonated with me, and still does. She said that for those who suffer greatly, maybe their pain is of their own choosing, which I interpreted as meaning choosing of the soul, since the deeply subjective body immersed in pain will never choose it. Parenthetically, days later when I asked her to elaborate on this concept, she could not remember what she had said. Perhaps proof that profound thoughts come in a variety of banal, innocuous packages.

Christianity is based on and often criticized for its emphasis on sacrifice. Resurrection in atonement for our sins is why Christianity exists, and despite the rise of secularism in the modern Western world, it has been remarkably robust and resilient for two thousand years. Christianity is singular among religions for its emphasis on forgiveness and redemption, not because we deserve to be forgiven and redeemed but because of the notion of sacrifice.

People without a religious foundation increasingly have a problem identifying abstract Christian concepts of forgiveness and sacrifice, though the same people identify strongly with tangible examples evident every day in their lives. If God is not, why would anyone ever sacrifice anything for anyone? This is not an abstract question. People, and often people who do not identify with having any religious belief or who profess an active disbelief in God, make sacrifices that do not jive with the self-interested secular animal. Soldiers in war, mothers with children in danger and people who discover strangers needing an organ transplant make sacrifices without question, without concern for self, without hesitation in the face of their inevitable obliteration. If God isn't, if Christianity is not, if survival and self-interest rule, the question is, why sacrifice? Why?

Most people know the liberating freedom of forgiveness. Ancient hatreds are never about what was originally contested but about entrenched views and scapegoating of those who have become the enemy. And though we may forgive because we are willing to move past that which another has done to us, forgiveness has more to do with liberating oneself from the prison of recrimination than with the person who has offended. To forgive is divine and, more to the point, necessary to save ourselves. We know this and recognize scenarios played out everywhere, every day of our lives. Maybe the Christian concepts of sacrifice and forgiveness are not archaic and irrelevant today. Maybe God is, and that is why we are.

So redemption is based on sacrifice, that is, the repayment of debt, and not our sparkling personalities. There is of course free will, but if Jesus was sacrificed for our sins, it follows that man is not capable of redemption on his own. Maybe the Christian concept of sacrifice is paralleled by the possibility of redemptive sacrifice by the soul. Though for many there will never be a satisfactory answer to the inevitability of pain and suffering, perhaps our souls—separate from our free will as individuals—have the potential to choose a disproportionate burden of suffering as a sacrifice for the rest of us. Outrageous as this proposition is in the material world, the prospect of arbitrary pain and suffering is more outrageous.

I have always resisted the belief that people who suffer greatly must be on some level, or in some other life, responsible for their own fate. People talk easily about karma in this way as a kind of social justice in perpetuity, without looking too deeply into what this might look like. In *Night*, Elie Wiesel writes of witnessing children being thrown alive into burning fire pits by the Nazis. These children had not yet started their life, were not responsible for it, and certainly were not responsible for another life lived before they got to the one just forfeited. The concept of a repayment plan for previous lives lived has troubled me my whole life. Every twitch and tick of my angst-ridden being says it is wrong.

I've worked with persons with disabilities for 30 years, and it cannot be that disability is a reflection of what one did in a former life. For many, disability has given perspective and a dose of reality, making them far less likely to be pulled into the hollow vortex of the modern world. The experience of adversity, the development of resiliency and the perspective of humility can help assuage, or at least give meaning to, suffering. Generally people suffer more from the loneliness of stigma than the actual condition, but the point is, what happens in life is less important than how we deal with it. Life is uneven and unfair, but in the final analysis not entirely, or perhaps even primarily, outside of our control. Maybe life is more than the limited sample before our eyes and in which we live.

Choosing to be a holy sacrifice is a choice that few of us as individuals would ever make. Perhaps the vague notion of *higher self* has specific meaning. Our higher selves are what we strive to become, even if with all our human weakness we most often fall short. There is grace and there is sacrifice, and our debts will be paid, if not by ourselves then by others whose higher self has been achieved. Before rejecting the radical notion of the soul's choosing, consider for one minute the world as it is, and ask yourself what better explains the human dilemma of pain and suffering. What?

If Dawkins can allow the world of possibility to creep into his atheist world of containment, then the concept of the soul's choosing is no less likely than our mind-numbing sheep-to-slaughter acceptance of loss and pain as the inevitable ticking down towards doom and gloom and death. And I humbly submit, it is far, far more satisfying. Maybe we are more than our failing bodies and broken hearts. Maybe time is not the final arbiter.

We believe that time is of the essence. Time separates us from our loved ones and ourselves; it is why we regret, are depressed and become anxious. The question of time is better stated as the problem of time. We are obsessed with time, and for good reason: in time it is going to kill us. Time is loss. Time is death.

The problem of time is that it is fixed and cannot be altered. Which is apparently why we dream up the absurdities of heaven and eternity, world without end. If Hitchens and Dawkins are to be believed, these fantasy states are merely our pathetic psychological crutches, dreamt up to get us from one regretful angst-ridden day to the next.

So we obsess over exactness of time. In the Olympics, sprint races were traditionally measured by hundredths of a second, but once a tie occurred they began to measure by thousandths of a second. We split and order time but still cannot alter it. At least, this is the assumption of our ordered lives.

In modern life, there is a movement to increase the value of time. We all know that we regret the past, are anxious over the future and don't spend enough time in the present. So the new mantra is to savour the present, to always stay in the moment and not stray back to unpleasant events that have passed and cannot be changed, and certainly not to unpleasant events that will come to pass. When we're always in the present, past and future dissolve into unnatural, unprogressive constructs of the human mind. Mindfulness books and workshops, the psychology of the here and now, are just one example of the many ways in which new progressive secular movements are supplanting religion. And it's no wonder; modern movements don't agonize over unpleasantness, death, conscience and consequence. Besides, with the right workout clothes, they can be super inspirational.

The problem is that the religion of non-consequence has consequences. Though there is nothing wrong with appreciating the present moment, mindfulness does not address our spiritual needs. Learning to dwell on the intake of your breath and appreciate the smell of flowers and the feel of the chair on your backside is fine, but presence without context or meaning is still a prelude to death; even if fixed on the workshop moment, it screams probable deniability. Workshops cannot disabuse us of what we know in our souls. Chicken soup does not actually help the soul.

For years I've had this vague, undefined and prevalent thought about time. It's a dumb thought, not for polite company, so read on. Though dumb, it is no more than much of what we accept as conventional wisdom. It started when I read that time—constant, immutable time—may, according to theoretical physicists, be mutable; that is, it may be possible to change time, or perhaps our rigid notions of linear ordered time may not be quite what we assume, live for and die by. Certainly, Einstein, no slouch in his musings about time, felt that sequential time was only fixed in our assumptions. He wrote, "Now he has departed from this strange world a little ahead of me. That means nothing. People like us, who believe in physics, know the distinction between past, present and future is only a stubbornly persistent illusion." Even more powerful, physicists Albert Einstein and Erwin Schrodinger are both credited with talking about the "dethronement of time as a rigid tyrant." So the door of possibility is open.

Fundamentally, I think that faith is about connection and relationship with God and family, the ones that matter. Time, at least the version we live with, is the great disconnect between ourselves and others, those we have loved who are gone, those we have never known. But what if one of the mysteries that will be revealed is that sequential time, which separates us from ourselves and others, will be repealed for perpetual time, which connects and makes one?

In *My Bright Abyss*, a poignant book on faith, Christian Wiman is confronted with a diagnosis, a death sentence, on his 39th birthday, and rather than experience mindfulness in the extreme as is expected of him, "not only was the world not intensified, it was palpably attenuated, because remove futurity from experience and you leach meaning from it just as surely as if you cut out a man's past."

He, with his intensity and insight, and me, with my nostalgia and angst, share a need and a timeless faith, as do all others who yearn for connection and reconnection without the constraints of time. "And if we can live out of time in our daily lives indeed, if apprehending and inhabiting our daily lives *demands* that we in some imaginative sense live out of time—then is it a stretch to imagine the fruition of existence as being altogether outside of time?"

If God is, if afterlife is, they are nothing that can be imagined (thank you, Mr. Dawkins). We can live with deep ambiguity, not knowing what, how or when, as long as we have faith that it is. And if God is, then love continues in perpetuity, was never broken, and the arch-enemy time no longer holds sway. Angst-ridden seculars clinging to the moment, ever mindful of coming death, as well as sentimental fools ever looking backward for those who have gone will continue their fear and foolishness in vain.

My relationship with my parents has changed over the years. Time has changed us. My sense of nostalgia has not lessened; in fact, I'm ashamed to admit, it has grown. I'm now older than my dad was when he died. We should all meet and get to know our parents as equals, that is, around the same age. That would change our relationship, clarify and clear up misunderstandings. My dad died over 35 years ago and missed getting to know any of his grandchildren. He was a decent, if distant, father but would have been a better—no, fantastic—grandfather. It is a role he was made for. I know because we talk, and our relationship is better now. We were fine before he died, but we did not talk much. Couldn't really, but not for lack of feeling. Now we talk all the time, even if few words are exchanged. There is still plenty of time.

———————

Mom pulls the plastic cap off her half-consumed bottle of porter. We are watching TV together, Carol Burnett and Harvey Korman. She sips the black liquid, a half bottle lasting the whole show. She still doesn't like it much but drinks the requisite amount on doctor's orders.

"Will you come to church with me tomorrow?" she asks beseechingly.

This is something I've not done often enough; not sure why, but I just haven't much, much as I'd done much else with her while she was alive.

"Sure."

"Really?"

"Promise."

"And then can we go to the restaurant for breakfast?"

"Sure."

"Is it okay if Archie comes too? He'll expect to, you know."

"I wouldn't have it any other way."

"Because if it's not okay, I'd still like you and I to go to church."

"It's fine, Mom. I like Archie."

Mom seems satisfied and uncharacteristically reaches out and grabs my hand. But then she sighs, and her expression changes, becomes strangely flat, as if bracing for a difficult task. Her voice is unsure; she feels her words before they become certain. "I didn't pick you up or play with you enough."

"Excuse me?"

"When you were a little boy."

I laugh. "Well, I might be a tad much for you now, but if it helps, gimme a lift."

Mom rarely ignores my jokes. "I never had time, but that really wasn't it. I just don't know."

"I don't know what you're talking about; you were always a great mom."

"I don't know what made me think of that just now."

Trembling, she knocks over the near-empty bottle of porter. We watch as a few dark drops soak into and stain the white tablecloth. She is annoyed at herself for her clumsiness, and her eyes tear up.

"It's okay, Mom." Inexplicably, I feel like crying too, but we both know it's only a few drops of spilt porter.

"I know," she says, "It's just that..." She is starting to fade.

"It's not time yet," I try to say, but she is gone. For now.

*"The Child is father of the Man:*
*And I could wish my days to be*
*Bound to each by natural piety."*

WILLIAM WORDSWORTH, "ODE: INTIMATIONS OF IMMORTALITY
FROM RECOLLECTIONS OF EARLY CHILDHOOD"

# AFTERWORD
## THE END IS THE BEGINNING

I'VE BEEN EDITING, NITPICKING MOSTLY THESE WEEKS, FAR REMOVED FROM WRITING during weeks of café life and the wilting heat of Europe, in the cold and snow of Ottawa days before Christmas. Time to finish with a few thoughts, so, both weirdly and naturally, I have one of my rare and vivid dreams. Out go my few thoughts for a few others.

I am back in my old neighbourhood with my five-year-old daughter, Cait. I don't know why I know she is five, and as I look at her closely, though she bursts with personality, I am not even sure if she is Cait, my youngest, now 22, or Kristen, my middle, now 32, or Shannon, my ultra-responsible eldest at 34. My five-year-old grabs my hand as we walk; she steers me to a street vendor, and we buy pizza slices, she insisting on pepperoni. I am fully attentive and completely connected to this daughter, specific identity unknown. We do not talk; she does not gush or emote at me, for me. She just does what five-year-olds do, more preoccupied with pizza than with me. The image is vivid, the content bland, unlike the other two defining dreams of my life. It doesn't matter; I am wholly anchored to this child, in this moment, until shaken back to the waking moment, delivered into false dawn with a searing sense of loss. Where is my five-year-old daughter?

I grew up in a large family of mainly boys, and I always wanted, and was blessed with, daughters. Given the fact that Cait is 10 and 13 years younger than Kristen and Shannon respectively, I had a little pal by my side unbroken for about 25 years. My little pal is both gone and always with me; I suppose my dream an archetypal expression of longing for home.

I miss her, but I am not pining. Last night I made dinner for my girls and their guys. After hanging a few decorations on the tree, the boys settled into *How the Grinch Stole Christmas* while the girls sat at the table immersed in high-octane animated conversation. Cara, a whirling dervish while preparing for dinner and tree decorating, now barely an hour later is asleep on the rug in front of the fire, with the form and consistency of a bag of milk. I watch from the couch, as I watched from the kitchen table at my parents' house, the unfolding of the ornate blandness of my daughters' lives, in the holy moment. They are perfect in a way they will never allow from me. I am not feeling shut out, unloved or regretful. So why this dream? Of course parents have these thoughts—that is, our kids as kids, before they became fully grown—that we do not pester our no-longer-kids with. It is our inarticulate speech of the pathetic parental heart.

My temporary sense of loss over the maturation of my little pal is more than bolstered by my gratitude for the reality of what they have become. And then another thought. The little pal pulling at my heartstrings that I've conjured may be any or all of my daughters, may include the *trailing clouds of glory* of all five-year-olds, and then, looking at the cover of this book, may be Mom as she once was, the child we never knew. Child is mother to the man. The bliss of bland, caring and in the care of a five-year-old, with echoes of timelessness, connection in perpetuity.

———————

And now the frenzied countdown to Christmas. Work details winding down, persnickety preparation for hosting dinners underway, with family far and wide about to descend upon us. Death by a thousand trips to the mall. Cara hates shopping, won't go this time of year, can't face the crowds, consumerism, bittersweet sensation of holiday fervour and palpable loneliness. My fiction is that I go to the malls because she won't. But this is disingenuous. Against pressing need and better judgment I find myself in the mall again, without plan or direction, and I have to admit that I often do this. I stroll, watch people, listen to excitement, strife, a symphony of humanity, a range of bland. This is not ideal community; it is highly imperfect human theatre; it just is, and all human clustering is to be held in wonder. People saunter, stroll, pass by with or without purpose, and for all exteriors, we all hold and withhold hellish passions sight unseen; for him, a double calamity of debt and regret; for her, a troubled relationship; over there a failed job; another with cancer; for everyone, loss, exacerbated by the season, or worse, those who pass through this life without acknowledging loss, who do not grieve, lament, feel for someone, for anyone, for themselves. All people, even Scrooge, want to connect, feel special to someone, exit the smallness of their lives, of the mall, but we are tethered to small compromise and defeat, all exacerbated by the season, the holy season that is intended to celebrate love and connection.

But there are glimpses when least expected. The discord of a thousand separate voices is stilled as I step out into the night air. Parking lot full, mind emptying, too much detail to make into any one discernible thing. Except snow. Each flake unique, a metaphor for separateness coming together into one discernible, now indivisible, whole. It is snowing great clumps, which began as separate flakes, each unto itself, then clinging couples, bunches and pods gathering momentum, colliding and coagulating into monstrous flakes spiralling downward, until a cradled landing, layer upon layer, piled high and thick beyond what should accumulate in so short a time, if anyone is paying attention. But I am the parking lot's lone flake, even as they cluster along my arms and eyelashes, and, yes, the ten-year-old within feels each barely perceptible landing, a millisecond on my tongue before its complete transformation. I look around at covered cars, scant trees, white expanse where road used to be, back to the mass of humanity that is the mall. I think human separation and see uniform whiteness, a colossal blanket covering all strife, decay and misunderstanding with comfort, security and love. It all seems so simple and complete. For all the complexity of life in the modern anxious world, there is the possibility of faith, blanketing all human pain and acrimony, simple and complete.

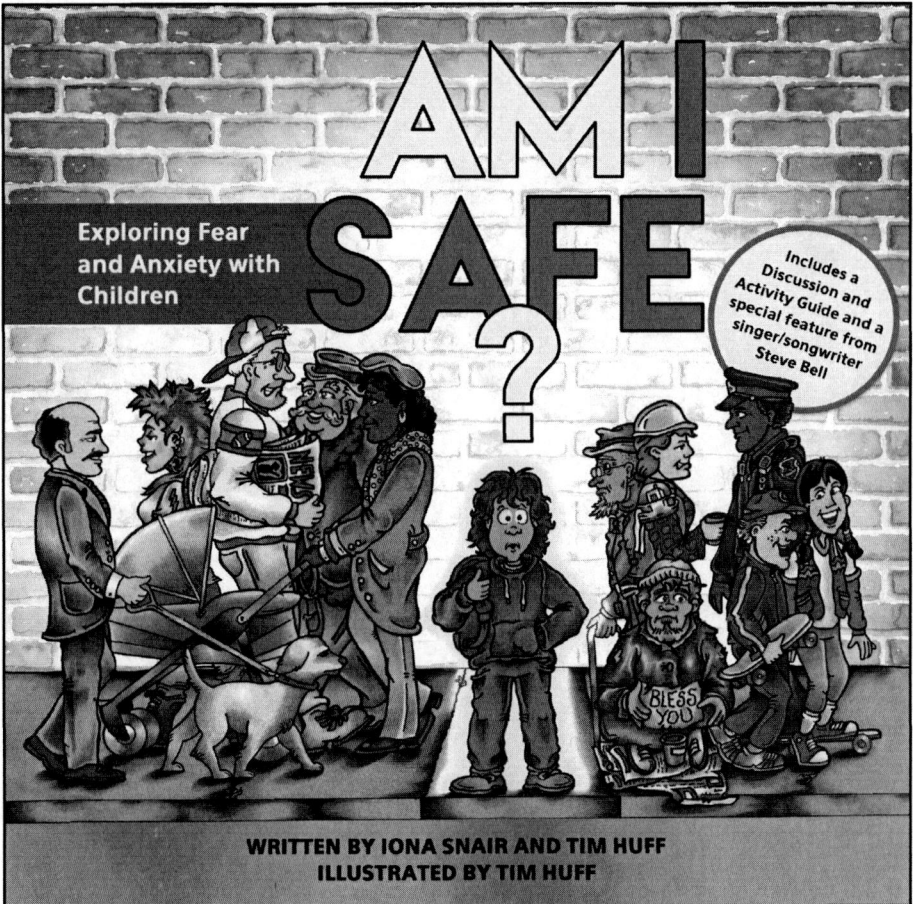

Compassion Series

BOOK 2

FOREWORD BY THE HONOURABLE DAVID C. ONLEY

IT'S HARD
NOT TO
STARE

HELPING
CHILDREN
UNDERSTAND
DISABILITIES

WRITTEN & ILLUSTRATED BY TIM HUFF
PARENT & TEACHER DISCUSSION GUIDE BY JAN FUKUMOTO

# Faith, LEADERSH✝P and Public Life

## Leadership Lessons from Moses to Jesus

### Preston Manning

# THE

# TRUE STORY

## OF CANADIAN HUMAN

# TRAFFICKING

BY PAUL H. BOGE
FOREWORD BY PAUL BRANDT